CAMBRIDGE STUDIES IN EIGHTEENTH-CENTURY
ENGLISH LITERATURE AND THOUGHT 7

Space and the Eighteenth-Century English Novel

In this challenging and original illustrated study, Simon Varey relates the idea of space in the major novels of Defoe, Fielding and Richardson to its use in the theory and practice of eighteenth-century architecture. Concepts of divine design, expressed in the work of philosophers and theologians, introduced an ideological element to the notion of space which gave it a heightened significance in contemporary thought. Professor Varey's central argument is that space becomes a political instrument used to establish conformity, assert power and give form to the aspirations of social classes. He draws on a wide range of architectural books, both English and European, and on the example of Bath (focusing in particular on its chief architect in the eighteenth century, John Wood). The discussion of the novels examines narrative as a form of spatial design, the use of architectural imagery to describe people, and the political control of social space. The result is a work which makes fertile conjunctions between literary criticism, architecture and the history of ideas.

CAMBRIDGE STUDIES IN EIGHTEENTH-CENTURY
ENGLISH LITERATURE AND THOUGHT

General Editors   Dr HOWARD ERSKINE-HILL, FBA, *Pembroke College, Cambridge*
                     and Professor JOHN RICHETTI, *University of Pennsylvania*

Editorial board   Morris Brownell, *University of Nevada*
                     Leopold Damrosch, *Harvard University*
                     J. Paul Hunter, *University of Chicago*
                     Isobel Grundy, *Queen Mary College, London*
                     Lawrence Lipking, *Northwestern University*
                     Harold Love, *Monash University*
                     Claude Rawson, *Yale University*
                     Pat Rogers, *University of South Florida*
                     James Sambrook, *Univeristy of Southampton*

The growth in recent years of eighteenth-century studies has prompted the establishment
of this series of books devoted to the period. The series is designed to accommodate mono-
graphs and critical studies on authors, works, genres and other aspects of literary culture
from the later part of the seventeenth century to the end of the eighteenth.

Since academic engagement with this field has become an increasingly interdisciplinary
enterprise, books will be especially encouraged which in some way stress the cultural context
of the literature, or examine it in relation to contemporary art, music, philosophy, histori-
ography, religion, politics, social affairs, and so on. New approaches to the established
canon are being tested with increasing frequency, and the series will hope to provide a
home for the best of these. The books we choose to publish will be thorough in their methods
of literary, historical, or biographical investigation, and will open interesting perspectives
on previously closed, or underexplored, or misrepresented areas of eighteenth-century
writing and thought. They will reflect the work of both younger and established scholars
on either side of the Atlantic and elsewhere.

Titles published
The Transformation of The Decline and Fall of the Roman Empire, by David Womersley
Women's Place in Pope's World, by Valerie Rumbold
Sterne's Fiction and the Double Principle, by Jonathan Lamb
Warrior Women and Popular Balladry, 1650–1850, by Dianne Dugaw
The Body in Swift and Defoe, by Carol Flynn
The Rhetoric of Berkeley's Philosophy, by Peter Walmsley
Space and the Eighteenth-Century English Novel, by Simon Varey

Other titles in preparation
Plots and Counterplots: Politics and Literary Representation, 1660–1730, by Richard Braverman
The Eighteenth-Century Hymn, by Donald Davie
Richardson's Clarissa *and the Eighteenth-Century Reader*, by Tom Keymer
Reason, Grace and Sentiment: A Study of the Language of Religion and Ethics in England,
1660–1780, by Isabel Rivers
Defoe's Politics: Parliament, Power, Kingship and Robinson Crusoe, by Manuel Schonhorn

Space and the Eighteenth-Century English Novel

SIMON VAREY

Department of English,
University of California at Los Angeles

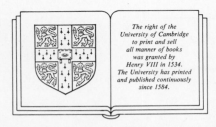

The right of the
University of Cambridge
to print and sell
all manner of books
was granted by
Henry VIII in 1534.
The University has printed
and published continuously
since 1584.

CAMBRIDGE UNIVERSITY PRESS

Cambridge

New York   Port Chester

Melbourne   Sydney

Published by the Press Syndicate of the University of Cambridge,
The Pitt Building, Trumpington Street, Cambridge CB2 1RP
40 West 20th Street, New York, NY 10011, USA
10 Stamford Road, Oakleigh, Melbourne 3166, Australia

First Published 1990

Printed in Great Britain at the University Press, Cambridge

British Library cataloguing in publication data
Varey, Simon, 1951–
Space and the eighteenth-century English novel. – (Cambridge studies in eighteenth-century
English literature and thought; 7).
1. Fiction in English, 1702–1800 – Critical studies I. Title
823'.5'09

Library of Congress cataloguing in publication data applied for

ISBN 0 521 37483 9

GG

Contents

Illustrations

Illustrations 1, 7, 8, 10, 11, 12, 15, are reproduced by permission of the William Andrews Clark Memorial Library, University of California, Los Angeles; 9, 13: by kind permission of Country Life; 2, 3, 4: from the collection of the Getty Center for the History of Art and the Humanities; 6, 14, 16: by permission of the Henry E. Huntington Library, San Marino, California; 5: author's collection.

Acknowledgments

In New York City on 1 May 1984, a thief took every one of my notes for an earlier incarnation of this book. I refer him to *Tristram Shandy*, book 3, chapter 11. Because of him I have written a different book, and probably a better one, but I wish I had not been forced to do so much of the research twice.

By contrast, it is my pleasure to thank ZWO, the Netherlands Organization for the Advancement of Pure Research, for a most welcome travel grant for research in England in 1982. For the privilege of short-term fellowships in 1982 and 1984, I am delighted to acknowledge the generosity of the Henry E. Huntington Library, San Marino, and William Andrews Clark Memorial Library, University of California, Los Angeles. I have done most of the work for this book at these two wonderful libraries. I have also benefited from the collections at the Bath Reference Library, the British Library, the City of Bristol Record Office, and the Library of the Getty Center for the History of Art and the Humanities, Santa Monica. Special thanks are due to the Clark for giving me my own cubicular space in the library these last few years, and for enabling me to move so far into the computer age that I can no longer use a pencil.

For all kinds of assistance I offer my gratitude to: Paul Alkon, Martin Battestin, Jerry Beasley, John Bidwell, Benjamin Boyce, Carol Briggs, Peter Delvaux, Jim Force, Larry Green, Susan Green, John Dixon Hunt, Richard Kroll, Tom Lockwood, Pat McCloskey, Caren Meghreblien, the late Ron Neale, Max Novak, Bill Park, Dick Popkin, John Porter, Virginia Renner, Martin Ridge, Nancy Shea, Carol Sommer, Mary Therese Bernadette Stancavage, Hugh Thompson, Carol Varey, Richard Varey, Van West, and Cal Winton. Many of these incredibly patient people have also put up with my ramblings on the subject of space for longer than I care to admit. As Lord Bolingbroke said when he thought he was a poet, 'I think myself obliged to own the debt, though I am unable to pay it.'

The eccentricities and errors are my doing.

Note on translations

In a few places I quote from works written or published originally in Dutch, French, German, Greek, Italian, or Latin. If there is an available English translation in the Loeb Classical Library editions for the Greek or Latin, I use that. In other cases I use English translations which British eighteenth-century authors could be expected to have read. Failing that, I use modern English translations. If no published translation in English is available, I quote the original language and follow it with my own fairly literal version.

Introduction

This book is about space in eighteenth-century Britain. The book is organized in three sections. Part I discusses conceptions of space expressed mainly by architects and writers about architecture; it also discusses concepts of divine design, expressed mainly by philosophers and theologians. Part II discusses that spatial thinking in practice, in the city of Bath. Part III discusses spatial concepts in the major novels of Defoe, Richardson and Fielding. This introduction explains the scope and purpose of each of these sections and the argument that connects them.

More convincingly than anyone else, Andrea Palladio had interpreted Vitruvius' *De Architectura* for the modern western world in 1570, but still he was just one of many interpreters of the only surviving classical treatise on architecture. Leon Battista Alberti's *De Re Aedificatoria*, first published posthumously in Latin in 1485, had already been translated into Italian and French before Palladio's *Quattro Libri dell'Architettura* appeared.[1] Among Palladio's contemporaries, his countrymen Sebastiano Serlio (1537–47), Giacomo Barozzi, known as Il Vignola (1563), Pietro Cataneo (1567) and Vincenzo Scamozzi (1615) wrote renowned architectural books that included responses to Vitruvius. French theorists, meanwhile, were developing their own architectural book industry, with major tracts first by Jacques Androuet du Cerceau (1559) and Philibert Delorme (1567), and later by Pierre Le Muet, who translated Palladio in 1645, Roland Fréart de Chambray (1650), Abraham Bosse (1664), René Ouvrard (1677), Pierre Bullet (1691), and Augustin Charles D'Aviler (1693–6). There was no comparable proliferation of English architectural books at the same time. Britain boasted only two slight treatises, by John Shute (1563) and Sir Henry Wotton (1624), before John Evelyn set matters right in 1664 by translating Fréart's *Parallèle*, which anthologized ten Renaissance authors. Since 'the British Palladio', Inigo Jones, at his death in 1652 had left buildings but no published theory, British connoisseurs relied on continental rather than native theoretical writing.[2]

---

[1] Alberti's treatise appeared in Latin again in 1541, Italian in 1546 and 1565, French in 1553, and English in 1715.

[2] The most authoritative general account of British Palladian architecture is John Summerson, *Architecture in Britain, 1530–1830*, Pelican History of Art, 7th edn (Harmondsworth: Penguin, 1983), esp. pp. 319–48. For the view that British Palladianism is indebted more to Inigo Jones than to Palladio, see Summerson, *Inigo Jones* (Harmondsworth: Penguin, 1966, reprinted 1983),

The many continental treatises published between the mid sixteenth and late seventeenth centuries almost all attempted to define architecture and locate its historical origins, and to establish 'correct' standards for the proportions of the Doric, Ionic, and Corinthian orders.[3] The authors inevitably fed on each other's work, notably in their agreement that the original purpose of architecture was, as Vitruvius defined it, to provide primitive man with shelter against bad weather.[4] When Vitruvius was writing, early in the reign of Augustus Caesar, architecture had already become a conspicuous means of glorifying the Roman Empire: the state, said Vitruvius, 'was not only made greater' through the Emperor's conquests, 'but the majesty of the empire also was expressed through the eminent dignity of its public buildings.'[5] In the stream of architectural books from Renaissance Italy and France, that imperial theme is rarely lost. When a few Englishmen started to write architectural treatises of their own soon after the Restoration in 1660, they too adopted this theme, to express their optimism over the expected political rehabilitation of their nation. Although the hopes faded quickly, the function of architecture as a means of glorifying monarchy and empire continued to appear in all kinds of books and buildings.

Far from developing a genuinely vernacular architecture, after the Restoration British architects and patrons designed their houses and public buildings in a conspicuously classical idiom for just about a century. Vernacular or classical, architecture confers spatial form on human aspirations. Architects and patrons transformed ideas into structures and spaces, occasionally idiosyncratic, but usually representative of the collective ideals and values of the wealthiest classes. Concepts of space and its uses were thus both personal and publicly sanctioned. Space is the basis of architecture, of cottages, country mansions, town houses, theatres, inns, streets, squares, and cities, but although it was a common subject of philosophical speculation and debate, space was rarely the explicit subject of architectural theory. Space does occur, but for the most part indirectly, as a topic in several kinds of commentary on architecture, especially on its origins, history, proportions, organization, and functions, none of which, I should say, is a result of the 'instinctive correctness' that Siegfried Giedion considered 'the secret of the architecture of the middle eighteenth century',[6] for that 'correctness', though not itself programmatic, is the product of systematic thought rather than instinct. In the first section of this book I use this architectural discourse, in books and

---

p. 138.

[3] The Tuscan and Composite orders were sometimes similarly discussed, but they were not usually accepted as strictly classical.

[4] *De Architectura*, II, i, 1–2.

[5] *Ibid.*, I, preface, 2.

[6] *Space, Time and Architecture: The Growth of a New Tradition*, 5th edn (Cambridge, Mass.: Harvard University Press, 1967), p. 147.

buildings, not to rewrite architectural history but to explore the spatial thinking of men who designed places where people would live and work.

My second section may seem quixotic, because I have taken as an example of the practical side of British architectural discourse not the most obvious choice, London, but a city that is both representative and aberrant: Bath. The ring of buildings constructed around the medieval centre of Bath was one of three substantial urban extensions built in eighteenth-century Britain. The other two were the Harley-Cavendish estate north of Oxford Street in London and the new town on the north side of Edinburgh. London and Edinburgh are only partly Georgian cities, but Bath is dominated by its eighteenth century accretions.[7] While the new districts of London and Edinburgh remained districts or suburbs, intimately connected to, but still distinct from the older areas, Bath's new buildings redefined the old town, so that Bath became virtually a purpose-built new city.

Georgian Bath today looks like everybody's idea of a neoclassical city, a compact cluster of strictly Palladian buildings. Although Bath is Palladian, the city's principal designer and developer, John Wood the Elder, had in mind more than Palladian theory. Aiming to outdo Palladio, and arguing forcefully against Vitruvian principles, Wood gave orthodox neoclassical theory relatively little prominence as he planned the new city on the basis of a theory of British history that has been dismissed from time to time as idiosyncratic, arcane, bizarre or insane. Wood's argument about his country's past was unhistorical, but not esoteric, since he drew much of it from the readily available published writings of historians, antiquaries and philosophers. What is perhaps oddest about Wood's theory is that it had never before been put explicitly into practice by an architect in Britain. That, together with Wood's willingness to carry his theory to an implausible extreme, is probably the reason for the dismissive reactions to his thinking.

Largely under Wood's self-appointed tutelage, Bath was designed as a playground for the 'great', the 'rich' and the 'middle sort', to use Defoe's terms.[8] Fashionable Bath was the most famous social symbol of the leisured classes in the eighteenth century and its disposition of space was a symbol of those classes. I go into the intellectual origins of Bath – however eccentric at times they may seem – in detail, in order to illustrate the ideology that could create the social spaces of a Georgian city.

A reader might reasonably expect that I should then discuss in part III the theory of architectural space and the buildings of Bath as they appear in the novels. I do not do so exactly, for two reasons. First, I do not discuss the

---

[7] New squares affected the character of Glasgow, Manchester, and Dublin but did not transform the topography of the whole city.

[8] In the *Review*, vol. 6, no. 36 (25 June 1709), p. 142, Defoe divided the population into seven groups: the great, the rich, the middle sort, labourers, farmers, the poor and the miserable. For analysis of Defoe's commentaries on class, see Peter Earle, *The World of Defoe* (New York: Atheneum, 1977), pp. 162–66.

theory because I know of no evidence to suggest that the novels of Defoe, Richardson and Fielding are somehow contrived as conscious responses to architectural writers, individual buildings, or particular theories of space. It would be an indefensible contrivance of my own to suggest that, say, Richardson's treatment of space is the same as Palladio's, is expressed in the same terms, or uses precisely the same concepts. The architectural books and novels with which I am familiar did not share the same views or methods of interpretation: an architect's spaces and a novelist's are rarely identical. But, divergent as their concepts of space are, the writers discussed here share a habit of spatial thinking. That thinking is what I concentrate on. Second, I do not discuss Bath's architecture and society in the novels because, although there is a case for a new critical study of this subject, it would be irrelevant here, because my subject is neither architectural history, nor the relations between architecture and the novel, but space.

My main purpose in part III is to investigate conceptions of space and place in writing that is usually not concerned with architecture at all. The principal uses of space that I seek to identify in the literature are: narrative as spatial design; the language of architecture employed to describe people; the exploitation of personal spaces, in such experiences as imprisonment, isolation and alienation; and the constitutive control of human activity that occurs when a particular function is assigned to a social space. My argument is that the spaces created (in theory or practice) by architects and those created by the novelists – whether or not they are the same spaces – express specific ideology and are therefore political.[9] I use political concepts of space to investigate the nature of a subject in relation to society in the major fictions of Defoe, Fielding, and Richardson. For one who resists the pressure to conform as for one who does not, the self is defined, to a remarkable degree, by space.

The last chapters concentrate on literature that was extremely popular in its day. This book is certainly not a survey of all the bestsellers of eighteenth-century Britain, but an attempt to locate in contemporary spatial discourse some of the most important and popular writing, which has continued to be considered important, if not necessarily popular, in the twentieth century. I am therefore dealing with some of the most familiar passages in eighteenth-century fiction, where many have been before me. Numerous other novels and poems have just as good a claim to inclusion, but one cannot have everything because there would be nowhere to put it.

---

[9] For commentary on spatiality as a part of the aesthetics of the novel, involving such concepts as 'chapter architecture' and spatial secondary illusion, see Philip Stevick, 'The Theory of Fictional Chapters', in *The Theory of the Novel*, ed. Philip Stevick (New York: Free Press, 1967), pp. 171–84; and Joseph A. Kestner, *The Spatiality of the Novel* (Detroit: Wayne State University Press, 1978).

PART I

1

Space, architecture, and politics

Woe unto them that join house to house, that lay field to field,
till there be no place.   Isaiah 5:8

Or, de toutes les actes, le plus complet est celui de construire.
Paul Valéry, *Eupalinos, ou l'architecte*

I

Many people, particularly city-dwellers, know the experience of crossing a
street from one range of buildings to another range that looks similar but has
an entirely different atmosphere. One might sense carefree gaiety on one
side of a New York street, tension and menace on the other. And yet all one
has done is pass through an empty space, from the shadow of one building
to that of another. Various factors, such as street lighting, garbage, or street
furniture of some kind, can contribute to such a change, but the most significant factor is surely what other people do in the spaces on each side of the
street. Perhaps one area is devoted to making money by legal means, the
other, illegal, or one might be a centre of power, the other of powerlessness.
The empty space that is the street (occupied only temporarily by passing
traffic) is sometimes the line that divides two communities. Most people, I
imagine, would probably not acknowledge this to be a function of the street
itself, that is, of the space. In Berlin or Belfast, everyone recognizes the
bounding and divisive function of the infamous walls, which are in any case
intended to prevent anyone from crossing the street at all, but in less eccentric
circumstances than these we can identify the diverse human activities on each
side of the street without even looking for a physical boundary such as a
wall. Some urban spaces, such as London's Hyde Park, appear from certain
vantage points to be limited only by perspectives, rather than by buildings or
streets. Paul Zucker's example, the Place de la Concorde in Paris, may suggest
boundaries by no more than an illusion, but there are other, far from illusory,
boundaries that have no tangible existence.[1] As Joseph Rykwert has

[1] Paul Zucker, *Town and Square from the Agora to the Village Green* (New York: Columbia University
Press, 1959), p. 186.

7

explained, the Roman augural *templum* might have had 'visible and permanent physical bounds, but its real boundaries were not fixed by them,' since
they were 'fixed' by the verbal assignation of a function to the space of the
templum itself.[2] A boundary can be defined by the function which people
attach to an empty space: not all boundaries have to be marked by walls,
fences, and hedges. Contiguity need not suggest continuity of subculture.

In our everyday lives, most of us interpret some particular spaces, which
we visit or use so habitually that interpretation is unconscious. People who
use banks scarcely need to interpret the space inside a bank, for instance,
although that is precisely what they do when they enter a bank building in
order to cash a cheque. We know that the place is a bank, either because we
think we have always known, or because it happens to be the bank we have
been using for four years, or because a sign outside the building tells us
that this is a branch of the First Pacific Bank of California. The interior
arrangements will usually suggest *bankness*: that is, they will include counter
tops with supplies of printed forms for various transactions, windows where
customers speak with cashiers, an informal desk or two where one can open
new accounts, and so forth. We would recognize all these familiar features
of a bank at a glance, irrespective of differences in their disposition between
one branch and another. The familiarity given us by experience enables us
therefore to 'read' the internal arrangement as a statement rather like: 'This is
a bank. People conduct financial transactions here.' In this entirely mundane
example of interpretation of interior space, a visitor defines the space by the
activity that occurs within its limits. The exterior of a typical modern bank in
a western. nation will probably not suggest, by its design, the activities that
take place inside. We are likely to need the sign outside to indicate those
activities. This is not to say that all modern banks look like all other modern
buildings, but rather to say that *bankness* is no longer as likely as it once was
to be implied by the shape of the building or the disposition of its wall sur-
faces, pillars, or windows. Some decoration, such as dollar signs carved into
brickwork, might suggest to one observer the function of the building, or to
another the cost of its construction. Alternatively, a conspicuous, massive
classical portico might imply solidity and weight, or tradition and empire,
none of which may be inherent in *bankness* but in which financial institutions
might be thought somehow to participate. Such inferences about an individual building are simpler to posit than reactions to outside space, to the block,
the street, the town, the city, or whatever space surrounds the building.
Outside space may be more difficult to interpret because it is less easily divis-
ible into discrete functions than the interior space of a single building usually
is. An individual building thus makes a more readily comprehensible state-

---

[2] *The Idea of a Town: The Anthropology of Urban Form in Rome, Italy and the Ancient World* (Princeton: Princeton University Press, 1976), p. 48. What is more, *templum* originally meant (1) an open place, and (2) the extent of the heavens (Varro, *De Lingua Latina*, VII, 6).

ment about itself than it does about the space outside it, even though it contributes to a definition of that outside space.

The builder of the first hut, if ever there was such a thing, defined not one but two spaces: the space outside the hut, and the space inside it. If we imagine the surface of the earth as a single space, the first edifice – be it a hut or a palace – divided that space into two new spaces. The second edifice divided the remaining outside space, and so on. Anyone who builds divides space. To create a building is to create a space, or more precisely to limit a space and, by limiting, to define it. To build a wall, a fence, or a street where none existed before is to divide one visible space into two, to violate infinite though knowable space by marking boundaries. An interior space remains inviolate until interior walls are erected, converting a single space into rooms. Rooms themselves are converted less definitely into smaller units of space by the addition of a fireplace, an alcove, or furniture. But definitions of space require the participation of designers, builders, inhabitants, and other users and visitors. The 'builder' of a nutshell may define the space it encloses as narrowly confined, while its 'user' may, like Hamlet, imagine counting himself a king of infinite space.[3] Interpreting space involves interpreting the use or uses to which space can be put, and it also involves differences of individual perception. One individual's sprawling and impersonal metropolis may be another's compact and intimate town.

Neoclassical theorists did not contemplate space, architectural or cosmic, in such ways as these. Instead, their favourite themes are oriented around other human needs and desires. Since space is man's inescapable element, the history of architecture is the history of man.[4] Together with the need for food, there is no human necessity more fundamental than shelter. Architecture, said Antoine Yves Goguet in 1758, in an unexceptionably orthodox Vitruvian remark, was born of necessity as shelter against the weather and wild animals.[5] And yet to speak of the crudest imaginable shelter as 'architecture' is almost heretical in view of architecture's long history as an art. Writing after centuries of emphasis on the aesthetics of architecture, the neoclassicists often distinguished between the origin of building and the origin of architecture as two entirely different things. If architecture was not mere building, what did neoclassicists think architecture was? Vitruvius had said originally that it was the arts of building, dialling (i.e. clockmaking) and mechanics.[6] Most later commentators ignored the last two and stuck to building. With his customary pragmatism the learned Dean of Christ Church, Henry Aldrich, defined architecture in 1710 as 'the art of building well,' adding that the

[3] *Hamlet*, II, ii, 260–61.
[4] Cf. Andrew Saint, 'A Plan without a Maze', review of Spiro Kostof, *A History of Architecture: Settings and Rituals* (New York: Oxford University Press, 1985), *TLS*, 14 February 1986, 168.
[5] *De l'origine des loix, des arts, et des sciences et leur progrès chez les anciens peuples* (Paris, 1758), I, p. 126.
[6] *De Architectura*, I, iii, 1.

architect could 'be considered in three views:' patron, designer, and builder.[7] Had Aldrich's contemporaries had access to a published text of his book, few would have dissented from his view. After Vitruvius it was orthodox to recognize two branches of building: public and private; and three classes of the public branch: civil, military, and religious. Writers with this passion for dividing and subdividing their subject would then duly account for the origins and characteristics of each class and branch. It was orthodox also to identify the fundamental principles of architecture as utility, strength, and beauty. By this route architecture could be defined then as a harmonious union of these three principles, with beauty arriving later than the other two as the inutile sophisticating factor that transforms a mere building into 'architecture'.[8]

With this perspective Robert Anthony Bromley suggested in the 1790s that ancient Persian architects were building

long, very long before any ideas of regular order in architecture had taken possession of the human mind. We shall consequently find the Persians acting on those notions for the obtaining of strength, and duration, and conveniency in buildings, which common sense with some future assistances from studious individuals must supply. It must be remembered that the buildings, which are now seen in ruins at Persepolis, were not intended to be inhabited, but were formed for a temple.[9]

The distinction between building and architecture was nicely expressed in 1674 by André Félibien, who wrote in his *Principes*:

Bien que les Bastimens soient considerez entre les premiers ouvrages des hommes, l'Architecture neanmoins n'est pas un des Arts les plus anciens. Elle a eu comme tous les autres de foibles commencemens, & ne s'est perfectionée qu'aprés un long usage.[10]

Although buildings are considered among the first works of men, architecture is nevertheless not one of the oldest arts. Like the other arts, it was weak at first, and was not perfected until it had been in use a long time.

---

[7] *The Elements of Civil Architecture, according to Vitruvius and other ancients, and the most approved practice of modern authors, especially Palladio*, translated by Philip Smyth (Oxford, 1789), p. 1. A portion of Aldrich's Latin manuscript was published in 1750, the whole of it in 1789 together with Smyth's English translation.

[8] After Vitruvius, *De Architectura*, I, iii. See Jacques-François Blondel's article on 'architecture' in the *Encyclopédie* (1751), I, p. 617, and Diderot's prospectus (1751). Eric Bentley reminds us 'of the man who, having watched for weeks the construction of a modern Gothic building, cried one day: "Oh, look, they're putting the architecture on now!" ' (*'The Importance of Being Earnest'*, in *The Playwright as Thinker* [New York: Reznal & Hitchcock, 1946], reprinted in *Oscar Wilde: A Collection of Critical Essays*, ed. Richard Ellmann, Twentieth-Century Views [Englewood Cliffs, N.J.: Prentice-Hall, 1969], p. 114).

[9] *A Philosophical and Critical History of the Fine Arts, Painting, Sculpture, and Architecture*, I (London, 1793), pp. 145–46. Bromley's own source was P. F. Hugues d'Hancarville, *Recherches sur l'origine, l'esprit, et les progrès des arts de la Grèce*, 3 vols. (London, 1785).

[10] *Des Principes de l'Architecture, de la Sculpture, de la Peinture, et des autres arts qui en dépendent* (Paris, 1674). I quote from the 2nd edition (Paris, 1690), p. 1.

And indeed Goguet recognized that 'c'est du luxe qu'elle a reçu ses embellisse-mens' (it is from luxury that architecture received its embellishments).[11]

'Building' did not have artistic principles, but 'architecture' did. These beautifying principles would dignify building by raising it above its obvious level of manual skill to one of high artistic achievement. Such 'improvement' was inseparable from growing political organization and sophistication: in antiquity, said Germain Boffrand, 'les habitations rustiques ont reçu une nouvelle forme, toujours fondée sur le besoin & sur l'utilité' (rustic habitations were given a new form, still based on necessity and utility), but only after societies had been united by the introduction of civil laws.[12] Beauty and mag-nificence, D'Aviler had argued, follow utility as a direct result of the increas-ing power and wealth of great men.[13] In such an historical perspective necessity and utility begin to lose some of their dominance. As societies grew more sophisticated, trees were still used for columns, but by giving them bases and capitals, art made them more elegantly contoured than trees are naturally: the classical orders, whose cohering feature is the column with its capital, traditionally merge 'nature' as expressed by a tree with 'nature' as found in the proportions of the human body.[14] Who discovered and devel-oped these principles of beauty is another question: evading it, the revolution-ary Etienne-Louis Boullée was certain that anyone seeking the origins of architecture could conclude that the principles were either unknown or undeveloped.[15]

As for the origin of building, almost every writer apparently felt obliged to preface his theory of architecture with an account of the origin, rise, and progress of building. One loses count of the number of writers who express the Vitruvian view that the first buildings were primitive huts: typically, these authors relate how, from a hut of mud and leaves, perhaps animal skins too, assembled rather like a lean-to supported by a standing tree, the earliest primitive shelter would gradually grow in sophistication, until it was replaced by a sturdier structure built exclusively from hewn wood. Once these struc-tures acquire neighbours, for reasons of security and communication, the origins of a city are established. From considerations of strength, utility, and a freer choice of site, the huts become houses with solid foundations; as soon as they acquire ornaments, they begin symbolically to represent the goals and desires of their inhabitants. The theory of the primitive hut does not rely

---

[11] Goguet, *De l'origine*, I, p. 126.

[12] *Livre d'Architecture* (Paris, 1745), I, p. 5.

[13] Augustin Charles D'Aviler, *Cours d'Architecture qui comprend les ordres de Vignole*, I (Paris, 1696), preface, sig. i, verso.

[14] Boffrand, *Livre*, I, p. 5. Cf. Isaac Ware's suggestively titled *A Complete Body of Architecture* (London, 1756), p. 135: 'Nature has formed the trunk of no tree square, therefore there could be originally no such thing as a square pillar.' The basic text is Vitruvius, *De Architectura*, III, i.

[15] *Architecture. Essai sur l'art*, ed. Jean-Marie Pérouse de Montclos (Paris: Hermann, 1968), p. 52. Boullée's treatise was composed no later than 1793.

on any serious expectation that the archaeological remains of any such hut will ever be found.[16] The search for the origins of building was not conducted in the hope of actually finding them: the search itself mattered most, because it could throw into sharper focus the practice of the modern architect. So even when 'building' and 'architecture' are kept separate, the theory of the primitive hut supports a progressive view of history, using architecture as a paradigm.

For the origins of architecture as an art, the authors of the major architectural treatises of sixteenth- and seventeenth-century Italy and France usually acknowledged Vitruvius as authoritative if fallible. One of the most respected and influential of these authors, Sebastiano Serlio, was mildly censured (as was Palladio) for his inaccurate measurements, but not for his customary endorsement of Vitruvius: 'the Greeks were the principall founders and inuentors of good Architecture.'[17] Such an attitude hardened into an orthodoxy passed on by Boffrand and D'Aviler.[18] The Earl of Shaftesbury's disciple, Robert Morris, even offered scholarly 'proof' from Pliny that the Greeks must have invented architecture.[19]

Occasionally the Egyptians rather than the Greeks were credited with the invention of the principles that changed building into the art of architecture. In his monumental *Description of the East*, the erudite tourist, Richard Pococke, reported that 'The architecture of Egypt may be look'd on as among the first essays in that noble art. It was in a style peculiar to themselves, in which, notwithstanding, we may trace the origin of many things we see in the most improved architecture.'[20] And repeating the judgment of his teacher, Jacques-François Blondel, Pierre Patte began his dissertation on the proportions of the classical orders by remarking that trees '& non la proportion humaine' were the origin of columns, and that the ancient Egyptians were the first people to make use of them in architecture. Egyptian columns were coarse, however, and it was left to the Greeks to refine them and devise the three classical orders.[21] Patte's view had already been given the stamp of approval in England by Isaac Ware in 1756. The Greeks, said Ware,

were the people who reduced [architecture] to a science: the orders, which are the

---

[16] See Joseph Rykwert, *On Adam's House in Paradise: The Idea of the Primitive Hut in Architectural History*, 2nd edn. (Cambridge, Mass.: MIT Press, 1981), esp. pp. 13–14.

[17] *The Book of Architecture*, translated by Robert Peake (1611; reprinted New York: Arno Press, 1980), bk 3, ch. 4, fol. 44, recto. The 'censurer' of Serlio and Palladio was Antoine Desgodetz in 1682.

[18] Boffrand, *Livre*, I, p. 4; D'Aviler, *Cours*, preface, sig. i, verso.

[19] Robert Morris, *An Essay in Defence of Ancient Architecture* (London, 1728), p. iv.

[20] (London, 1745), I, p. 215.

[21] *Mémoires sur les objets les plus importans de l'Architecture* (Paris, 1769), p. 71. Blondel had expressed the same view in lectures at his Ecole des Arts in Paris from 1750. The lectures were printed as *Cours d'Architecture*, 9 vols. (Paris, 1771–77). Patte completed the text (vols. 5–6) and the accompanying plates (vol. 9).

ornament and glory of the art, are all of *Greek* invention, but without this knowledge of a peculiar form and proportion in their columns, the *Ægyptians* arrived at great magnificence in their edifices.[22]

The art of architecture may involve adding beauty to strength and utility, but the implicit purpose of beautifying a building – as remarks like these remind us – is to create magnificence, to be impressive and suggest greatness, that is political greatness. The origin of architecture, 'when it happened, or in what quarter of the world, are points that dreaming monks might better study than people who enjoy the present advantages of science,' said Ware.[23] Anyone sharing Ware's rather dismissive view nearly always cited the Greeks the way he did, as architecture's beautifiers and developers, but did not trouble to determine whether or not they were its inventors. The standard view was that the Romans then brought architecture to a new refinement, but with the fall of the Roman empire the Goths replaced classical idiom with their own vernacular barbarisms, and finally, as soon as the glories of classical Rome were rediscovered in the fifteenth century, northern Europe proceeded to imitate Roman perfection. The bare outlines of the story are repeated with remarkably few variations by architectural writers all over western Europe from the Renaissance onwards. The 'historical' origins of building thus precede not only modern architecture but also modern discourse about architecture. The inescapably influential Vitruvius began it all with his account of the progress of architecture running in parallel with the progress of civilization from primitive origins to the glorious monuments of imperial Rome. Whatever modifications of Vitruvius they may introduce, seventeenth-century French architectural treatises and eighteenth-century English ones repeatedly show their authors' devotion to a progressive view of history.[24] Neoclassical writing about architecture usually aims to conserve principles of classical taste, with the political overtones that were represented in classical public buildings.

Architecture, then, is more than 'mere' building, but architectural writers hesitated to denominate architecture an art or a science, because most of them seem to have wanted it to be both. Many writers begin their introductions, prefaces, or dedications with some statement to the effect that architecture is 'the Queen of the Fine Arts,' in Sir John Soane's phrase. Such an image had been portrayed graphically in a frontispiece to one of Abraham Bosse's works, and was still being touted as recently as 1927 when Martin S. Briggs called architecture the 'Mistress Art.'[25] If we disregard the many definitions

---

[22] *Complete Body of Architecture*, p. 338.

[23] *Ibid.*, p. 290. See Morris, *Essay in Defence of Ancient Architecture*, p. 19, for a similar sentiment.

[24] For example, Julien Mauclerc, *A New Treatise of Architecture, according to Vitruvius*, translated by Robert Pricke (London, 1669), preface, sig. A2, recto.

[25] Soane, *Designs for Public Improvements in London and Westminster* (London: James Moyes, 1827), dedication, sig. B, recto. Bosse, *Traité des Manieres de dessiner les O'rdres [sic] de l'Architecture antique en toutes leurs parties* (Paris, 1664), part 2, title page. Martin S. Briggs, *The Architect in*

of architecture that amount to little more than panegyric, we still find most eighteenth-century writers nodding deferentially to Vitruvius, and then explaining the origins and proportions of the classical orders before distinguishing the 'science' of designing the appropriate geometrical proportions from the 'art' of matching the appearance to the function of a building, that is exercising what Vitruvius called 'decor,' 'propriety' or 'decorum.'[26] Distinguishing easily between the art and the science, Boullée was one of the unconventional few who dismissed Vitruvius by asking

Qu'est-ce que l'architecture? La définirai-je avec Vitruve l'art de bâtir? Non. Il y a dans cette définition une erreur grossière. Vitruve prend l'effet pour la cause. . . Il faut concevoir pour effecteur. . . L'art de bâtir n'est donc qu'un art secondaire, qu'il nous paraît convenable de nommer la partie scientifique de l'architecture.[27]

What is architecture? Am I to define it, with Vitruvius, as the art of building? No. There is a gross error in this definition. Vitruvius mistakes effect for cause. One must conceive in order to realize. The art of building is thus only a secondary art, which it seems reasonable to call the scientific part of architecture.

Applied to painters, architects, or poets, the related idea that an artist (of any sort) grasps wholes while lesser mortals see only parts, had become commonplace in England too.[28] Unlike a bricklayer, an architect was required to envision a whole building, to know the theory that lay behind the design. To be able to conceive a whole design, architects were supposed to have fair knowledge in a wide range of disciplines, but in reality hardly any of them ever did. It was easier to get by with 'A Redundancy of superficial Talk, with the Addition of Freedom, otherwise Confidence, in the Behaviour'.[29] Vitruvius had recommended that the architect be 'a man of letters, a skilful draughtsman, a mathematician, familiar with historical studies, a diligent student of philosophy, acquainted with music; not ignorant of medicine, learned in the responses of juriconsults, familiar with astronomy and astronomical calculations.'[30] It was a short step from there to agree with Blondel or D'Aviler that architecture embraced 'toutes les connoissances qui servent tant à la Construction qu'à la Décoration des Edifices' (all the branches of knowledge that contribute as much to the construction as to the decoration of buildings),[31] or even to assert that architecture was the original art, from which most or all others are derived. Mathurin Jousse confidently declared

History (Oxford: Clarendon Press, 1927), p. 1.

[26] *De Architectura*, I, iii. An exception was Bosse, who pointed out that Vitruvius included some things contrary to the order of nature (*Traité*, pl. II).

[27] *Essai*, p. 49.

[28] Cf. Joshua Reynolds, *Discourses on Art*, ed. Robert R. Wark (San Marino: Huntington Library, 1959), p. 192.

[29] Morris, *Essay in Defence of Ancient Architecture*, p. 99.

[30] *De Architectura*, I, i.

[31] D'Aviler, *Cours*, I, p. 190. Also Blondel, *Cours*, I, p. 3, and I, p. 128.

that geometry and architecture ranked highest among the liberal arts, and Soane thought of painting and sculpture as architecture's 'handmaids.'[32]

Starting his treatment of specific arts with architecture because it had been accorded this supremacy and because it predated the others, Hegel decided that architecture comprised everything in a building that did not suggest utility. Bernard Tschumi points out the difficulty that would have faced Hegel had he tried to develop his argument any further, for it is hard 'to conceive of a building that escapes the utility of space, a building which would have no other purpose but 'architecture.' '[33] The obvious orthodoxy was that art and utility were inseparable. D'Aviler decided that

ny l'érudition, ny les discours, ny les voyages, ny mesme enfin les desseins quelques beaux qu'ils soient, ne servent que de peu de chose, si on ne les sçait mettre en œuvre: C'est cette pratique qui fait le veritable Architecte, & qui luy fait remarquer la grande difference qu'il y a entre les desseins & l'ouvrage.[34]

erudition, discourse, travel, finally even designs – however beautiful they may be – help only very little, if one cannot put them into practice: this practice is what makes the true architect, and what enables him to see the great difference between the designs and the work.

Echoes of Vitruvius are audible here, as one would expect of a book that is fundamentally a commentary on Vignola: the architect is distinguished from the mere workman by his ability to put theory into practice. More than a century earlier Philibert Delorme had lamented that too many so-called architects were no better than master masons because they had too little theory to add to their practice, that is, too little 'art' to add to 'utility.'[35] This would become a familiar complaint. Pierre Bullet expressed it in another form in 1691 by saying that too many writers claimed to know about architecture when all they had done was read a little and look at famous buildings. Bullet's point was that they lacked the necessary theory.[36] But there were dissenting voices too, such as the German architect Georg Andreas Bockler, who did not doubt that all theory and no practice was equally impossible: 'Dann die Baukunst bestehet nicht in Worten, sondern in einer sichtbaren und handgreifflichen Demonstration' (Architecture does not consist of words, but of visible and palpable realization).[37]

Although architecture was often taken to be a mixture of art and science,

---

[32] Jousse, *Le Secret d'Architecture* (La Flèche, 1642), dedication, sig. a ii, recto; Soane, *Designs for Public Improvements*, dedication, sig. B, recto.

[33] Hegel, *The Philosophy of Fine Art*, translated by F. P. B. Osmaston (London: G. Bell & Sons, 1920), III, pp. 25–31; Tschumi, 'Questions of Space: the Pyramid and the Labyrinth (or the Architectural Paradox),' *Studio International*, 190, no. 177 (September/October, 1975), 137.

[34] D'Aviler, *Cours*, preface, sig. i, recto.

[35] *Le Premier Tome de l'Architecture* (Paris, 1567), fol. 1, verso.

[36] *L'Architecture pratique* (Paris, 1691), preface, n.p.

[37] *Architectura Civilis Nova & Antiqua* (Frankfurt, 1663), preface, n.p.

of aesthetic and geometric considerations, art and science were rarely taken to correspond to theory and practice. This was not the issue. It is more significant that Soane's queen of the arts, attended by painting and sculpture, 'naturally addresses herself to the SOVEREIGN for protection and support.'[38] Similarly George Marshall opens his dedication to George III by announcing that architecture is the 'Science of Kings.' What matters most is not that Soane calls architecture an art and Marshall calls it a science, but that they both recognize the indispensable role of royal and aristocratic patronage: designs are 'called forth to real effect by regal liberality. . . from the erection of the Egyptian pyramids to the present time, the world has owed to the magnificence of Monarchs the grandeur of its buildings.'[39] Marshall's dedication precedes his translation of Antoine Desgodetz' classic work on the ancient buildings of Rome, which was dedicated not to Louis XIV, but to Jean Baptiste Colbert, who had conceived 'le dessein' of Desgodetz' book and thought it 'peut contribuer à la gloire de notre grand monarque' (might contribute to the glory of our great monarch; my translation).[40] Overcome by loyalty to his king, Desgodetz went on, 'les grands hommes qui les [modern buildings] ont élevés, les Augustes, les Trajans & les Antonins, ont cédé la premiere place dans ce temple de la gloire, à l'invincible, au grand & au magnanime Louis' (the great men who built them [modern buildings], like Augustus, Trajan or Antoninus, have lost the first place in this temple of glory to the invincible, great, and magnanimous Louis; my translation).[41] Though Marshall did not translate Desgodetz' dedication, but wrote his own, Marshall's dedication to George paralleled Desgodetz' to Colbert.

This instance shows an attitude to architecture that had been common since the obsequious flattery of Augustus by Vitruvius and Suetonius.[42] In 1771 William Newton prefaced his English translation of Vitruvius with these prophetic words: 'We many observe also that the course of the arts, as well as of empire, has been directed westward [from Italy]; and they may not yet have arrived at the full zenith of our isle. They however now appear to be advancing apace, and there is a prospect that they will reach their utmost heighth [sic] and perfection in this nation.'[43] Political sophistication, especially in the preferred form of imperial expansion, does not merely allow architecture to flourish, but endows architecture with its characteristic function as a glorifier of imperial achievement, of monarchy, and sometimes of the vanity

[38] *Designs for Public Improvements*, dedication, sig. B, recto. Architectural books were usually dedicated to royal or aristocratic patrons.

[39] George Marshall, translator, *The Ancient Buildings of Rome* (London, 1795), dedication, n.p. This edition printed parallel texts.

[40] *Les Edifices Antiques de Rome Dessinés et Mesurés Très Exactement* (Paris, 1682), dedication, n.p. [1795 edn, p. vii].

[41] Desgodetz, *Les Edifices Antiques* (1795 edn), p. vii.

[42] Vitruvius, *De Architectura*, II, preface. Suetonius, *Lives of the Caesars*, II, xviii.

[43] *The Architecture of M. Vitruvius Pollio*, translated by William Newton, I (1771), iii.

of a ruler.[44] Just as emphatically, Sir Christopher Wren believed that 'Architecture has its political Use . . . makes the People love their native Country, which Passion is the Original of all great Actions in a Common-wealth,' and much later John Claudius Loudon praised Holkham Hall and Woburn Abbey for their 'patriotic exhibitions of agricultural skill and produce,' but Charles Augustus Busby would strike a more judicious and pragmatic note when, with apparent approval, he noted the close links between despotic governments, their systematic looting of countries defeated in war, and magnificent building.[45] The memory of some heroic military victory would supposedly be perpetuated by a monument, in much the same way as statues of Roman heroes were sometimes placed in conspicuous domestic locations as exemplary reminders of appropriate virtues, as Lord Bolingbroke liked to recall.[46]

Devoted to the same view of the political function of architectural space, Blondel told his students that everyone knew they had architecture to thank for 'les Palais des Rois, les Places publiques, les Monuments durables à la gloire des Héros' (royal palaces, public squares, permanent memorials to the glory of heroes), and as an afterthought 'des demeures particulieres pour les differentes classes de Citoyens' (private houses for the various classes of citizens).[47] 'A picture or a statue too may be a moral or political lecture, as well as a poem,' said Dr Pococke, after noting that 'A taste for architecture has had effects very much to the honour of our country.'[48] Although it is worth remembering that London's architecture had always been (as it still is) more restrained than the flamboyant splendours of Paris or Rome, it was a rhetorical commonplace of the neoclassical period in England as well as France or Italy that architecture was a source of national pride and glory.[49] Some, like Boullée, thought that this ostentatious function, even in domestic buildings, distinguished architecture from the other arts.[50] Despite its origins

[44] Perhaps implied by Vitruvius' preface. And cf. Lewis Mumford, *The Culture of Cities* (New York: Harcourt Brace Jovanovich, 1938), p. 61.

[45] Christopher Wren, *Parentalia* (London, 1750), p. 351; Loudon, *Observations on Laying Out Farms in the Scotch Style, adapted to England* (London: for John Harding, 1812), pp. 101–02. Busby, *A Series of Designs for Villas and Country Houses. Adapted with Economy to the Comforts of Modern Life* (London: J. Taylor, 1808), p. 9.

[46] Henry St John, Viscount Bolingbroke, *Works* (1844; reprinted, London: Frank Cass, 1967), II, p. 179.

[47] Blondel, *Cours*, III, p. xiii.

[48] *A Description of the East and Some Other Countries*, II (1745), p. 277, and cf. Bromley, *Philosophical and Critical History*, I, p. 130.

[49] See: Smyth's introduction to Aldrich, *Elements*, p. iii; Bromley, *Philosophical and Critical History*, I, p. 237; Charles Cameron, *The Baths of the Romans Explained and Illustrated* (London, 1772), p. 3; Desgodetz, *Les Edifices Antiques*, dedication; Goguet, *De l'origine*, II, p. 127; John Gwynn, *An Essay on Design* (London, 1749), pp. vi, 23; Patte, dedication; Uvedale Price, *Essays on the Picturesque*, rev. edn (London, 1810), II, p. 342; Abraham Swan, *A Collection of Designs in Architecture* (London, 1757), II, iii; George Wither, *A Collection of Emblemes* (London, 1635), p. 78.

[50] Boullée, *Essai*, pp. 148–49.

in private wealth, architecture was in a pragmatic sense for Boullée actually public property.

The tendency of repeated accounts of the origins, principles, and public functions of architecture is to emphasize the antiquity and respectability of architecture as a science and an art, its perfectibility and, perhaps most significantly, its function of conferring visible spatial form on imperial conquest, wealth, and glory. By merging this vision of architecture with a contemporary British taste for the classical, writers could easily make suitably patriotic assertions of national greatness. Taking Brunelleschi to be the leader of the revival of architecture early in the fifteenth century, Aldrich saw architecture as having progressed continuously until it reached a peak in Europe during his lifetime (he died in 1710).[51] It is appropriate that mid-eighteenth-century Britain should acquire buildings, particularly country houses, which self-consciously symbolize imperial achievements. An obvious example is Syon House, a fifteenth- and sixteenth-century construction whose interior Robert Adam rebuilt for the first Duke of Northumberland in the 1760s, with an uncompromisingly classical entrance hall, filled with classical statuary, leading to sumptuously classical rooms. The most imposing of these spaces is the circular Grand Saloon, whose form Adam described as 'new and singular: it is a circle within a circle', decorated with classical statuary.[52] Adam's war on neoclassical dogmatism resulted in a revival of what he considered pure classicism, so that specific forms and spaces would not be repeated slavishly but, as at Syon, would be reinterpreted to suit specific needs and occasions. One way of interpreting Syon is to say that Adam and Northumberland evidently thought (as for instance John Gwynn did) that mercantile Britain had reached a zenith of prosperity comparable to that of imperial Rome, and this conspicuously classical display of wealth – until the Duke called a halt to Adam's extravagance – was a means of expressing their view.[53] The interior spaces of Syon were thus political.

Adam's professed aim was 'to render [Syon] a noble and elegant habitation, not unworthy of a proprietor, who possessed not only wealth to execute a great design, but skill to judge of its merit':[54] the house represented the social status of its owner. Even though Adam had to leave the old exterior of Syon alone, his aim was a specific case of a political commonplace, as William Newton expressed it in 1771, 'that every building should by its appearance express its destination and purpose, and that some character should prevail therein, which is suitable to, and expressive of, the particular end it is to

[51] *Elements*, p. 12. Colen Campbell said the same sort of thing in *Vitruvius Britannicus*, I, p. 1.
[52] *The Works in Architecture of Robert and James Adam*, ed. Robert Oresko (London: Academy, and New York: St Martin's, 1975), pp. 48–49.
[53] Gwynn, *London and Westminster Improved* (London, 1766), p. xv; Adam, *Works*, p. 30; Busby disapproved of Adam's work (*Series*, p. 10).
[54] *The Works in Architecture*, p. 48.

answer.'[55] This had been a familiar notion since Vitruvius had illustrated the meaning of decorum by saying that a solid Doric design was appropriate only for temples dedicated to Minerva, Mars, and Hercules, 'for to these gods, because of their might, buildings ought to be erected without embellishments.'[56] Complaining that the facades of French 'grandes maisons' were scarcely distinguishable from those of artisans' houses, Boffrand insisted that 'des Palais & des Edifices publics . . . doivent être distingués des maisons des marchands & des artisans' (palaces and public buildings should be distinct from the houses of merchants and artisans).[57] But the concept could be applied just to interiors too: in Charles Etienne Briseux's view, the grandeur of interior rooms 'doit être réglée suivant l'état du Maître, & l'étendue du Bâtiment' (should be proportioned according to the status of the master of the house and the extent of the building).[58] The general idea, that buildings represent the human temperament, originated in the traditional derivation of architectural proportions from those of the human body, for as Aldrich's posthumous translator and editor, Philip Smyth, interpreted Palladio, 'His Villas speak themselves the retreats of nobility, veiled but not hid. – If analogy between the human and material fabrics (much resorted to by writers on architecture) be allowable here, perhaps we may not unfitly say that the general effect of Palladio's edifices is similar to that of personal dignity well dressed'.[59] The modernized version of Vitruvian decorum extends the analogy to a point where a house represents the wealth, class and occupation of its owner. So what a monument does for the state, a domestic building does for the private individual.

The demand for this kind of decorum could be heard in numerous areas of eighteenth-century life: architecture merely reflected it. Timothy Nourse, for example, complained, ''Twould be much more suitable to the Gravity of a Court of Justice, were it kept in some Town-House or Market-House' instead of a pub, which he felt lacked the dignity of a magistrate, who should 'not be oblig'd (as may be seen sometimes) to hold a Glass in one hand, whilst he signs a Warrant with the other; tho' much more Eminent was he, who to shew the stediness of his Hand, writ and sign'd a Warrant upon the heaving Belly of a boggy Hostess.'[60] Less colourfully, Aldrich made the obvious observation that a merchant would choose to build a house 'near the exchange, the trader in the principal street; and every other citizen in the same manner would chuse his dwelling according to his occupation', and Blondel knew well that a man of taste 'sçait associer le style de son Architecture à la convenance

[55] Newton's *Vitruvius*, I, vii.
[56] *De Architectura*, I, ii.
[57] *Livre*, pp. 32, 41.
[58] *L'Art de Bâtir des Maisons de Campagne* (Paris, 1743), I, p. 21.
[59] *Elements*, p. lix.
[60] *Campania Fœlix. Or, A Discourse of the Benefits and Improvements of Husbandry* (London, 1700), pp. 166–67.

du Bâtiment' (can accommodate the style of his architecture to the convenience of the building).[61] Even more emphatically and intriguingly, Aldrich thought that

> In marking the proportions of [rooms] the architect should have an eye to the office and dignity of the possessor. Men of ordinary fortune want not houses either large or magnificent. Money lenders and inn holders wish to have them convenient, showy, and well secured from thieves. Lawyers build them with more elegance and space to receive their clients. Merchants require rooms to stow their goods in. Men in office and noblemen demand houses large, lofty, ornamented, and in short princely.[62]

Aldrich merges commercial pragmatism with the inhabitant's desire to let the spatial design of his house represent its purpose.

Aldrich's point had been made before, and continued to be made, unequivocally by Robert Morris, Batty Langley, and Germain Boffrand, who thought it simply common sense that a house should represent the status of its owner, by its site, size, and ornaments.[63] There are numerous examples of this idea in practice. Vanbrugh's castellated design for Blenheim, with its almost forbidding military air of a fortress, alluded to the achievements of its owner, the Duke of Marlborough, as commander of the allied forces during the War of the Spanish Succession.[64] Boullée's planned spherical cenotaph for Newton was intended to represent the great philosopher: 'O Newton! Si par l'étendue de tes lumières et la sublimité de ton génie, tu as déterminé la figure de la terre, moi j'ai conçu le projet de t'envelopper de ta découverte. C'est en quelque façon t'avoir enveloppé de toi-même' (O Newton! If by the extent of your enlightenment and the sublimity of your genius, you have determined the shape of the earth, for my part I have conceived of enshrining you in your own discovery, in a way to envelop you in yourself).[65] Raising the idea from this personal level to a universal one, Palladio had said the Pantheon was so called either because 'it was consecrated to all the gods; or perhaps (as others will have it) because it is of the figure of the world, that is, round'.[66]

Until 1759, when Sir William Chambers introduced the term 'character' into English architectural discourse, the word that was used to indicate this matching of external appearance to the status or temperament of the owner was 'convenience,' a translation of 'convenance.' Confusingly, 'convenience' meant other things as well, such as commodiousness and amenity.[67] One part

[61] *Elements*, pp. 43–44; *Cours*, IV, p. xliv.
[62] *Elements*, p. 45.
[63] *Livre*, p. 11.
[64] Calling the palace the 'House of Pride', Swift thought Blenheim matched Marlborough in quite another way (*Prose Works*, XIV [Oxford: Blackwell, 1968] p. 10).
[65] *Essai*, p. 137.
[66] Palladio, *Four Books of Architecture*, translated by Isaac Ware (London, 1738), p. 99.
[67] See, for instance, Matthew Brettingham, *The Plans, Elevations and Sections, of Holkham in Norfolk*, 2nd edn (London, 1773), p. vii; Blondel, *Cours*, I, pp. 389–90.

of Palladio's own platitude on this ancient ethical and aesthetic topic was that a house should be suited to the condition of its inhabitant and to the place where it is to stand. Batty Langley and Isaac Ware expanded the master's idea, pointing out not only that a law court should be 'grave and solemn' in appearance (Langley) but that 'he would be mad who should build a shed in *Grosvenor Square*, or a palace in *Hedge Lane*; and thus far he will be able to proportion the building to the tenant, or purchaser, though unknown' (Ware).[68] But the concept was not necessarily realized in practice: Thomas Brown noted in 1700 that the foremost 'Amusement' of Bedlam was that 'so stately an Edifice' was built 'for Persons wholly unsensible of the Beauty and Use of it: The Outside is a perfect Mockery to the Inside.'[69] Robert Morris would remind his readers that the architect must take due account of the purpose and use to which a building is put, and therefore must judge the suitability of ornament (or lack of it), a good foundation, 'well-chosen and proper *Materials*, of proportionate Magnitude, and of skilful *Artists* to connect and put them together'.[70] But Balthazar Gerbier had argued for convenience in these terms back in 1662:

Builders ought also to be very curious and carefull in the choice of the place to Build a Seat on, for good Prospect, well Garnisht with Woods, and the Water at hand, not too near, nor too far from a City or Town . . . I must wish all Princes and Noble Persons who are resolved to Build Pallaces and Seats answerable to their quality, to imitate those who in the Heathen age were so carefull in the ordering of the Structure of their Stone Images, especially of their *Saturn, Jupiter, Apollo, Mars, Nepttune,* (and all their Fry of wanton Godesses) as to empannel a Jury of Philosophers, Naturalists, Physiognomists and Anatomists, who were to direct the Sculptors how to Represent those Images.[71]

For Morris, following Vitruvius, the most important aspect of convenience is the suitability of the site: small or irregular sites hamper an architect's design, but a well-chosen site satisfies Gerbier's demands by having suitable supplies of air, sunshine, shade, water, and so on; convenience 'is the just supplying of Wants; it is the Handmaid to Nature, assisting us to what is necessary in Life'.[72] Ware carefully distinguished between city and country houses:

When we speak of a situation we naturally mean that of a house in the country. In cities and great towns business is more regarded than pleasure, and men are confined

[68] Palladio, *Four Books of Architecture*, pp. 37, 46; Langley, *Ancient Masonry, Both in Theory and Practice* (London, 1736), p. 7; Ware, *Complete Body of Architecture*, p. 291. Most of Langley's book is plagiarized from Morris' *Lectures on Architecture*.

[69] *Amusements Serious and Comical, calculated for the Meridian of London* (London, 1700), p. 34. Bedlam – Bethlehem Hospital – had been built in the 1670s to Robert Hooke's design.

[70] Morris, *The Archhitectural Remembrancerr* (London, 1751), p. vi.

[71] *A Brief Discourse concerning the Three Chief Principles of Magnificent Building. Viz. Solidity, Conveniency, and Ornament* (London, 1662), pp. 15–16.

[72] *Lectures on Architecture*, I (London, 1734), p. 81.

to do not what they chuse, but what they can. They are cramp'd for room, and must conform to the method of other buildings: what regards a situation therefore in this respect, concerns rather the placing of streets and squares than of private houses.[73]

In addition to this distinctively spatial concept of convenience (which few sites in a city could ever offer), Palladio thought of a convenient house as one 'whose parts correspond to the whole and to each other': *ordinatio*, as Vitruvius had called it, or ordonnance, as it had become known when Evelyn complained that the word was voguish.[74] As Ware defined ordonnance, 'The composition of a building, and the disposition of its several parts,' though vital, was given no prominence at all by Morris or Langley, but was absorbed in their overall conceptions of Palladianism.[75]

In his *Treatise of Human Nature* (1739) David Hume introduced to his discussion of aesthetics just one architectural analogy, and a telling one, which explicitly employs one of these meanings of 'convenience':

A man, who shews us any house or building, takes particular care among other things to point out the convenience of the apartments, the advantages of their situation, and the little room lost in the stairs, anti-chambers and passages; and indeed 'tis evident, the chief part of the beauty consists in these particulars. The observation of convenience gives pleasure, since convenience is beauty. But after what manner does it give pleasure? 'Tis certain our own interest is not in the least concern'd; and as this is a beauty of interest, not of form, so to speak, it must delight us merely by communication, and by our sympathizing with the proprietor of the lodging. We enter into his interest by the force of imagination, and feel the same satisfaction, that the objects naturally occasion in him.

This observation extends to tables, chairs, scritoires, chimneys, coaches, sadles, ploughs, and indeed to every work of art; it being an universal rule, that their beauty is chiefly deriv'd from their utility, and from their fitness for that purpose, to which they are destin'd. But this is an advantage, that concerns only the owner, nor is there any thing but sympathy, which can interest the spectator.[76]

Hume's aesthetic here is founded entirely on a conception of 'convenience' as amenity. Amenity itself is utility and thus beauty. This pragmatic interpretation of beauty, as Hume makes clear, is of consequence to the spectator only through the medium of 'sympathy' with the owner. As a result, the owner's social status and occupation are of prime importance not only to his own conception of his house, but also to his visitor's interpretation of it. But Hume is not interested in finding that status reflected in the external design, since he describes only the interior of a house. 'Convenience' in the sense of outer and inner harmony is transmuted into an expression of the owner's taste, in

---

[73] Ware, *Complete Body of Architecture*, p. 95.

[74] Evelyn's translation of Roland Fréart, *A Parallel of the Ancient Architecture with the Modern*, 2nd edn (London, 1707), p. 11; Palladio, *Four Books of Architecture*, p. 37; Vitruvius, I, ii, 2.

[75] *Complete Body of Architecture*, p. 27.

[76] *Treatise of Human Nature*, II, pp. 154–55.

this case his taste in furnishings. Hume's example also necessarily implies that the visitor will be of roughly the same social standing as his host, for otherwise he would not be shown around the house.

II

Such writing as I have surveyed so far reveals a conception of architecture as political, especially as it reflects class, wealth, taste, and power. What then of architectural space, specifically? At the end of the eighteenth century, Bromley, noting with his customary intelligence that space had been neglected as a subject in architecture, thought

It cannot be denied that architecture must not found it's [sic] fame merely in the perfection of external design; the interior disposition of the edifice to the purposes for which it is raised constitutes an important part of that fame, although it has not been sufficiently studied, but has indeed been too much overlooked by the best architects in every age.[77]

Bromley was dismayed that ancient Greeks 'occupied a very great, and what should seem a very needless, space in their houses; they appear to have been at the pains of very little contrivance in the distribution of the whole according to art or the best convenience.'[78] Bromley's observations are unusual for the time in calling attention explicitly to space, which he nevertheless perceives as part of the customary concepts of utility and convenience.

Instead of emphasizing space as such, neoclassical theories and definitions of architecture usually find value in utility and convenience, in proportions, in the relationship of ornamental detail to overall design, in architecture's symbolic representations of human temperaments and professions, and broadly in the harmonious relation of parts to wholes. 'For,' as James Gibbs said, 'It is not the Bulk of a Fabrick, the Richness and Quantity of the Materials, the Multiplicity of Lines, nor the Gaudiness of the Finishing, that give the Grace or Beauty and Grandeur to a Building; but the Proportion of the Parts to one another and to the Whole, whether entirely plain, or enriched with a few Ornaments properly disposed.'[79] In such an academic conception of architecture space is important, as it is for Hume, if only in the sense that utility must be a major consideration, but the theorists tend to restrict their commentaries on space to rather generalized questions of relative scale: of large and imposing spaces, such as grand entrance halls and staircases, or small and 'convenient' spaces, such as bedrooms. French and British theorists offer designs that show elevations and floor plans, which together provide a

[77] *Philosophical and Critical History*, I, p. 399; for Bromley's reaction to the opposition his work aroused, see II, preface.
[78] Bromley, *Philosophical and Critical History*, I, p. 399.
[79] Gibbs, *A Book of Architecture, containing designs of buildings and ornaments* (London, 1728), pp. ii–iii.

two-dimensional sense of a building's external appearance and its layout. The experience of penetrating the space of a building is not – perhaps cannot be – suggested by drawings. The same goes for the experience of seeing a building in its environment, whether urban or rural, since the physical surroundings are not usually conveyed by the drawings. Despite the type of depiction known as an 'architect's impression,' which often does include some sense of the immediate environment of a planned building, no one can experience space until a building is constructed. But spatial concepts must be the very foundation of the designs.

It is sometimes difficult to perceive behind all these words about theory and practice, beauty and utility, the political assumption that spaces can determine human actions, rather than vice versa. Baron Haussmann did not invent this assumption in the 1860s and bequeath it to the modern west, as Richard Sennett says, but Haussmann's transformation of modern Paris certainly did harden the assumption into the orthodoxy that

it is a good idea to plan physical space for predetermined social use; that is, instead of assuming that changes in the social structure of the city should be accomplished first in order to change the physical appearance of the city . . . it is somehow better, and certainly easier, to change the physical landscape in order to alter the social patterns of the metropolis.[80]

Framing a space with buildings in a particular idiom expresses a political point about the space. More generally than that, provided spaces do determine activities, then if a theatre is somehow known as a place of entertainment, its users will not treat it as a temple, and so will conform to the activity prescribed by the confederation of owner, designer and builder. Such conformity is really obvious. If labourers are kept in overcrowded, insanitary conditions, they will (it is assumed) adapt to their 'homes' rather than riot or otherwise protest.[81] In Defoe's Newgate Moll Flanders realizes 'how Time, Necessity, and Conversing with the Wretches that are there Familiarizes the Place to them; how at last they become reconcil'd to that which at first was the greatest Dread upon their Spirits in the World.'[82]

The function of a space therefore tends to be more important than the dimensions, proportions, or architectural idiom. In eighteenth-century England interior spaces such as single living rooms in labourers' dwellings were used for virtually all aspects of 'living,' but in larger and more expensive houses with more rooms, each space could have a discrete function, such as one for dining, another for sleeping, and so on.[83] This did not make indivi-

---

[80] Richard Sennett, *The Uses of Disorder: Personal Identity and City Life* (New York: Vintage, 1971), pp. 90–91.

[81] Lewis Mumford, *Culture of Cities* (New York: Harcourt Brace, 1938; reprinted 1970), p. 123.

[82] *Moll Flanders*, Shakespeare Head Edition (Oxford: Blackwell, 1927), II, p. 101.

[83] Robert Adam, *Works* p. 48, noted how the decoration of French and English dining rooms differed, because the French used the room for eating, the English for male conversation about

dual rooms any more private, but effectively marked off boundaries. Exterior 'public' spaces such as city squares were frequently very narrowly defined not by what they were actually used for, but by what someone – patron or designer, usually – restrictively said they should be used for. Analogous to the example of the augural *templum*, assembly rooms were used for assembly, and churches for worship, but there were counter-examples, even if they represented only violations of verbally assigned functions. In a simple way, Hogarth's print, *The Sleeping Congregation* (1736) suggests two unofficial functions of the interior space of a church: sleeping and ogling. Other common examples would be any places used for illegal activities, such as gaming.[84] A single officially or legally sanctioned function might commonly be assigned to a specific space, but the function of an ancient architectural model was not always transferred to a modern building. A church might be designed to resemble a particular reconstruction of Solomon's Temple, but so too might a private house, in which case the functions could scarcely be reconciled. Whatever the Scotsman Robert Adam said about the narrow dogmatism of contemporary architects, a neoclassical building did not necessarily reproduce the style of its classical predecessors, nor imitate the function of its space, since the symbolism of the ancient building could be ignored, adapted, or modernized, and a new function assigned to the new space.[85] Whatever idiom an architect chose to give his building, assigning a specific function to a space immediately limited it, supposedly by limiting the human activity for which the patron intended it. Whether verbal or physical, limitations of space are necessarily political.

A single large focal point, such as the spaces before the steps of St Paul's Cathedral or the Royal Exchange, or the space enclosed in the centre of a typical square in the west end of London, is limited by both the function assigned it and the actual use to which it is put. Perhaps the most extreme case of space that is political in this sense is a Quaker meeting house, whose architecture suggests neither numinosity nor awe, but assembly: it is not a house of God but of God's congregation. In a nearly analogous way, Christopher Wren's galleried churches in the City of London are at least as secular as they are religious, since the churches were superfluous additions to the devotional life of the city.[86] Two connected pragmatic reasons for Wren's almost theatrical galleried interiors are not hard to find: small spaces between

---

politics and for 'the enjoyment of the bottle'. Cf. Mumford, *Culture of Cities*, p. 115; also, Witold Rybczynski, *Home: A Short History of an Idea* (New York: Viking Penguin, 1986).

[84] Cf. Pope, *Dunciad in Four Books*, I, l. 310, note.

[85] Examples of 'modernized' classical temples are John James' St George's, Hanover Square (1720–5), and Nicholas Hawksmoor's St George's Bloomsbury Way (1716–31), two of London's earliest churches to be fronted with classical porticoes. Cf. Bernard Tschumi, 'The Violence of Architecture', *Artforum*, 20, no. 1 (September 1981), 46.

[86] Horton Davies comments on Wren's churches (*Worship and Theology in England: from Andrewes to Baxter and Fox, 1603–1690* [Princeton: Princeton University Press, 1975], pp. 24–29).

existing buildings, which obliged him to build upwards rather than sideways, and money. Obviously, the physical limits of any building, in any environment, are determined by the available land and the amount of money spent on the construction. Once a sophisticated network of credit was established in Britain after the settlement of 1688, the desire for political and financial power could be more easily satisfied if the city could expand above its existing limits, and so rents could rise without the landlord's having to acquire more land. As Swift put it, 'The God of Wealth was therefore made / Sole Patron of the building Trade.'[87] The limits of a square, a street, a group of streets, and a village are similarly determined by those who have access to and control of wealth.

In a residential or commercial district, the political space of the square is especially important. The Greek agora, as Pierre Lavedan suggests, is a physical expression of *polis*, whether the agora be the kind that is divided by streets, which Pausanias describes, or the Ionian, which consists of self-contained space. In Lavedan's view, because the agora is a public meeting place, the primary function of the space is political.[88] As political space, the agora anticipated the Roman forum, itself adapted by urban developments elsewhere in western Europe in the seventeenth and eighteenth centuries. In 1789 Philip Smyth drew a significant distinction by noting that English speakers often misuse the word *piazza* 'by employing it to signify the surrounding Porticos, e.g. of Covent Garden, instead of the large Area they inclose, where the market is held, which is the real Piazza, or Place.' (One writer was making this 'mistake' in the same year.)[89] Wealth determines the limits of the square but the space itself, not the limiting buildings, defines it.

Medieval European city squares, as Leonardo Benevolo points out, were not merely self-contained open spaces, but were integral to larger street plans: 'Only the lesser streets were intended to act purely as thoroughfares: all the other ones were designed to be used as places to stop, to conduct business or for holding meetings.'[90] By means of such enclosed areas the medieval city bequeathed to modern urbanism spaces that were more public and more organized than the classical precedent as interpreted in the eighteenth century ever did. But as the modern city began to adapt itself to more wheeled traffic, streets began to be designed for transport rather than meet-

87 *Poems*, ed. Harold Williams, 2nd edn (Oxford: Clarendon, 1958), p. 79. And see Mumford, *Culture of Cities*, p. 93.
88 *Histoire de l'urbanisme* (Paris: Henri Laurens, 1926–41), I, pp. 112, 135, 169; Pausanias, *Description of Greece*, VI, xxiv, 2.
89 Smyth, introduction to Aldrich, *Elements*, p. xv; *The Rudiments of Ancient Architecture* (London, 1789), p. 79.
90 *The History of the City*, translated by Geoffrey Culverwell (Cambridge, Mass.: MIT Press, 1980), p. 308, and cf. Mumford, *Culture of Cities*, p. 56. Nourse lamented the degeneration of the inn from a meeting place for business to a site of 'Drunkenness and Debauchery' (*Campania Fœlix*, pp. 163–64). The typical meeting place in the country was enclosed, like an inn, but that in the city was an open street.

ing. The new word for the modern function of these streets, paradoxically, was 'communication.' The London square, in particular, was tending to become an oasis in a city relentlessly on the move.

Writing at the end of the seventeenth century, D'Aviler recognized two distinct types of square, implicitly consonant with the different activities that took place within them: the place of residence (usually the more splendid), and the market.[91] By combining both public streets and private parks in a single space, many of the new squares of fashionable Georgian London seem to have been a compromise between public function and private usage, but with the overriding purpose of being residential areas, not markets (which might be situated nearby as part of the local development). The central areas of Grosvenor Square or St James's Square may have been intended as symmetrical showpieces, but instead of imitating an Athenian agora or Roman forum or eighteenth-century Covent Garden, they were exclusive places for private residents and so were reserved for only very limited public assembly.[92] Complete with grass, trees, and shrubs, the space in the centre of a new London square shows how easily *rus in urbe* could be realized, and, vice versa, William Mason extolled Chambers for impressing upon his fellow pleasure-takers that the perfect garden 'must contain within itself all the amusements of a great city; that *Urbs in rure*, not *Rus in urbe*, is the thing, which an improver of true taste ought to aim at.'[93] The wealthy and leisured classes did indeed bring the country into town. These central areas were spatial luxuries in the sense that they were destined to be used neither for actual residence nor for trade, but for pleasure, sometimes only the residents' negative pleasure of seeing them empty of people who had no right to use them. Spaces like these were therefore expressions of social division.

Even with such limited social use, the space in the middle of a typical square in Mayfair or Bloomsbury expresses communal will. Although delimiting space as these squares do is a statement of private ownership and a display of wealth, it is also the product of collaboration, however fragmented, of an exclusive group of landowners, designers, builders, and residents. Residents were relatively unlikely to have much interest in the disposition of space in a neighbouring district unless they owned land in it. As a result, the design of an eighteenth-century city or of major extensions to it was usually the product of discrete units of collaboration, linked – sometimes adventitiously – into a larger urban complex by the dominant tastes of landowners, designers, and builders. There is of course no role for the disenfranchised poor in making decisions about any urban space, least of all an expensive one like Grosvenor

---

91 *Cours d'Architecture*, II, p. 198.

92 Covent Garden had previously been the Bedford family's private garden. See Robert Thorne's brief account: *Covent Garden Market: Its History and Restoration* (London: Architectural Press, 1974).

93 *Heroic Epistle to Sir William Chambers* (London, 1773), p. 4; Mumford, *Culture of Cities*, p. 138.

Square. This disposition of private property in Georgian London enabled the city eventually to become, like Second Empire Paris in Benevolo's phrasing, 'a vast discriminatory apparatus, which confirmed the dominion of the strong over the weak.'[94] The environments of modern cities were shaped by the interests of minorities of owners, like London's handful of wealthy families, rather than by majorities of tenants.[95] The spaces of modern central London became a collective emblem of the ideology of the wealthy, and have remained so.

Delorme had no recourse to specific examples, but thought that houses and cities, 'qui equipollent à vn petit Royaume' (which are equivalent to a little kingdom), comprised individual parts and members in precisely the same way as the body economic and the body politic with the proportions of the human body ('Belle comparaison') providing the model.[96] The body politic and the body architectural are analogies of one another, because they both express the same hierarchy, a point deftly made by pageants and festival programmes, which show how architecture is the theatre for human activity.[97] The political structure of the household is presumably the sort of analogy Palladio had in mind when he wrote that 'the city is as it were but a great house, and, on the contrary, a country house is a little city',[98] which might imply that houses and cities evolve in parallel. Palladio recognized that one of the joys of country life was that 'we are not confined (as commonly happens in cities) by publick walls, or those of our neighbours, to certain and determinate bounds.'[99] Beyond sharing a common origin in contemporary taste, they hardly could be analogous in any physical way. The boundaries of the country, the city, and the house are dissimilar forms of limitation.[100] It was often no more than a *jeu d'esprit* to interpret Suetonius as Blondel did, 'on auroit pris . . . l'étang pour une mer, & l'assemblage de ces édifices [at Nero's palace] pour une Ville' (the pond would be taken for a sea, and the collection of buildings for a town).[101] Facile parallels between the house and the city neglect the economy of the city's spaces, but they emphasise a habit of conceiving structures as microcosms, particularly (but not exclusively) of the state.[102]

Cities have themselves often been taken as microcosms. Robert Burton loved poring over maps, especially 'those books of cities, put out by Braunus and Hogenbergius', who thought their own important collection of urban

[94] *History of the City*, pp. 786–87.
[95] Mumford, *Culture of Cities*, p. 26.
[96] *Premier Tome*, preface, fol. 3, recto.
[97] Alan J. Plattus, 'Emblems of the City: Civic Pageantry and the Rhetoric of Urbanism,' *Artforum*, 20, no. 1 (September 1981), 48–52; see also Rykwert, *Idea of a Town*, pp. 188–89.
[98] *Four Books of Architecture*, p. 47.
[99] *Ibid.* p. 46.
[100] Cf. Lavedan, *Histoire de l'urbanisme*, I, p. 59.
[101] Blondel, *Cours*, I, p. 50. Suetonius said only that the pond was 'like a sea, surrounded with buildings to represent cities' (*Lives of the Caesars*, VI, xxxi, 1).
[102] Rykwert, *Idea of a Town*, p. 24.

maps provided 'the universal form of the earth,' so even a map of a city was not so much referential as microcosmic.[103] From their vantage point in the mercantile northern Europe of the 1570s Braun and Hogenberg concluded that Greek civilization proved that 'nobilissima Architectura, in summo collocata fastidio, totius Vniuersi ornamentum, iure nominatur' (the noblest architecture, put together with the finest taste, may justly be called the ornament of the entire universe).[104]

The idea of the city as microcosm is common in Utopian writing, too. Johann Valentin Andreae's ideal city, Christianopolis, was to be on an antarctic island, its form a triangle, its perimeter about 30 miles: 'a whole world in miniature', a marriage of heaven and earth in peace.[105] Utopists did not usually imagine triangular cities: the typical plan would be circular (symbolic of harmony) or star-shaped (for efficient defence), and a few cities were actually laid out according to these shapes.[106]

Perhaps the most commonly cited example of an urban microcosm was the city of Rome, which was often said to be not just the centre of the Empire, but a whole world, for the Empire was a city and 'Rome' was metonymy for 'Empire'.[107] When 'Athenian' Stuart said that 'From beginnings by no means splendid,' the Roman Empire's policy had raised a 'stupendous . . . superstructure',[108] he did not need to labour the point that the political structure was inseparable from the spatial structure that contained it.

Analysis of houses and cities as microcosms of political structures and as images of social structures frequently results in the negative conclusion that architecture is passive as soon as a building is completed, and therefore cannot act as a political instrument.[109] This conclusion suggests that architectural *design* embodies a political expression, of the will of designer and patron, and so of the society to which they belong, but to say this is to take too little account of space. The microcosmic analogies show strikingly that architectural space, inherently passive, is filled with the actions of people. Space is not passive if people can change its function at will. Therefore human action determines the nature of spaces, and their relationship, especially in a city. This may be

---

[103] Georg Braun and Frans Hogenberg, *Civitates Orbis Terrarum*, 6 vols. (Cologne, 1572–1617); reprinted in 3 vols (Cleveland and New York: World Publishing Co., 1966), I, p. vii.

[104] *Ibid.*, sig. E, recto.

[105] *Christianopolis: An Ideal State of the Seventeenth Century* [1619], translated by Felix Emil Held (London: Oxford University Press, 1916), p. 143.

[106] For example, Freudenstadt, Karlsruhe, Mannheim, Grenoble, Naples, Nancy. One might think also of the semi-circular plan of Amsterdam, and innumerable districts of other cities. Cf. Siegfried Giedion, *Space, Time and Architecture: The Growth of a New Tradition*, 5th edn (Cambridge, Mass.: Harvard University Press, 1967), pp. 41–54, and Norman J. Johnston, *Cities in the Round* (Seattle and London: University of Washington Press, 1983).

[107] *History of the City*, p. 140.

[108] James Stuart, *The Antiquities of Athens*, III (1794), p. i. For Stuart, see David Watkins' concise study, *Athenian Stuart: Pioneer of the Greek Revival* (London: George Allen and Unwin, 1982).

[109] Tschumi, 'Questions of Space', 141.

a good reason why Utopias are almost always political statements, which indeed frequently consist of objections to the political status quo, because they suggest not only ideal human behaviour but also new ways of symbolising human behaviour in the disposition of buildings. Robert Fishman argues that 'To build the ideal city is to create the utopian society. . . . The ideal city . . . does not challenge the limits imposed by power so much as ignore them',[110] but ignoring them *is* challenging them, because it is radical defiance of the political values that impose those limits. Utopists make their most overtly political statement by acknowledging that their ideal city 'has no history; indeed, it is an escape from history.'[111] Unlike Utopian cities, a real city is usually the product not of a single mind, but of a dominant social group's diverse and vital aspirations: the city is therefore limited and shaped by the history of its political structure.[112]

Whatever the relationship between public areas and private property, however much or little it changes, the city expresses the relationship itself, and so expresses human life within the city. The city is the history of 'civilization'.[113] The history of cities is consequently the most important aspect of the human use of space. Looking at the ruins of ancient Athens, Charles Cameron thought in 1772 that 'we collect into one point of view the succession of Empire, and the progress of the Arts'.[114] In the eighteenth century, as in other periods, the origins and history of cities – especially Rome, but also Paris, Athens, Babylon and Jerusalem – were crucial to the development of an architectural purpose and idiom, since these cities provided an historical sanction and justification for modern practice.[115]

The origin of the city, as Benevolo puts it, lies in the expansion of a class of people who were released, for one reason or another, from the obligation to work the land, and 'who were supported by the surplus produced by the cultivators': the city was the 'hub' of the development of 'two distinct social classes – the ruling elite and the subordinates'.[116] There is no doubting that the eighteenth-century western city reinforced this political distinction in practice, but published theory rarely offered any serious alternative to the account of the origins of urbanism put forward by Vitruvian commentators. Cities were taken to have developed from rural settlements whose site and size were determined by the potential for cultivation of the land, and the location of the markets in which the settlers could dispose of their produce. Adapting this pedigree, Patte found the origin of cities in the proximity of

---

[110] 'Utopia in Three Dimensions: The Ideal City and the Origins of Modern Design,' in *Utopias*, ed. Peter Alexander and Roger Gill (London: Duckworth, 1984), p. 95.
[111] *Ibid.*, p. 96.
[112] *Ibid.*, p. 98.
[113] And since 'civis' means 'citizen', 'civilization' is semantically associated with the city.
[114] *Baths of the Romans*, p. iii.
[115] Cf. Mumford, *Culture of Cities*, p. 92.
[116] *History of the City*, p. 16.

the houses of parents and children, who would then move on together in search of new land to cultivate.[117] It was generally agreed that the earliest villages and towns were 'inorganic', meaning that the design of the settlement was determined by the terrain, not by the conscious art of men with a firm grasp of 'design'. Loudon would add: 'Such is the superiority of rural occupations and pleasures, that commerce, large societies, or crowded cities, may be justly reckoned unnatural. Indeed, the very purpose for which we engage in commerce is, that we may one day be enabled to retire to the country.'[118]

As Loudon's words imply, the city has always been a fiscal and political structure. The Vitruvian argument cannot conceal the political origins of the city simply because it associates political organization uniquely with the flourishing of the arts under imperial Rome. A city consists of people first, walls, streets, and buildings second. As the vast cities of modern history grew, people ceased to know even their neighbours, and began to pursue such unimaginably numerous, diverse, and separate ends, that the community was replaced with millions of individual, independent units. This was Baudelaire's impersonal Paris and, often, Dickens's London, but it was also the Georgian London that did away with the street's spaces as meeting places.[119]

These political aspects of architectural space, rather than some appreciation of proportion and ornament, support one of the most familiar formulations in eighteenth-century English literature. The city – nearly always London – is contrasted with the country in poem after poem, and novel after novel. Ian Donaldson summarizes conveniently:

Since classical times it has been a common rhetorical pastime to play upon these neuroses: to deplore the iniquities of the city and speak affectionately of the virtues of the country life; and (alternatively) to deplore the uncouthness and boredom of the country life, and speak affectionately of the civilizing excitements of the city.[120]

In eighteenth-century England, the attitudes that Donaldson recognizes are based primarily on patterns of social intercourse, and only secondarily on space.[121] But space is crucially important for social life, and thus for the attractions of city and country, because the longer distances between houses in the country had a direct influence on the frequency of social visits, and the

---

[117] Patte, *Mémoires*, pp. 1–2.

[118] John Claudius Loudon, *A Treatise on Forming, Improving, and Managing Country Residences* (London: Longman, Hurst, Rees and Orme, 1806), pp. 4–5.

[119] Benevolo, *History of the City*, p. 798. See also Max Weber, *The City*, translated by Don Martindale and Gertrud Neuwirth (New York: Free Press, 1958), p. 61. Rykwert, *Idea of a Town*, p. 23, refers to Hobbes's translation of Thucydides, VII, section 63, to credit Nicias (in his speech to the Athenian troops) with a definition of a city as people first. Nothing close to it appears in Nicias' speech, nor can I find the sentiment elsewhere in Thucydides or in any edition of Hobbes's translaton, from the first (1629) to the most recent, ed. Richard Schlatter (New Brunswick: Rutgers University Press, 1975).

[120] 'The Satirists' London', *Essays in Criticism*, 25 (1975), 107.

[121] See, for instance, Wycherley, *The Country Wife*, IV, i.

correspondingly shorter distances in the city meant more frequent social contact. Also, assembly rooms and theatres were ostensibly public but, like the central space of St James's Square, were actually exclusive. The excitements of the city might easily be connected intimately with the socially exclusive, truly 'private' nature of supposedly 'public' space. The country offered little or nothing of this kind.[122]

Like its individually exclusive spaces, the whole city is an emblem of enclosure, for enclosed spaces shut some people in just as effectively as they shut others out. The country encloses too, just as conspicuously. Between 1714 and 1820, the incredible number of 3,602 acts of enclosure passed through Parliament, most of them after 1760, but common land always had been enclosed, by the spaces around it.[123] Farmers and landowners, the advocates of enclosure, were seeking not only to boost their profits at the expense of labourers and smallholders, but also to bolster an existing social structure. Loudon's praise of 'the progress of improvement' necessitated enclosure 'over the greater part of the country. This would lead to a progressive step of refinement, in order to preserve the proper distinction.'[124] Back in 1700 Timothy Nourse had viewed enclosure as simultaneously aesthetic and political: 'a Common, upon the matter, is nothing but a Naked Theater of Poverty, both as to Men and Beasts, where all things appear horrid and uncultivated, and may be term'd, not improperly, the very abstract of Degenerated Nature' and yet commons could be preferable to enclosure because they support more people. And, Nourse condescended to admit, poverty does not matter if it is not so dire as to cause parish relief, for 'were it not for these poor Labourers, the Rich themselves would soon become poor; for either they must labour and Till the Ground themselves, or suffer it to ly waste, and in the end Common'.[125] Enclosure was obviously a matter of marking boundaries for political purposes as well as profit.

Although social spaces in the country and the city are different in kind, the literary obsession with the contrast shows that both country and city are organizations which impose a distinct political order on their inhabitants by limiting space. Social spaces in the country tend to be country houses for the relatively wealthy, cottages for the poor, village pubs, churches, churchyards, and market places. Social spaces in cities fall roughly into two types: the apparently private spaces of houses, and rooms within houses, and the apparently public spaces of streets, squares, and the interiors of 'public' buildings such as assembly halls. Numerous factors must qualify such terms as 'private'

[122] On 'country' entertainments, see Mark Girouard, *Life in the English Country House: A Social and Architectural History* (New Haven: Yale University Press, 1978), pp. 191–94.

[123] William Holdsworth, *A History of English Law*, XI (London: Methuen and Sweet & Maxwell, 1938), p. 625.

[124] Loudon, *Treatise*, p. 8. W. A. Speck cautions that too much importance can be attached to enclosure (*Stability and Strife: England, 1714–1760* [London: Edward Arnold, 1977], p. 131).

[125] Nourse, *Campania Fœlix*, pp. 99–100.

and 'public'. Naturally using his own modern interpretations of 'private' and 'public', Bromley found the disposition of ancient Greek city houses odd, but accountable as soon as one remembered the Greek style of living, which allotted every individual a separate space.[126] Bromley also detected a disparity between the Greeks' frugality in private life and space and their ostentation in public building.[127] Richard Pococke made a similar observation about the Egyptians.[128] Such considerations of private and public are just as important in eighteenth-century British life. If privacy means the opportunity to withdraw into voluntary isolation, few eighteenth-century British individuals enjoyed much privacy in their entire lives. Although interior space within the house was beginning to be specialized, individual members of a family still shared their spaces in two senses. Bedrooms and beds were often still shared and, at least in the more expensive new houses, apparently individual spaces (like bedrooms and 'closets') were connected by a corridor. This internal 'communicating' space fulfilled a function analogous to the space of a street: as house doors give on to the street, so room doors give on to the corridor. To families in such houses, privacy seems to have meant limited community rather than complete isolation. Even solitary confinement in prison was rare: it was more likely for lunatics than for criminals.[129]

III

Late in the eighteenth century and early in the nineteenth, plans for new cities were being published as frequently as ever, but plans for country dwellings and model villages were also beginning to emerge in such considerable numbers that 'Some persons have thought the public taste has been vitiated', and that pattern books have replaced architects: 'This is an erroneous opinion', announced Busby.[130] Some of these plans proposed public spaces that were meant to be 'common'. One such scheme was John Plaw's model village, which enclosed an oval space in the centre, where 'a Church or Chapel would be both convenient and picturesque'.[131] Plaw was one of a growing number of British architects and planners who were giving their professional

[126] Bromley, *Philosophical and Critical History*, I, p. 400.

[127] *Ibid.*, I, p. 405.

[128] Pococke, *A Description of the East*, I, p. 220.

[129] Lawrence Stone, *The Family, Sex and Marriage in England 1500–1800* (New York: Harper & Row, 1977), pp. 253–56; Philippe Ariès, *Centuries of Childhood: A Social History of Family Life*, translated by Robert Baldick (New York: Knopf, 1962), pp. 398–400; Mumford, *Culture of Cities*, pp. 40, 115. See also Michel Foucault, *Discipline and Punish: the Birth of the Prison*, translated by Alan Sheridan (1978; New York: Vintage, 1979), esp. p. 11. John Bender, *Imagining the Penitentiary: Fiction and Architecture of Mind in Eighteenth-Century England* (Chicago: University of Chicago Press, 1987) convincingly argues that authority is expressed in prison design (especially later in the century) and in fictional narrative, both being part of one discourse.

[130] Busby, *Series*, p. 12.

[131] *Ferme Ornee, or Rural Improvements* (London: I. & J. Taylor, 1796), commentary on plate 33.

attention to *all* types of building, and so for the first time to designs for individual cottages for labourers.[132] Model villages had been in existence since at least the 1720s, when the cottages adjacent to Robert Walpole's Houghton estate were built,[133] but only in the 1790s did the interior disposition of the cottages that constituted such villages begin to receive serious scrutiny.

The purpose behind the design of either the cottage or the village was still the same as it had been when Leonardo da Vinci offered his proposals to the Duke of Milan for mass-produced workers' housing: to build a cheap, reproducible habitation. Robert Lugar calculated his sketches of cottages 'for those persons whose liberal minds may lead them to accommodate their peasantry and dependants with dwellings, and at the same time to embellish their domains with a variety of picturesque buildings, which shall be both ornamental and useful'.[134] Once a basic plan for a single cottage was established, a uniform village required no further effort of design. Writing in or before 1781, John Wood the Younger turned his attention to cottages, perceiving a regular gradation from a 'simple hut' to a 'superb palace': and besides, he said, 'a palace is nothing more than a cottage IMPROVED'.[135] Improvement, in Wood's view, meant proper materials, a healthy site, good lighting, heating, and ventilation. We can recognize the politics of his proposals easily by hearing what Lugar had to say about materials: 'Bricks and tiles may be considered as not suitable for a peasant's Cottage; the costliness of the materials exclude [*sic*] lowliness from the mind, destroys simplicity, and consequently character'.[136] Countering the usual practice of the wealthy, who imprisoned their poor tenants in uncomfortably cramped cottages made from flimsy materials, Wood proposed sturdy structures, each with a garden, outside toilet and – most radically – a minimum ceiling height for rooms. The height he recommended, 7ft 6in, is the standard legal minimum for rooms in all new houses in the United States today. At the time Wood was writing, the ceiling of a drawing room in a country house might be as high as eighteen feet, thus tending to 'superhumanize' the inhabitants, as Auden said.[137] At first Wood's advice went unheeded in the city and the country: there are many all too depressing examples of cramped dwellings, however good the planners' intentions may have been on occasion. Auden was right: 'a pen / for a rational animal / is no fitting habitat for Adam's / sovereign clone.'[138]

[132] Blondel too thought architecture included all types of building (*Cours*, III, p. xiv).

[133] Begun in 1724, the new village was built outside the walls of the Houghton estate.

[134] *Architectural Sketches for Cottages, Rural Dwellings, and Villas, in the Grecian, Gothic, and Fancy Styles* (London: J. Taylor, 1805), preface, n.p.

[135] *Series of Plans for Cottages or Habitations of the Labourer*, 2nd edn (London: J. Taylor, 1806), p. 3. Although the engraved plates are dated 1781, the year of Wood's death, the first edition was not published until 1792.

[136] Lugar, *Architectural Sketches*, p. 7.

[137] W. H. Auden, 'Thanksgiving for a Habitat: Prologue: The Birth of Architecture', *About the House* (New York: Random House, 1965), p. 6.

[138] *Ibid.*, p. 6.

In cities, but not in the country, overall heights of buildings had been recommended or legally restricted as long ago as Augustus's edict that *insulae* accommodating Rome's proletariat were to be no higher than six stories, about seventy feet. Trajan had ordered a reduction of one story, to a total height of about sixty feet.[139] Apart from London's post-Fire legislation of 1667, which included an attempt to limit heights as a safety precaution, there is scant evidence before Wood's book of any interest either in minimum heights of rooms as conducive to health, or in consideration of personal space. The few comments on heights of buildings and rooms refer usually to an aesthetic conception of visual uniformity. Alberti, for instance, wanted all buildings in his ideal city to be the same height. In Lavedan's persuasive view, such a desire as this is an attempt at harmonization but above all a political act, because uniformity suggests conformity among the subjects of the state.[140] Additional upper stories also pragmatically prevented expanding cities from spilling out beyond their walls, accommodated an increasing population, and therefore gave landlords another opportunity to increase income from rent. It had happened in Augustan Rome, and at the end of the sixteenth century the same thing had happened again in London, when John Stow wrote that buildings were rising to four and five stories 'for winning of ground'.[141] The tendency continued during the seventeenth and eighteenth centuries, particularly in London, Edinburgh, and Paris.

In 1792, when Wood the Younger's book was published posthumously, it was revolutionary that anyone should consider the conditions of a mere rural labourer's dwelling individually important at all. The climate of opinion against which Wood was working is perhaps best illustrated by the attitude of John Gwynn, who came up with a plan for redesigning and rebuilding parts of London in 1766. In Gwynn's scheme, the 'most deplorable objects that human nature can furnish', the wretched inhabitants of a notorious slum district, Broad St Giles, were simply to be removed, but Gwynn does not suggest where they could be expected to go.[142] The reason for his proposal was that the main road curved there, taking the reluctant traveller through a slum, hard by Hogarth's Gin Lane, which the fashionable eye would rather not be forced to see.[143] Gwynn's preference for wide, straight boulevards, rather like Haussmann's in Paris a century later, was determined only by the

139 Benevolo, *History of the City*, pp. 176–77.
140 *Histoire de l'urbanisme*, II, p. 32.
141 *A Survey of London*, ed. Charles Lethbridge Kingsford (Oxford: Clarendon Press, 1908), I, p. 194.
142 *London and Westminster Improved*, p. 9. Without intending to be whimsically even-handed, Gwynn also recommended the demolition of Burlington House (p. 82). See also John Archer, *The Literature of British Domestic Architecture 1715–1842* (Cambridge, Mass.: MIT Press, 1985), p. 111.
143 Gwynn, *London and Westminster Improved*, p. 9. Gwynn's plan was realized in 1847, when New Oxford Street was built to join High Holborn and Oxford Street.

need for 'a quiet and easy communication' between the east and west ends of the 'great commercial city'.[144] His new thoroughfares would help merchants to conduct their business more rapidly and profitably, but the poorer inhabitants of districts that got in the way of his straight lines were to be swept aside and ignored.

The mere fact that the more democratic ideology of John Wood the Younger came into existence is of considerable consequence. Wood's successors claimed to satisfy 'the humane desire of increasing the comforts and improving the condition of the Labouring Poor', as Joseph Gandy said, but rather than the altruism that these words might suggest, Gandy's main aim was 'the advancement of Public Taste', which dictated 'that we should combine convenience of arrangement with elegance in the external appearance; a point of much consequence to the general aspect of the country'. Busby and Lugar said much the same.[145] At least these men had made some advance on the repugnant philosophy of Timothy Nourse, who approved of 'poor Cottages' because their 'lazy' inhabitants,

inur'd to all manner of Hardships, prove excellent good Labourers, where they are kept in order; and as they are exceeding serviceable for the Country Affairs in Times of Peace, so are they most useful in Time of War, for the same reason of being bred hardy, and when reform'd by Discipline will make good rough, cross-grain'd Soldiers enough, fit to kill or be kill'd.[146]

Wood's concern with decent living conditions for the rural labouring poor was initially motivated not by any wish for picturesque pretty views, nor obviously by any wish to breed men for slaughter, but by a humane desire to relieve his fellow men from serious, unnecessary distress. Tourists sometimes think a cottage is picturesque because they walk down a step or two to enter by the front door, but the steps have to be there, as Wood knew, only because inadequate foundations cause the building to sink, thus encouraging rising damp.[147] Wood's warm humanity was affected by profit, as well as altruism, for if 'that useful and necessary rank of men, the LABOURERS' lived in an unhealthy situation they themselves would be unhealthy, unproductive, and unprofitable to their employers: since Wood was of course trying to persuade employers to adopt his building schemes, his argument was judicious.[148]

While several authors made Wood's point in one way or another, a few clung to the nostalgic and misleading image of the benevolent landlord gra-

[144] *Ibid.*, p. 7.

[145] Gandy, *Designs for Cottages, Cottage Farms, and Other Rural Buildings* (London: John Harding, 1805), p. iii. Busby, *Series*, p. 13; Lugar, *Architectural Sketches*, preface, n.p. See Summerson, 'The Vision of J. M. Gandy', in *Heavenly Mansions, and other Essays on Architecture* (1948; New York: Norton, 1963), pp. 111–34.

[146] Nourse, *Campania Fœlix*, p. 100.

[147] Wood, *Series*, p. 4.

[148] *Ibid.*, p. 3.

ciously providing a pleasant residence for his loyal servants, and taking pleasure in 'promoting the happiness and prosperity of an industrious peasantry'.[149] Similarly, William Mason's sentimental verses associated the impoverished peasantry with God's bounty.[150] In Lugar's view, the purpose in giving labourers 'a comfortable habitation' was to 'afford real satisfaction to the benevolent mind', that is, the mind of the landlord.[151] Some other writers – William Gilpin, for example – associated benevolence more broadly with general taste, rather than with individual landowners. In *Three Essays on Picturesque Beauty* Gilpin says benevolence is 'nearly allied' to 'that complacency of mind' which nature's 'tranquil scenes' can inspire.[152]

Complementing this sentimental concept of benevolence, Delorme had judged 200 years earlier that architecture kept vagrants off the streets, and similar justifications of expenditure on building recurred in the seventeenth and eighteenth centuries. Sir William Temple maintained that both gardening and building helped to 'employ many hands, and circulate money among the poorer sort and artisans', and were therefore 'a public service to one's country'.[153] Roger North echoed Temple, adding that 'superfluous mony cannot be better imployed'.[154] North does not say what happens when there is no superfluity of money, but intones: 'To maintaine idly mean men and their familys, is to nourish vice and imorality, as will happen if their time be not filled with drudgery for a lively hood.'[155]Such justification of building – even of Timon's Villa in Pope's *Epistle to Burlington* – had become a standard theme by the time Richard Pococke concluded in 1745: 'A taste for architecture has had effects very much to the honour of our country: Painting and sculpture are such embellishments as are not without their use, circulate the money of the great among the ingenious, and from them to the lower rank of people, and encourage arts and sciences.'[156] Predictably, new buildings in eighteenth-century Britain often expressed the ideology of emergent capitalism in the guise of benevolence: the predominant neo-Palladian style was classical, conservative, representative of the affluence of a prosperous trading nation. And certainly the architects, masons, carpenters, plasterers, and

---

[149] Loudon, *Treatise*, p. 6.
[150] *The English Garden* (York, 1783), II, ll. 409–16.
[151] Lugar, *The Country Gentleman's Architect* (London: J. Taylor, 1807), p. 3.
[152] (London, 1792), p. 47.
[153] 'Upon the Gardens of Epicurus', in *Five Miscellaneous Essays*, ed. Samuel Holt Monk (Ann Arbor: University of Michigan Press, 1963), p. 31.
[154] *Of Building: Roger North's Writings on Architecture*, ed. Howard Colvin and John Newman (Oxford: Clarendon Press, 1981), p. 4. North wrote the manuscript in 1698.
[155] *Ibid.*
[156] *A Description of the East*, II, p. 277; Sir William Chambers said that architecture introduces commerce, wealth, and luxury (*A Treatise on Civil Architecture* [London, 1759], p. i). Pope, *Epistle to Burlington*, lines 169–72, in *Epistles to Several Persons*, ed. F. W. Bateson, Twickenham Edition of the Poems of Alexander Pope, III, ii (London: Methuen, and New Haven: Yale University Press, 1951), pp. 148–49.

unskilled labourers involved in the construction of houses of all sizes could expect to be paid reasonably well as long as the work lasted.[157]

Putting labourers in cottages ranged in a pleasing geometric pattern, such as Plaw proposed, had little genuine connection with benevolence in the 1790s, and even less with the needs and desires of the labourers themselves. Unlike Plaw, Wood the Younger deliberately set out 'to feel as the cottager himself', for 'no architect can form a convenient plan, unless he ideally places himself in the situation of the person for whom he designs', so he went 'to enquire after the conveniencies he [the labourer] wanted, and into the inconveniencies he laboured under'.[158] One of Wood's footnotes records a row of cottages in Dorchester 'in which there has not been the least attention paid either to the principles of sound building, or to decency, or conveniency'. These cottages were dreadfully cramped and indecently overcrowded, too hot in summer, too cold in winter, in danger of collapse, and at a shilling a week, exorbitantly expensive to rent.[159] Wood's increasingly depressing, first hand observations reveal that 'the poor man wishes for conveniency, but knows not how to remedy himself; and would be decent, was it in his power'.[160] Labourers might have put thoughts of a dry, warm house before any plan like Plaw's for the tidy disposition of their own and their neighbours' houses around a village church, but the interest of most planners who proposed model villages was only incidentally to meet the needs of labourers, and was mainly to make individual houses conform to a more comprehensive spatial design, which, like their urban equivalents, in turn implied the inhabitants' conformity to the authority that imposed the design.

For as long as labourers' cottages had been excluded from the professional architect's interest, only more spacious houses, 'for Persons of more independent circumstances' than labourers, needed to be treated with any seriousness,[161] but as soon as Wood demanded proper consideration of workers' cottages, he spoiled the humanistic conception of buildings as objects to be seen from the outside, because he brought 'architecture' into the lowest social stratum, where 'building' had previously been considered sufficient.[162] In

---

[157] A General Description of all Trades (London, 1747), pp. 36–37, 55, 136: 'Master-builders', that is, architects, 'obtain good Estates', and might turn over £500 per annum. Bricklayers earned 1s 8d or 2s per day; journeymen made 2s 6d to 3s 6d a day, and 'to set up a Master' required £200 or more. R. Campbell Esq. of London advised that stonemasons could expect to be unemployed for the four winter months, bricklayers for five or even six months, 'and, in and about London, drink more than one Third of the other Six' (The London Tradesman [London, 1747], p. 159).

[158] Wood, Series, p. 3.

[159] Ibid., p. 7. Even Nourse objected to such exploitation by voracious landlords (Campania Fœlix, p. 103).

[160] Wood, Series, p. 7.

[161] Plaw's design was intended to be adaptable to any scale (Ferme Ornee, commentary on plate 33).

[162] Cf. Lise Bek, Towards Paradise on Earth: Modern Space Conception in Architecture, a Creation of Renaissance Humanism, Analecta Romana Instituti Danici IX, supplement (Odense: University

the case of larger, more imposing and impressive houses, the spectator who remained a spectator, and not a participant, was excluded from the intimacy of the interior, so that exteriors could be used to emphasize the alienating role of authority and rule. The answer to Wood's awkward proposals was to emphasize the organized, regular pattern of a village of workers' houses, so that interior space would remain less important than a gentleman's perception of the exterior.[163]

Concepts of both interior and exterior space depend to a great degree on perception, especially that of wholes rather than parts. Samuel Johnson pragmatically recognized the contrast between a distant view of a city and a view of it from within: it is the contrast between splendour and wretchedness.[164] Gwynn quoted Johnson on the title page of his *London and Westminster Improved*, for which Johnson wrote the dedication to the king. Planners like Gwynn and Wren in the city or Plaw and Gandy in the country sought to impose a comprehensive scheme on the inhabitants: they tended to be remote spectators seeing only the splendour. Such distant perception is a variant of the idea of seeing wholes rather than parts.[165] As Swift showed in Gulliver's encounter with Laputa's mad architects, who try to build from the roof downwards, the most important of all the theoretical considerations for the neoclassical designer was the emphasis on understanding the whole, even if the whole is so hard to perceive, harder still to imagine from drawings.[166] What then did neoclassical theorists mean when they talked of the desirability of understanding the whole?

Gwynn's scheme for 'improving' London depended on a conception of the city as a whole that would then determine the distribution of its parts. Gwynn's idol was Wren, whose plan for rebuilding the city after the Great Fire in 1666 had been frustrated by 'the interested views of ignorant, obstinate, designing men'.[167] Gwynn did more than just imitate Wren. Gwynn's scheme required that the existing boundaries of London be recognized and somehow marked, because the approach roads disgraced such 'a great and opulent city'.[168]

Press, 1980), p. 93.

[163] Other writers did not take issue with Wood, but ignored him. Besides Gandy, Plaw, and W. F. Pocock, others who proposed significant village plans and designs for country and farm houses included: Edmund Bartell, Busby, John Crunden, Edward Gyfford, David Laing, Loudon, and Lugar.

[164] *Rambler*, 14 (5 May 1750), in *The Rambler*, ed. W. J. Bate and Albrecht B. Strauss, The Yale Edition of the Works of Samuel Johnson, I (New Haven and London: Yale University Press, 1969), p. 80.

[165] Tourists visiting William Beckford's Fonthill Abbey were shown 'the grand architectural features' only 'gradually', so that their sense of the whole would be delayed until they had seen all the parts (John Rutter, *Delineations of Fonthill and Its Abbey* [Shaftesbury: the author, and London: Charles Knight & Co., 1823], p. 8).

[166] *Gulliver's Travels*, bk 3, ch. 5 (*Prose Works of Jonathan Swift*, XI, rev. edn. [Oxford: Blackwell, 1959], p. 180). See also Bernard Tschumi, 'Questions of Space', p. 140.

[167] *London and Westminster Improved*, p. vi.

[168] *Ibid.*, pp. xi, 78.

Gwynn expresses his understanding of space by means of the relation of individual districts to the limits of the whole city. That relation is itself determined by his desire that the whole should represent the status quo of a political hierarchy:

In settling a plan of large streets for the dwellings of the rich, it will be found necessary to allot smaller spaces contiguous, for the habitations of useful and laborious people, whose dependance on their superiors requires such a distribution; and by adhering to this principal [sic] a political advantage will result to the nation; as this intercourse stimulates their industry, improves their morals by example, and prevents any particular part from being the habitation of the indigent alone, to the great detriment of private property.[169]

By integrating local populations in such ways, Gwynn would have broken down the whole city into a large number of small images of the whole. Within each community space is organized as a forcible reminder of social hierarchy, a point that is reinforced by Gwynn's gratuitous assumption that the morals of the rich are worth emulating. The moralizing of Gwynn's treatise emphasizes repeatedly his conception of spatial wholes and parts, like the social ones that give them existence, as political.[170]

Unlike France, where Claude Nicolas Ledoux was offering a radical programme of change, England did not adopt theories such as Gwynn's that were supposed to lead to edification. English theory at the end of the eighteenth century tended instead to lay greater stress on the affective function of architecture. Ledoux may have erased French neoclassicism's legacy of spatial feeling, ending 'any possibility of conceiving of a group of buildings and even less of an entire town quarter as a totality in three dimensions', but he had no such effect in England.[171] Ledoux's influence was evidently forgotten by the 1860s, when Haussmann redesigned Paris by thinking first of the whole city, and then altering individual areas to suit his overall scheme. Haussmann's broad boulevards linked public monuments, not social groups, and served military needs, not social ones. In Britain as late as 1796 and 1805, when Plaw and Gandy published their plans, conceiving of towns and villages as totalities was normal, but often the places would be perceptible as totalities only on maps. Like the architecture of individual buildings, English neoclassical town planning was based on symmetry and uniformity, which suggest a coherent entity, so that an urban quarter would be 'planned' only if its buildings approached uniformity in their outward appearance, often at the expense of demolishing some medieval arrangement whose spatial relations suggested dispersal, disorder

---

169 *Ibid.*, p. viii.
170 See, for example, pp. 1–2.
171 Zucker, *Town and Square*, pp. 193–94. See John Archer, 'Character in English Architectural Design,' *Eighteenth-Century Studies*, 12 (1979), 347.

and fragmentation to the eighteenth-century mind.[172] The new, coherent disposition of space is both an organizing principle and a political instrument.

---

[172] See Mumford, *Culture of Cities*, pp. 13–14, 53; and Donald J. Olsen, *Town Planning in London: the Eighteenth and Nineteenth Centuries*, 2nd edn (New Haven & London: Yale University Press, 1982), pp. 27–96.

2

Space, the architect and the design argument

Nature that fram'd us of foure Elements,
Warring within our breasts for regiment,
Doth teach us all to have aspyring minds:
Our soules, whose faculties can comprehend
The wondrous Architecture of the world: . . .

Christopher Marlowe,
1 *Tamburlaine the Great*

Car Dieu est le seul, le grand, & l'admirable
Architecte, qui a ordonné & crée de sa seule parole
toute la machine du monde tant celeste que elementaire
& terrestre . . .

Philibert Delorme, *Premier Tome*

As London began to recover from the disaster of the Great Fire of September 1666, an Italian visitor, Giovanni Torriano, thought the rebuilt city appeared 'with a greater and more sublime splendor, than before, by the addition of many Streets and Lanes; again, by the contiguity, variety, and thickness of Houses, Courts, and Markets, from place to place, very well contrived and ordered, it makes a better show. . . . a Phenix, having been burnt down, and afterwards sprung up from its own ashes, so that the whole World doth ring of it'.[1] The fire had presented Londoners with a rare opportunity to plan a purpose-built city, yet few contemporaries found any evidence that the urban community had built an environment appropriate to its pursuits. The enthusiastic Torriano belonged to a minority. To most, the rebuilding was an opportunity missed.

The best known of the many schemes for rebuilding London is Christopher Wren's grandiose plan, which proposed wide streets, regular squares, and two adaptations of Vitruvian radial layout. But Wren was thwarted by bureaucracy and the law's delays. Like the protesters who rejected the Greater London Council's 1971 proposals for redeveloping Covent Garden

---

[1] Cited by Frances Yates, 'An Italian in Restoration England', *Journal of the Warburg and Courtauld Institutes*, 6 (1943), 217.

as an 'attempt to impose a neat intellectual exercise on to a diverse and uniquely untouched part of the city', Londoners in 1666 responded in similar terms when they ignored Wren and rebuilt their houses where they had stood before the fire.[2] Wren threw up his hands in frustration, as planners do when they are unable to force their designs on reluctant clients. And yet, despite its rejection, in one important respect Wren's thwarted scheme does express the will of the expanding middle class. The largest of his planned piazzas, the focal point of his new city, was to be around the Royal Exchange, not the cathedral, and on paper at least it looks far more imposing than the narrow triangular space he had in mind for St Paul's.[3] Wren would have symbolized the city's role as a major commercial and mercantile centre. But with all its borrowings from Alberti, Vitruvius, and the star and fan shapes of French and Roman city planning, Wren's plan looks remorselessly cerebral. Much the same might be said of the equally feasible plans devised by John Evelyn and Robert Hooke, which also seem to take little account of the spatial needs of city dwellers.[4] Evelyn shared Wren's enthusiasm for a methodically planned city, approving in particular the 'divaricated' form of the Strand, 'like a Pythagorean Y', a symbolism for which the average Londoner cared not a fig.[5] By the time the new St Paul's Cathedral began to rise in the 1670s, smaller houses had already encroached on Wren's planned open spaces, spoiling his intended piazza by recreating the disorganized sprawl that had evolved there once before. The resulting area was an irregular space that embodied the ideals not of one mind, but of many.

For reasons like this Evelyn lamented that London had lost a chance to become 'as far superior to any other city in the habitable world for beauty, commodiousness, and magnificence . . . as it has hitherto been somewhat inferior to many imperial cities in Europe, for want of improving those advantages, which God and Nature have dignified it withal above them'.[6] Travellers had often condemned London on moral grounds, and now they complained that London was 'inconvenient', dirty, and neglected. One anonymous visitor was 'amaz'd at the *genius* of these People', that in only forty years, Inigo Jones's

[2] Colin Amery, 'Save the Garden', *Architectural Review*, 152 (July 1972), 20, quoted by Robert Thorne, *Covent Garden: Its History and Restoration* (London: Architectural Press, 1980), p. 108; cf. Richard Sennett, *The Uses of Disorder* (New York: Vintage, 1970), p. 99.

[3] Bernard Adams, *London Illustrated 1604–1851* (Phoenix, Ariz.: Oryx Press, 1983), plate 6, shows a Dutch engraving of the Royal Exchange in 1699. See also Lawrence Worms' useful illustrated account of the Royal Exchange, 'Mapsellers at the Royal Exchange, Part One: Before the Great Fire', *The Map Collector*, no. 34 (March 1986), 2–9.

[4] Cf. Paul Zucker, *Town and Square from the Agora to the Village Green* (New York: Columbia University Press, 1959), p. 198.

[5] John Evelyn, *London Revived: Considerations for its Rebuilding in 1666*, ed. E. S. de Beer (Oxford: Clarendon Press, 1938), p. 45. Known, after the birthplace of Pythagoras, as the Samian letter, 'Y' symbolizes the choice of the roads of Virtue and Vice. See Persius, *Satires*, III, 56; Pope, *The Dunciad*, IV, 151; and Fielding, *A Journey from this World to the Next*, ch. 5.

[6] *London Revived*, p. 30.

two masterpieces, St Paul's, Covent Garden, and the Banqueting House in Whitehall, should be 'so sordidly obscur'd and defac'd': such contempt for fine architecture betokened great 'Avarice, Malice, Meanness, and deformity of Mind.'[7] Yet besides this sort of lament came enthusiastic praise for the city in the early years of the eighteenth century: Torriano's praise, unusual for the 1660s, was quite restrained in comparison with the hyperbole later heaped upon the greatest trading centre in the entire world by Nourse and Stow, by Thomas Shadwell, who called on 'all Europe's cities' to 'bow' to the 'height' of London, 'Thou great support of princely dignity', and by Defoe, who deplored London's 'straggling, confus'd' expansion, 'out of all shape, uncompact, and unequal', who cared little for the new symbolic spaces and regular streets, but who was excited by the mercantile activities that made London (allegedly) the foremost city in Europe.[8]

Like Jones and Wren, Evelyn accepted the idea that architecture, already an emblem of civilization, has the political function of expressing 'the pride of sovereigns and the boast of nations' (as Philip Smyth said) so that cities, particularly capitals, become the focus and symbol of empire.[9] John Wood the Elder would add later that this function of architecture was the very reason why Alexander the Great and Julius Caesar built at all.[10] Evelyn seems also to have taken one tentative step in a more democratic direction. He at least saw that architecture is a more collaborative effort than Wren apparently considered it. Evelyn knew that design had to be commonly the result of agreement between builders and occupants, but he went slightly further when he suggested that plans for the city 'ought to be the joint and mature contrivance of the ablest men, Merchants, Architects, and Workmen, in consort; and such as have a true idea what proprieties, and conveniencies, belong to so great a city.'[11] Nevertheless, such an appeal to a confederacy of experts

---

[7] *A Journey to England. With some Account of the Manners and Customs of that Nation* (London, 1700), p. 6, sometimes attributed to John Evelyn or William King. See also Max Byrd, *London Transformed: Images of the City in the Eighteenth Century* (New Haven and London: Yale University Press, 1978), pp. 21–22.

[8] Timothy Nourse, *Campania Fælix* (London, 1700), pp. 345–48; William Stow, *Remarks on London* (London, 1722), sig. A2, verso; [Shadwell], *The Medal of John Bayes* (1682), ll. 307–8, in *Poems on Affairs of State: Augustan Satirical Verse, 1660–1714*, vol. 3, ed. Howard H. Schless (New Haven and London: Yale University Press, 1968), p. 92; Defoe, *A Tour thro' the whole Island of Great Britain*, ed. G. D. H. Cole (London: Peter Davies, 1927), I, pp. 316–17.

[9] Philip Smyth, introduction to *Elements of Architecture* by Henry Aldrich (Oxford, 1789), p. iii. For this interpretation of Jones, who wrote no systematic treatise on architecture, see Joseph Rykwert, *The First Moderns: the Architects of the Eighteenth Century* (Cambridge, Mass. & London: MIT Press, 1980), p. 139; for Wren, *Parentalia: or, Memoirs of the Family of the Wrens* (London, 1751), p. 351; Evelyn, dedication (to Charles II) of *Parallel of the Antient Architecture with the Modern*, 2nd edn (London, 1707), n.p.; and John Wilkins, *Mathematicall Magick. Or, the Wonders that may be performed by Mechanicall Geometry* (London, 1648), p. 69, applying the idea to ancient architecture in general, and the Temple of Solomon in particular.

[10] *The Origin of Building: or, the Plagiarism of the Heathens Detected* (Bath, 1741), pp. 3–4.

[11] *London Revived*, p. 31. Jacques Androuet du Cerceau advised all concerned to plan everything, inside and out, to avoid unexpected expense (*Livre d'Architecture* [Paris, 1615], fol. 4, recto).

still excludes the private interests and inclinations of the majority of the inhabitants. The lack of such agreement caused London to fall short of the standards set by its European neighbours.

Before the Fire, 'the Architecture of [London's] Buildings, both publick and private, were [sic] very ordinary and irregular', said William Stow, and Evelyn thought it was 'from the asymmetrie of our Buildings, want of decorum and proportion in our Houses, that the irregularity of our humors and affections may be shrewdly discern'd'.[12] Evelyn realized that another, related reason for what he took to be the low quality of British architecture was the lack of text books in English.

Architectural treatises in the vernacular were available to builders in Italy, France, Germany, and the Netherlands even if some, as Jousse thought, went over the head of the average architect.[13] Many of these treatises, such as Androuet's *Livre d'architecture*, were addressed to 'Seigneurs, Gentilhommes, & autres qui voudront bastir aux champs' (nobles, gentlemen, and others who would like to build in the country)[14] but some were meant specifically for people in the building industry rather than for their patrons alone. For instance, Jousse set out one explanation 'pour l'instruction de ceux qui n'y sont pas trop intelligens' (to instruct those who do not know too much about it), and Symon Bosboom compiled his simplified version of Scamozzi mainly for the benefit of 'de Jonge Leerlingen' (young pupils) and to be 'dienstich voor alle Ionge Liefhebbers der Bouw-Const' (useful for all young lovers of architecture), with the aim 'dat nu alle gemeene verstanden dit kunnen verstaen' (that now all mean understandings can comprehend it).[15] By contrast, complete editions of Vignola, Scamozzi, Serlio, Alberti, Palladio, and Vitruvius himself, whose unclassical Latin was notoriously difficult to translate, were scarce or not available at all in English.[16] 'Few Nations of any note', said Joseph Moxon in 1665, have not the works of Vignola 'translated into

---

[12] Stow's unctuous dedication (*Remarks on London*, sig. A2, verso) to the Prince of Wales – the future George II – speculated that the Fire was Providential, 'that Fate contriv'd the Magnificence of this great City by Fire, for the better Reception of a King, who may justly claim the Title of *Defender of the Faith*.' Evelyn, *A Parallel of the Antient Architecture with the Modern* (London, 1664), dedication.

[13] *Le Secret d'Architecture* (La Flèche, 1642), p. 3.

[14] Androuet, *Livre d'architecture*, title page.

[15] *Secret*, p. 115; Bosboom, *Cort Onderwijs van de Vijf Colonnen* (Amsterdam, 1736), title page and p. 5. For the English readership of architectural books, see John Archer, *The Literature of British Domestic Architecture 1715–1842* (Cambridge, Mass.: MIT Press, 1985), pp. 20–22.

[16] See William Newton, translator, *The Architecture of M. Vitruvius Pollio*, I (London, 1771), iii, 2, echoing Perrault's comment on Vitruvius' idiomatic Latin. In 1611 Robert Peake had translated Serlio's *Book of Architecture* from Pieter Coecke van Aelst's Dutch translation (Amsterdam, 1606, itself a reprint of an edition published in Antwerp, 1542): this soon became an extremely rare book; in 1663 Godfrey Richards put only the first book of Palladio's *Quattro Libri* into English; and in 1669 Robert Pricke published his translation of Julien Mauclerc's *New Treatise of Architecture, according to Vitruvius*, with additions from Scamozzi, Palladio, and Vignola. Pricke followed this in 1676 with his translation of Bosboom's Dutch simplification of Scamozzi.

their own Language: only we here in *England* (I know not whether it be through carelessness in Artists, or else covetousness) mind not those things which makes [*sic*] other Countries (that have nothing else to boast of) so famous among their Neighbours.'[17] The 1703 edition of Moxon's translation of Vignola was even more explicit than earlier editions in its aim to ensure that 'any that can but read, and understand English, may readily learn the proportions that all members in a building have one unto another'.[18] Even before the Great Fire, Evelyn, 'taking notice of our want of bookes of architecture in the English tongue, . . . published those most usefull directions of Ten of the best Authors on that subject, whose works were very rarely to be had, all of them written in French, Latine, or Italian, & so not intelligible to our mechanics'.[19]

Moxon seems not to have realized that Evelyn had already made a start by breaking through British insularity. By translating Fréart's *Parallèle*, Evelyn made ancient and modern architectural theory accessible, not only for 'Politer *Students* of this Magnificent *Art*', but also for 'the most Vulgar Understandings',[20] which suggests that Evelyn considered architects, rather than their better educated patrons, to be the designers of buildings. Together with his far-sighted zoning proposals and his exposure of London's air-pollution problem, Evelyn's introduction of continental European theory to Britain gave significant momentum to the development of architectural literature in English. Then within fifty years of Evelyn's pioneering work the feisty Scot, Colen Campbell, was polemically condemning 'Things that are Foreign' in British architecture.[21]

Evelyn's words show that design and building in 1664 were entrusted largely to 'mechanics'. In Britain there were plenty of architects, but as yet virtually no such thing as 'the important Profession of an Architect', as Sebastien Le Clerc called it.[22] That Britain should lag behind continental Europe in this respect was again due to insularity as much as anything,[23] if by 'architect' we accept Alberti's definition:

Him I call an Architect, who, by a sure and wonderful Art and Method, is able, both with thought and invention, to devise, and, with execution, to compleat all those Works, which, by means of the movement of great Weights, and the conjunction and

[17] Joseph Moxon, trans., *Vignola: or the Compleat Architect*, 2nd edn (London, 1665), preface, n.p.
[18] 5th edn (London, 1703), title page.
[19] Evelyn to Lady Sunderland, 4 August 1690, *Diary* [and] . . . *Familiar Letters*, ed. William Bray, revised by H. B. Wheatley (London: Bickers & Son, 1906), III, p. 464.
[20] *An Account of Architects and Architecture, Together with an Historical, and Etymological Explanation of Certain Terms Particularly Affected by Architects* (London, 1706), preface, n.p.
[21] *Vitruvius Britannicus, or the British Architect*, I (London, 1715), p. 1.
[22] *A Treatise of Architecture, with Remarks and Observations. Necessary for Young People, who would apply themselves to that Noble Art* (London, 1727). The quoted words may be the translator's.
[23] Cf. Rykwert, *The First Moderns*, p. 121, Martin S. Briggs, *The Architect in History* (Oxford: Clarendon Press, 1927), and Charles-Etienne Briseux, *L'Art de Bâtir des Maisons de Campagne* (Paris, 1743), I, p. v.

amassment of Bodies, can, with the greatest Beauty, be adapted to the uses of Mankind: and to be able to do this, he must have a thorough insight into the noblest and most curious Sciences. Such must be the Architect.[24]

Alberti proceeds with a hymn in praise of the architect as an extremely important and influential man, especially in the political context of building. Mastery of 'the noblest and most curious Sciences' is, of course, a requirement laid down by Vitruvius. The architect's special skill consists of design, since (said Alberti) 'the whole Art of Building consists in the Design, and in the Structure'.[25]

Brunelleschi was possibly the first to distinguish the architect as designer from the workmen who constructed. In Hanoverian Britain the architect was slowly becoming the designer who did not dirty his hands on a building site, but instead acted as an intermediary between his patron and his workmen: a well-proportioned building, said Robert Morris, was a 'Monument of Judgment to the *Gentleman* who builds, the *Architect* who designs, and the *Workmen* who execute'.[26] It would be absurd to suppose that before the Restoration there had been no architects but only surveyors incapable of 'design'. Design was, and would still continue to be, the province of gentlemen and scholars, of virtuosi, of 'earls of creation', only no longer exclusively so, because according to Batty Langley 'Builders and Workmen of all Kinds' were producing, by 1740, 'Works executed in a much neater and more magnificent Manner than was ever done in this Kingdom before'.[27] In 1756 Isaac Ware proposed his compendious *Complete Body of Architecture* 'as a library on this subject to the gentleman and the builder'.[28] The 'builder' had always meant a man employed by a gentleman to translate ideas into architecture. Ware's 'builder' now meant – or could mean – one who envisaged designs independently, a professional architect, who was sometimes his own patron, as John Wood the Elder became in Bath. Although an architect usually still worked for a patron, he was by mid-century 'the Person who draws the Design and Plan of a Palace, or other Edifice', and so 'gives his Employer a distinct View of the Design': very often now, the design came before the 'employment'.[29] Early in the eighteenth century, as the profession of architect began to establish itself as

[24] *The Architecture of Leon Battista Alberti*, translated [into Italian] by Cosimo Bartoli and [into English] by Giacomo Leoni (London, 1726), I, sig. a, verso.

[25] *Ibid.*, Bk I, ch. 1, fol. 1, recto.

[26] *The Architectural Remembrancer* (London, 1751), p. vi; this echoes André Félibien's *Dictionnaire in Principes*, 2nd edn (Paris, 1690), p. 482.

[27] *The City and Country Builder's and Workman's Treasury* (London, 1740), p. 2. Cf. John Harris, *The Palladians* (New York: Rizzoli, 1982), p. 37, James Lees-Milne, *Earls of Creation: Five Great Patrons of Eighteenth-Century Art* (London: Hamish Hamilton, 1962). See also James Gibbs, *A Book of Architecture, containing designs of buildings and ornaments* (London, 1728), p. i.

[28] *A Complete Body of Architecture* (London, 1756), preface, n.p.

[29] R. Campbell, *The London Tradesman* (London, 1747), p. 155.

the forerunner of the one we recognize today, it became democratized in a limited way by freeing itself partly from the command of the aristocrat.[30]

By the 1750s the practice of architecture had become increasingly the domain of professionals as well as amateurs, so that the professional architect figured more frequently and prominently as the individual at the head of a team of masons, carpenters, joiners, plasterers, and unskilled labourers. But, in Martin Briggs' view, this relationship must always have existed, for 'we' (he says) 'must know that the design and erection of every large and complicated building in the past involved the control of some master-brain, that no group or committee could have taken its place, and neither Salisbury Cathedral nor the Parthenon could have leapt from the ground at the behest of a handful of rustic craftsmen'.[31] Le Corbusier struck a more fundamental note when he said: 'There is no such thing as a primitive man; there are primitive resources. The idea is constant, in full sway from the beginning.'[32]

As the profession gradually became more democratic, so too did architectural literature, but more slowly. The books reveal the eighteenth century's paradox of democratization: an expression of Whiggish republicanism took classical, not vernacular, form. This paradox is still visible at the very end of the century even in the compromises scattered among John Crunden's designs for structures ranging from simple farms to grand villas. Crunden asserts that 'To be sparing of antique ornaments' reveals 'true taste', and that his own designs are 'entirely out of the common style of building', and yet one design is a conscious imitation of Inigo Jones' style, and another, for 'a villa in the Palladian style', is more than vaguely reminiscent of Wood the Elder's Prior Park or Campbell's neo-Palladian classic, Wanstead.[33] Crunden's was one of scores of pattern books that advertised the possibility of mass-produced architecture. Whig ideology accommodated the idea of both the aristocratic patron and the professional architect as individual designers, only now the architect's designs were more frequently published as a basis for negotiation with prospective patrons.

Emphasis on the individual designer, whatever his social status, is important. Wood the Elder's commendation in his *Origin of Building* of the twelve Vitruvian 'necessities' was more than an orthodoxy: it was also part of his effort to raise the status of the architect, whose public image was, to say the least, tarnished. Back in the 1690s Roger North depicted 'a profest architect' as 'proud, opiniative and troublesome, seldome at hand, and a head workman pretending to the designing part, is full of paultry vulgar contrivances', and

[30] John Wilkins said much the same in *Mathematicall Magick* (London, 1648), pp. 75–76.

[31] Martin S. Briggs, *The Architect in History* p. 2. See also Howard Colvin's lucid and compact history of the profession (*Biographical Dictionary of British Architects 1600–1840* [London: John Murray, 1978], introduction, pp. 18–41).

[32] Le Corbusier, *Towards a New Architecture*, translated by Frederick Etchells (1931; reprinted New York: Dover, 1986), p. 70.

[33] John Crunden, *Convenient and Ornamental Architecture* (London, 1797), plates 52–53.

always ready to overcharge his client.[34] So much for that man who (Blondel taught his students) was 'Juge-né de tous les Arts liberaux' (a born judge of all the liberal arts).[35] Wood was reminding his readers of the tradition that architecture had always been valued as a 'noble science', the *'Queen of Arts'*, the art that embraced all the others.[36]

The books' repeated, almost tiresome emphasis on the antiquity and respectability of architecture may have helped eighteenth-century architects to establish themselves as somehow respectable: in Bath at least, John Wood certainly succeeded in raising his own status, in which he proceeded to revel. The friend of such local notables as Dr Oliver and Dr Cheyne, and the partner and frequent guest of the renowned Ralph Allen, Wood was neither mere employee nor hired artisan. An archetypal self-made man starting his career in the 1720s, by 1744 plain Mr Wood had become 'J. Wood, *Esq.*,' a man of sufficient wealth and status to send his eldest son John, whom we have met as the champion of the labourer around 1780, to University College, Oxford.[37] Wood the Elder's contemporaries endorsed his new status: his obituary in the *Bath Journal* said that he had 'not only raised himself in the esteem of his superiors, but in the compass of a few years, by an honest and commendable industry, obtained an handsome competence for himself and family'.[38] Jerry Peirce, the surgeon for whom Wood built Lilliput Castle, told Sarah Clayton that 'except Lord Burlington, there was no person in England that had a juster and better taste in architecture' than Wood.[39] By constructing 'many useful and ornamental buildings'[40] to his own published designs, Wood was drawing attention to the importance of design, to his own abilities as a designer, and to his professional independence. The commodity he was selling was design. In *The Origin of Building*, Wood repeatedly envisions the architect not as a builder but as a designing mastermind. 'Geometry', said Le Corbusier, 'is the language of man': architecture, said Wood more pragmatically, was an effort of the mind.[41] What, asked Loudon, continuing the theme,

[34] British Library, Add. MS 32540, fol. 23, and *Of Building*, ed. Howard Colvin and John Newman (Oxford: Clarendon Press, 1981), pp. 23–24.

[35] Blondel, *Cours d'architecture*, 9 vols. (Paris, 1771–77), III, p. lxxiv.

[36] Isaac Ware, *A Complete Body of Architecture* (London, 1756), p. 91; Fréart, *Parallèle de l'Architecture Antique et de la Moderne* (Paris, 1650), p. 13; Wood, *Origin of Building*, pp. 68–69.

[37] 'J. Wood, *Esq.*' appears in the subscription list on Thomas Thorpe's map, *An Actual Survey of the City of Bath . . . Survey'd . . . in the Year 1742* (Bath, 1744). Wood the Younger matriculated on 10 March 1747, but apparently did not graduate. His father's status was listed as 'arm.', presumably meaning 'armiger', or gentleman (Joseph Foster, *Alumni Oxonienses* [Oxford: Parker, 1891–2], VIII, p. 1,598).

[38] *Bath Journal*, 15 July 1754; whatever Wood's social status, he certainly was comfortably off at his death. For details, see J. P. E. Falconer, 'The Family of John Wood, of Bath', *Notes & Queries*, 193 (1948), 403–08.

[39] Quoted by Walter Ison, 'A Show-Place of European Fame', *Apollo*, n.s. 98, no. 141 (November 1973), p. 345.

[40] *Ibid.*

[41] *Origin of Building*, p. 67. Le Corbusier, *Towards a New Architecture*, p. 72. Also Robert Morris,

'constitutes the difference between a pile of stones in a quarry, and the same pile formed into a house, but the *mind* displayed in the latter?'[42]

Glorifying the capacity of one mind (particularly his own) to create design, Wood's economic individualism in some measure countered the democratizing tendency of the profession, even though he was gradually becoming his own patron. A century before Wood, and contrary to Evelyn, Descartes had gone so far as to assert that buildings are better if left to one man, because otherwise the evolution of villages into towns creates indiscriminate, crooked, and irregular urban sites, so that 'you would say it is chance, rather than the will of men using reason, that placed them so'.[43] Until in a strange anticipation of the cult of the picturesque, Reynolds declared 'a regular built city or house' less 'pleasant' than 'a chance city or improved house', most commentators agreed that regular cities and houses were preferable, but that an urban population was regrettably unlikely to reconcile public and private interests in a unified design.[44]

Design was a question of organizing parts into wholes. Ware recommended that the young architect

consider the general design and purpose of the building, and then examine freely how far, according to his own judgment, the purpose will be answered by that structure. He will thus establish in himself a custom of judging by the whole as well as by parts; and he will find new beauties in the structure considered in this light.[45]

By 1756, when Ware was writing, such advice was standard. An equally standard complaint could be heard, that modern architects were so preoccupied with parts that they lost sight of total effects: but Ware pointed out, as did many others, that the ability to conceive of overall design distinguished the architect from the mere bricklayer.[46] Helped by Berkeley's recognition of perception, which provided a new vocabulary, the British neo-Palladian aesthetic was to be found in totalities, not details, since, as James Ralph commented, 'the eye is best satisfied with seeing the whole at once, not in travelling from object to object; for then the whole is comprehended with pain and difficulty, the attention is broken, and we forget one moment what we had

Essay in Defence of Ancient Architecture, p. 73.

[42] Loudon, *Observations on Laying Out Farms, in the Scotch Style, adapted to England* (London, 1806), p. 101.

[43] *Discourse on the Method*, part 2: *The Philosophical Writings of Descartes*, translated by John Cottingham, Robert Stoothoff, and Dugald Murdoch, I (Cambridge: Cambridge University Press, 1985), p. 116.

[44] *Portraits by Sir Joshua Reynolds*, ed. Frederick W. Hilles. The Yale Edition of the Papers of James Boswell (New York: McGraw-Hill; and London: Heinemann, 1952), p. 123.

[45] Ware, *Complete Body of Architecture*, p. 695.

[46] *Ibid.*, p. 406; and cf. Joseph Moxon, *Mechanick Exercises, or, the Doctrine of Handy-Works* (London, 1677–83), p. 154, and Palladio, *The Four Books of Architecture*, translated by Isaac Ware (London, 1738) p. 1.

observed another.'[47] As a result of the ascendancy of this kind of thought, neo-Palladian architecture in Britain often tended to be sparingly orna-mented. Anticipating by two centuries Adolf Loos's assault on ornament, North believed that Inigo Jones' work 'hath more majesty than anything done since' because of its plainness.[48] But it had long been true of academic architecture, such as Juan de Herrera's work at the Escorial, that simple or sparing ornamentation threw more emphasis on proportional relationships and made them more easily perceptible.[49] Although, unlike Herrera, John Wood was a professional architect, his designs owe a great deal more to academic books than to existing buildings. Wood's are among the most aus-tere examples of designs that dispense with ornamental detail for the sake of simplicity, elegance, and a total effect of structural harmony.

In a run-of-the-mill pattern book William Halfpenny would trot out: 'sim-plicity is the basis of beauty; as decoration is of magnificence; harmony is the result of the first, and proportion elegantly compos'd is the certain effect of the latter.'[50] And long before him Vignola explained that the most beautiful ornaments of the five orders in ancient Rome 'have a certain correspondence and proportion of Numbers among themselves not intricate, seeing that each of the lesser Members measure [sic] the greater, punctually distributing them into so many parts'.[51] Like music, architecture was seen to have arisen from Pythagorean geometry. In accordance with an ancient tradition the origin of architectural beauty in Palladian theory is the origin of geometry: universal proportion and harmony.

The Pythagorean concept of harmony as the product of geometrical pro-portion had long been accepted virtually without question.[52] From Pythag-oras a correlation could be derived between musical and spatial harmony, a correlation that the myth of Amphion conveniently expressed, and which

---

[47] *A Critical Review of the Publick Buildings, Statues and Ornaments in, and about London and Westminster* (London, 1734), p. 115; George Berkeley, *An Essay towards a New Theory of Vision* (London, 1709), esp. pp. 47–49.

[48] For discussion of Loos' essay 'Ornament und Verbrechen' (1908), see Rykwert, 'Ornament is no Crime', *Studio International*, 190, no. 977 (September/October, 1975), 91–97. Roger North, *Of Building, Roger North's Writings on Architecture* ed. Howard Colvin and John Newman (Oxford: Clarendon Press, 1981), p. 23, note.

[49] Catherine Wilkinson, 'The Escorial and the Invention of the Imperial Staircase', *Art Bulletin*, 57 (1975), 87–88. Cf. Colin Rowe's remarkable claim for the blank panel on Le Corbusier's Villa Schwob: 'the blank surface is both disturbance and delight; and it is the activity of emptiness [sic] which the observer is ultimately called upon to enjoy' ('Mannerism and Modern Architecture', in *The Mathematics of the Ideal Villa and Other Essays* [Cambridge, Mass.: MIT Press, 1976], p. 31).

[50] *A New and Compleat System of Architecture Delineated, in a Variety of Plans and Elevations of Designs for Convenient and Decorated Houses* (London, 1749), preface, n.p.

[51] Giacomo Barozzi, Il Vignola, *The Regular Architect: or the General Rule of the Five Orders of Architecture*, translated by John Leeke (London, 1669), preface, n.p.

[52] See Rykwert's convenient summary in *The First Moderns*, pp. 12–13, and Rudolf Wittkower's comprehensive treatment in *Architectural Principles in the Age of Humanism*, 4th edn (London: Academy, 1973).

Dryden perpetuated, so that architecture became, as René Guénon was to put it, 'la traduction spatiale des nombres et de leurs rapports' (the spatial translation of numbers and their correspondences).[53] Palladio made that correlation fundamental to his architecture: parallel to musical harmony, a visual 'harmony' became a microcosm of the universal. Therefore mathematics was the basis of architecture, and most importantly, the relation between the musical and the spatial 'seemed to Palladio and his contemporaries to indicate a universal Design'.[54] The concept belongs to the design argument, that enduring philosophical allegation that the order and harmony of the world are proof of the existence of a designing deity.

The repeated emphasis on that total effect of order and regularity led directly to the argument that architecture – the art of designing wholes – is a divine activity, and that God is not just a creator, but specifically an architect, a designer of universal harmony. This was one way of rationalizing fear of an infinite universe: 'How great is the house of God,' wrote Sir Walter Ralegh (quoting Baruch), 'how large is the place of his possession! it is great, and hath no end; it is high, and unmeasurable.'[55] And Ralegh went on to cite Procopius, who rather prosaically likened God's creation of light to a king's command for 'some goodly building to be erected'.[56] Just as lamely, George Cheyne sought to prove the existence of a designing deity by appealing to the example of a 'convenient' house. Cheyne posited a savage who had never seen a house before: from the existence of 'a *Noble Palace* neatly finish'd and finely furnish'd', and 'the Accommodations and Conveniences of this *Building* . . . exactly suited in every Circumstance to the Wants and Necessities' of its inhabitants, Cheyne's 'wild *Scythian* or *Indian* . . . wou'd have no difficulty in concluding that this House was built by some wise *Architect*'. For Cheyne this is the ideal analogy: 'Now this is the very Case betwixt us and the *System* of things about us.'[57] To prove divine organization, the first analogue to which Cheyne and many others turn is architecture, because it is the fundamental human art. (Cheyne also spoke of the journey from this world to the next as a passage 'from *this* to *that* Mansion.')[58] Batty Langley passed on the received wisdom that some ancient buildings 'so charm'd the Mind, and ravish'd the Eye, that the *Architects* themselves were, by the Vulgar, often thought to be *divinely inspired*.'[59] Even Cheyne's ignorant savage must see that. Architecture is the plainest illustration of divine design in the human world.

[53] 'Les arts et leur conception traditionelle', in *Mélanges* (Paris: Gallimard, 1976), p. 107.
[54] James S. Ackerman, *Palladio* (Harmondsworth: Penguin, 1966), p. 162. Wilkins argued that architecture was reducible to geometry (*Mathematicall Magick*, pp. 9–10).
[55] Ralegh, *History of the World*, 11th edn (London, 1736), p. 5.
[56] *Ibid.*, p. 8.
[57] Cheyne, *Philosophical Principles of Natural Religion* (London, 1705), II, p. 46.
[58] *Dr Cheyne's Account of Himself and his Writings: faithfully extracted from his Works*, 2nd edn (London, 1743), p. 17.
[59] *Ancient Masonry, both in Theory and Practice* (London, 1736), p. 7.

Arguments of this kind had been flourishing for some time. In his essay 'Of Atheism' (1613) Francis Bacon said he preferred to believe 'all the fables in the Legend, and the Talmud, and the Alcoran, than that this universal frame is without a mind. And therefore God never wrought miracle to convince atheism, because his ordinary works convince it.'[60] Later, opponents of Epicureanism and advocates of the design argument were similarly certain that chance alone could not have created *'The Orderly Regularity and Harmony of the Mundane System . . .* the *Regular Frame* and *Harmony of the Universe'*, just as 'the Fortuitous Projection or Tumbling out of so many Forms of Letters, confounded all together' could not have created *'Ennius* his *Annals*, or *Homer*'s Iliads [*sic*]'.[61] The evidence of nature was proof, to the convinced, that a supreme intelligence had created the world. With increasing frequency in the course of the late seventeenth century and the early eighteenth, that intelligence becomes the creative mind of an architect. There is plenty of evidence that such a conception of the supreme intelligence was habitual. A characteristic example is Edward Bysshe's translation of Xenophon (1712), where Socrates proves to Aristodemus the existence of a God by appealing to the usefulness or purpose of parts of the human body. Bysshe converts the Greek into a spatial vocabulary:

Is it not a wonderful Providence, that our Eyes, which are extreamly delicate, are cover'd with Lids, which like two Doors, open whenever it is needful, and are shut in our sleep? That there are short Hairs growing on the edges of our Eyelids, that the Wind may glide over, and do no hurt to the Eyes, and the Eye-brows are like two Penthouses to keep them from being incommoded by the Sweat that trickles down from the Forehead?[62]

The skeptical Aristodemus says he cannot imagine that an intelligent being created the universe, 'because I see not these Gods who you tell me make and govern all Things, as I see the other Artificers who are among us'.[63] Andrew Ramsay's paraphrase of the same passage has Socrates asking, 'Does blind chance work every thing, and is there no such thing as wisdom besides what you have?' Ramsay goes on: 'Aristodemus having reply'd, that he did not see that wise Architect of the Universe; Socrates answers him . . . Aristodemus at length acknowledging a supreme Being, is still in doubt as to Providence; not being able to comprehend how the Deity can see every thing at once.'[64]

[60] *The Works of Francis Bacon*, ed. James Spedding, Robert Leslie Ellis, and Douglas Denon Heath, VI (London: Longman *et al.*, 1861), p. 413.

[61] Ralph Cudworth, *The True Intellectual System of the Universe* (London, 1678), pp. 175, 421. See Cheyne, *Philosophical Principles*, II, p. 11.

[62] Xenophon, *The Memorable Things of Socrates*, translated by Edward Bysshe (London, 1712), pp. 30–31.

[63] *Ibid.*, p. 33.

[64] Ramsay, *A Discourse upon the Theology and Mythology of the Pagans*, p. 33, in *The Travels of Cyrus*, 4th edn (London, 1730).

Socrates and Xenophon did not speak of a divine architect: their translators did.

When neo-Palladian architecture was growing in Britain, the design argument received a new development, particularly from Newton, who 'argued that God is not merely a designer, but a designer with certain specific skills, i.e. geometry and mechanics'.[65] Really a revival of Plato's geometer-deity, the inference was well established. Cheyne was saying in 1705 that he understood 'nature' to mean 'this vast, if not infinite *Machin* of the *Universe*, the Perfect and Wise Production of Almighty God, consisting of an infinite Number of lesser *Machins*, every one of which is adjusted by Weight and Measure'.[66] Cheyne, indeed, was one of many who expressed the hoary comparison between the great machine of the universe and 'a finish'd Piece of Clock-Work, form'd upon *Geometrick* Principles'.[67] Relatively recent in Britain, such ideas had been commonplace since the Renaissance elsewhere in Europe. Scamozzi, yet another who considered architecture 'Scienza nobilissima', had confidently declared in 1615 that the 'machina del Mondo' had been created by 'LA MAESTA del grand'IDDIO sommo Architetto' (The Majesty of the great God the highest Architect).[68] In the late 1730s Wood the Elder took such arguments in his stride, accepting the Newtonian basis of the design argument, as well as the argument itself, without much question. That God should be a geometer suited Wood perfectly, as it suited almost all neo-Palladian theorists of architecture in Britain. But Wood gave a theological twist to his own argument about the origin of building, one that tends to align him with the mysticism of John Dee rather than Shaftesbury, Morris or Burlington's school of neo-Palladianism. For since, in Wood's view, Roman building is derived from the sacred buildings described in the Old Testament, his chosen Palladian idiom is finally not pagan, but sanctioned by God. R. S. Neale interprets this as Wood's tortured desire to satisfy his own conscience, to free himself 'from threatening pagan associations',[69] but Wood is also arguing that all architecture is one, and that all architects, provided they adhere to the proportions of sacred geometry, stand in relation to their work as the divine architect does to his 'building', the universe.

Of the four examples illustrating the meaning of *architect* in Johnson's *Dictionary* one is a quotation from John Ray, who refers to 'the Divine Architect of the Body',[70] whose creation of 'this stately Fabrick of Heaven and Earth' implies 'the Being and Operation of some intelligent Architect or

---

[65] Robert H. Hurlbutt III, *Hume, Newton, and the Design Argument* (Lincoln, Nebraska: University of Nebraska Press, 1965), p. 7. Cf. Palladio, *Four Books of Architecture* p. 79.

[66] *Philosophical Principles*, I, p. 2.

[67] *Ibid.*, I. p. 5.

[68] Vincenzo Scamozzi, *L'Idea della Architettura Universale* (Venice, 1615), p. 9.

[69] *Bath: A Social History 1680–1850: or A Valley of Pleasure, yet a Sink of Iniquity* (London: Routledge & Kegan Paul, 1981), p. 190.

[70] *The Wisdom of God Manifested in the Works of the Creation*, 2nd edn (London, 1692), II, p. 141.

Engineer'.[71] For *architecture*, Johnson cites Thomas Burnet's *Sacred Theory of the Earth*: 'The formation of the first earth being a piece of divine *architecture*, ascribed to a particular providence.' Burnet argued that the earth itself is 'a piece of Divine Geometry or Architecture': but just as the world is a building, so one particular building represents the world, for the Jews' 'first and second Temple represented the first and second Earth or World'.[72]

Johnson's examples suggest that his chosen authors were not striving to prove or establish the concept of a divine architect, because it had become a commonplace. The earliest occurrences of *architect* in English are in Peake's 1611 translation of Serlio, and in Henry Wotton's *Elements* (1624), which refers to a divine architect.[73] The concept of an architect – whatever his precise professional function – was already current but the word itself was not.[74] As soon as the word did gain wide currency, it was applied to the deity to indicate divine design. Later in the seventeenth century, Balthazar Gerbier attributed the creation of such diverse 'Fabrick[s]' as 'the Silk Worm and the Soul of Man' to 'the powers of the great Architect and Director of all things'.[75] Evelyn rejects the argument in Lucretius' *De Rerum Natura* that chance '(O wondrous chance!)' caused myriads of atoms to 'fall into that goodly Fabrick and admirable *Architecture* of the *Universe* or World, which with so much *Extasie* and wonder we daily contemplate'.[76] Evelyn also compares Charles II first to Augustus, and then to 'the *Divine Architect*', significantly because in his '*Majesties Plantations* . . . [Charles] has proposed . . . such a *Pattern* to [his] *Subjects*, as merit their imitation'.[77]

Of all the terrestrial buildings that showed the work of a divine architect, three stood apart because they had Biblical authority: Noah's Ark, the Tabernacle, and the Temple of Solomon, even though no one had a reliable idea of what any of them looked like. Of the three, Solomon's Temple was pre-eminent. There was a plentiful supply of 'reconstructions', on paper or in models, of the Temple: of Solomon's original, Ezekiel's vision of it, Zerubbabel's rebuilding according to the decree of Cyrus, and the enlarged, embellished temple authorized by Herod.[78] The Temple occupied the most

[71] *Ibid.*, I, p. 14.
[72] (London, 1684–90), pp. 65–66, 282.
[73] Peake's Serlio, *Book of Architecture* (London, 1611), dedication, n.p. Wotton, *Elements of Architecture* (London, 1624), p. 7. Derived from the Greek αρχιτεκτων, the Latin 'architectus' was widely used to mean a master-builder, and less commonly to mean a designer. Cicero applied the word to a deity (*De Natura Deorum*, II, 90), as did Apuleius (*De Dogmate Platonis* I, 11).
[74] *OED*'s earliest illustrative quotation for 'architect' as designer (especially the Creator), as opposed to 'master builder' is dated 1659. Cf. Frances A. Yates, *Theatre of the World* (Chicago: University of Chicago Press, 1969), p. 21.
[75] *A Brief Discourse concerning the Three Chief Principles of Magnificent Building* (London, 1662), p. 23.
[76] *An Essay on the First Book of T. Lucretius Carus de Rerum Natura* (London, 1656), p. 171.
[77] Dedication to Evelyn's translation of Fréart, *Parallèle*, n.p.
[78] See ch. 4, below. Also, the checklist in René Taylor, 'Architecture and Magic: Some Considerations on the *Idea* of the Escorial', *Essays in the History of Architecture presented to Rudolf Wittkower*,

inquiring minds, as in some quarters it still does. Monarchs grasped the opportunity to liken their most grandiose projects to the Temple, and themselves to Solomon: Justinian claimed to have surpassed Solomon by building Santa Sophia in Constantinople, Charlemagne was praised as Solomon by Notker the Stammerer for the Palatine Chapel in Aachen, and Philip II and Frederick II received similar praise.[79] Such churchmen as James Noyes conceived of 'the Militant Church of Christ upon earth' as 'one visible Body, one House, one Family, one Tabernacle, one Temple, one Candlestick, one Citie, one *New Jerusalem*': if 'the Universal Church' was visible, 'the mystical Church' was not, but it was 'resembled by the Temple'.[80] The Temple was subjected to all kinds of investigation: travellers tried to find its exact location; numerous interpreters of the Bible described the Temple's dimensions, ornaments, architectural style, social organization, cosmological symbolism, and its anthropomorphic aspects.[81] The underlying argument was always consistent: as the scriptures say, God gave the geometric proportions of these buildings to Noah, Moses, and Solomon, therefore they were all true examples of divine design. The Temple, however, was the most magnificent, the most beautiful, the great achievement to be imaginatively reconstructed by the architect.

In Britain the identification of the world as an edifice designed by the divine architect can be traced back to Homer, Plato, Pythagoras, and Cicero, by way of Bacon, Dee, and other British authors addicted to number symbolism,[82] and the concept is central to the design argument. Yet the idea of a divine architect is as rare in English architectural writing as it is common in continental. Apart from Wood, only Robert Morris among architectural writers uses the concept explicitly:

no Science but Architecture is, or has been permitted to contain the sacred Deity . . . [and temples have been built] not only that they might, by the Magnificence of the Building, invite the Deity to reside within it, but that such stupendous Works might

ed. Douglas Fraser, Howard Hibbard, and Milton J. Lewine (London: Phaidon, 1967), to which may be added: Helen Rosenau, 'Jacob Judah Leon Templo's Contribution to Architectural Imagery', *Journal of Jewish Studies*, 23, no. 1 (1972), 72–81, and the same author's *Vision of the Temple: The Image of the Temple of Jerusalem in Judaism and Christianity* (London: Oresko, 1979).

[79] Walter Cahn, 'Solomonic Elements in Romanesque Art', in *The Temple of Solomon: Archaeological Fact and Medieval Tradition in Christian, Islamic and Jewish Art*, ed. Joseph Gutmann (Missoula: Scholars Press [for the American Academy of Religion and the Society of Biblical Literature], 1976), pp. 57, 69–70. Also, Frances Yates, *The Valois Tapestries*, 2nd edn (London: Routledge & Kegan Paul, 1975), p. 25.

[80] James Noyes, *The Temple Measur'd: or, a brief Survey of the Temple mystical, which is instituted the Church of Christ* (London, 1647), pp. 1–3.

[81] For example: Cornelis de Bruyn, *A Voyage to the Levant: or, Travels in the Principal Parts of Asia Minor, the Islands of Scio, Rhodes, Cyprus, &c*, translated by W. J. (London, 1702); Henry Maundrell, *A Journey from Aleppo to Jerusalem*, 2nd edn (Oxford, 1707); Thomas Collins Overton, *The Temple Builder's Most Useful Companion* (London, 1774).

[82] Including Pope: see his translation of Homer's *Iliad*, I, 741, XVIII, 179.

at the same time be Competitors with the greatest Structures of Nature: Besides, it likewise opens the Mind to vast Conceptions, and fits it to converse with the Divinity of the Place; for every thing that is majestick, imprints an Awfulness and Reverence on the Mind of the Beholder, and strikes it with the natural Greatness of the Soul . . . God, the World's Architect, (as *Milton* and several other divine Writers frequently call him) has more than once been pleased to direct Mankind in the attainment of [the great achievement of Nature], as by the Example of *Noah* in Naval Buildings, and *Solomon* in Templar and Domal Architecture.[83]

The Bible says that God directed the 'architects' but, despite Félibien's confidence on the matter, does not actually speak of God as 'l'architecte souverain de l'Univers'.[84] While Milton (after a fashion) might suggest that the world is a building designed by God, and Dryden and Cowley adopt the idea,[85] the widely accepted concept of a divine architect is not to be found where one might expect it – in the writings of Colen Campbell, Batty Langley, or Isaac Ware. Yet it is, as Morris tells us, common among 'divine Writers'. Just as the design argument iself was embraced by people pursuing extremely diverse goals, so the concept of the divine architect was adopted by a wide range of writers who never agreed with one another on anything else.[86]

In Britain by far the most important and extensive kind of writing to exploit the idea of a divine architect is philosophical and theological. The Cambridge Platonists did more than anyone else to give the concept the currency it gained. One of them, Henry More, argues that as the soul is the architect of the body, which is 'the soul's own house', so 'the Soule of the World' is the 'perfective Architect' of the world.[87] Ralph Cudworth goes much further. In his immense, unreadable *True Intellectual System of the Universe*, Cudworth speaks of the Supreme Deity as opificer, architect, framer, creator, governor, maker, numen, sovereign, and first cause. He translates Plato's δημιοργος as '*Architectonick Framer of the whole World*', and also 'the Architect, Maker or Artificer of the whole World'.[88] In his commentaries and interpretations of Aristotle, Heraclitus, Democritus, Iamblichus, and other ancient

[83] *Essay in Defence of Ancient Architecture* (London, 1728), pp. 1–3. Cf. Wood's *Origin of Building*, pp. 59, 70, 72, 117.

[84] Félibien, *Entretiens sur les vies et sur les ouvrages des plus excellens peintres anciens et modernes; avec la vie des architectes* (Trévoux, 1725; reprinted Farnborough: Gregg Press, 1967), v, 51. See also William McClung, *The Architecture of Paradise* (Berkeley and Los Angeles: University of California Press, 1983).

[85] *Paradise Lost*, I, 714, and see William A. McClung, 'The Architecture of Pandemonium', *Milton Quarterly*, 15 (1981), 109–12; Dryden, *Absalom and Achitophel*, 801–04 and *Astraea Redux*, 165; Cowley, *The Garden* in Evelyn, *Sylva, or a Discourse of Forest-Trees and the Propagation of Timber in His Majesties Dominions*, 3rd edn (London, 1679), n.p. Bromley refers to architecture as the divinity that turns posts into porticos (*Philosophical and Critical History of the Fine Arts, Painting, Sculpture and Architecture*, II [London, 1795], p. 239).

[86] Hurlbutt, *Hume, Newton, and the Design Argument*, p. 95.

[87] *The Immortality of the Soul. So farre forth as it is demonstrable from the Knowledge of Nature and the Light of Reason* (London, 1659), pp. 216, 299.

[88] Cudworth, *True Intellectual System*, pp. 406, 408.

philosophers, Cudworth speaks of the universe as a fabric, an artificial frame, and as architecture. His vocabulary of creation shows his bias towards God 'moliminously' creating the vast 'Fabrick' of the universe. Paul Fussell has shown how the language of architecture, in which 'fabrick' and 'frame' are prominent, was absorbed with apparently unconscious ease by his strange quintet of Augustan humanists, Swift, Pope, Johnson, Burke, and Gibbon:[89] the same usage is second nature to Cudworth, too, and to dozens more writers who are neither Augustans nor humanists. Governing Cudworth's vocabulary is the concept of God – in whichever role he casts him – as a *designer*. In this respect Cudworth is a representative proponent of the design argument. Apart from those I have quoted, other significant or influential English writers who express the concept include Wilkins, Temple, Newton, Bentley, Cheyne, Shaftesbury, and Locke.[90]

Shaftesbury and Locke were especially important. Obstinately out of fashion now, Shaftesbury's complacent philosophy of human nature was certainly influential: his major work, *Characteristicks*, went through ten printings between 1711 and 1758, eight of them after his death. Shaftesbury too uses the concept of a divine architect without feeling any need to pause to justify it. He speaks of the world as 'this Mansion-Globe, this Man-Container' and of order in nature as the deliberate design of a '*divine Artificer*;' human desires and hopes he associates with the 'Proportions of this *living Architecture*'.[91] Architecture, in fact, provides Shaftesbury with his most favoured images; 'a just *Plan* or *Model*' of the '*Mechanism*' of the world would reveal 'what Proportion the *friendly* and *natural Affections* seem to bear in this Order of Architecture'.[92] Shaftesbury evidently provided a suitable philosophical source for Morris' architectural writing, but the most important and interesting proponent of an architect-deity was not Shaftesbury but Locke. Locke's use of the concept implies a static universe in the sense that buildings are static, 'put together out of separable, inorganic materials', in Fussell's phrasing.[93] Locke posits 'this Globe of Earth allotted for our Mansion, [by] the all-wise Architect',[94] and likens the human mind to that mansion. Throughout the *Essay Concerning Human Understanding*, Locke employs an architectural and spatial vocabulary, 'fabric' and 'frame' being two of his most trusted words.[95] Memory is a storehouse where ideas are 'lodged', the brain is the mind's

[89] Paul Fussell, *The Rhetorical World of Augustan Humanism* (Oxford: Clarendon Press, 1965), pp. 171–210.

[90] And cf. the second epigraph to this chapter, from Philibert Delorme, *Le Premier Tome de l'Architecture* (Paris, 1567), fol. 4.

[91] *Characteristicks of Men, Manners, Opinions, Times*, 5th edn (London, 1732), II, pp. 373, 347, 398.

[92] *Ibid.*, I, p. 115.

[93] Fussell, *Rhetorical World*, p. 177.

[94] *An Essay Concerning Human Understanding*, ed. Peter H. Nidditch (Oxford: Clarendon Press, 1975, reprinted 1982), bk II, ch. xxiii, par. 12.

[95] *Essay*, II, iii, 1; II, x, 2. Cf. Fussell, *Rhetorical World*, p. 177.

'presence-room', doctrines are 'the Basis and Foundation, on which [adults] build [children's] Religion or Manners',[96] and so on. Like More, Locke also speaks of the body as the 'house' of the soul.[97] One chapter explains that man has the ability to synthesize large numbers of simple ideas, thereby making 'collective *Ideas* of Substances, as a Troop, an Army, a Swarm, a City, a Fleet', and the next chapter argues that the mind absorbs the details of parts as only relative, thus grasping the larger structures, or wholes.[98]

These spatial concepts are significant. Locke's complex discussion of expansion and extension seeks to explain man's perception of infinity and eternity. Locke thinks people have more trouble conceiving of infinite space, because

Duration and Extension being used as names of affections belonging to other Beings, we easily conceive in GOD infinite Duration, and we cannot avoid doing so: but not attributing to him Extension, but only to Matter, which is finite, we are apter to doubt of the existence of Expansion without Matter; of which alone we commonly suppose it an Attribute. And therefore when Men pursue their Thoughts of Space, they are apt to stop at the confines of the Body: as if Space were there at an end too, and reached no farther. Or if their *Ideas* upon consideration carry them farther, yet they term what is beyond the limits of the Universe, imaginary Space: as if it were nothing, because there is no Body existing in it.[99]

Locke's own conception of space is certainly prominent in his explanation of human understanding: he is concerned with the mind's existence much less in time than in space. The mind, indeed, is a place: a space upon which light can be let in, a 'Cabinet' furnished with ideas by the senses, a *'dark Room'* illuminated through windows, for 'the *Understanding* is not much unlike a Closet wholly shut from light, with only some little openings left, to let in external visible Resemblances, or *Ideas* of things without'.[100]

Like the edifice that is the universe, human beings are 'framed' according to the same principles by the divine architect. Isaac de La Peyrère had spoken of 'the framing of *Adam*, and building of *Eve*', and of the world as a house spoiled by the corruptions of man.[101] The widespread image of the world *'as a large and stately Edifice'* (Cudworth's phrase), confirms an intellectual system of the universe, which a supreme designer created and over which he presides; the system is providential, the designer a benevolent deity.[102] The

[96] *Essay*, II, x, 2; I, ii, 15; II, iii, 1; I, iii, 22.
[97] *Essay*, II, xxvii, 6.
[98] *Essay*, II, xxiv, 2; II, xxv, 6.
[99] *Essay*, II, xv, 4.
[100] *Essay*, I, i, 1; I, ii, 15; II, xi, 17.
[101] *Men before Adam* (London, 1656). I am grateful to Richard H. Popkin for introducing me to La Peyrère's remarkable, and once controversial book. Popkin's *Isaac La Peyrere (1596–1676): His Life, Work and Influence* (Leiden: E. J. Brill, 1987) is definitive.
[102] Cudworth, *True Intellectual System*, p. 465. Like Cudworth, Thomas Browne writes of 'the great house of the world' ('The Garden of Cyrus' [1658] in *Religio Medici and Other Works*, ed. L. C. Martin [Oxford: Clarendon Press, 1964], p. 165). Hume would use the same evidence to posit

design argument, together with its variations, is pervasive in the natural philosophy and the literature of the earlier eighteenth century, and just as common in the writings of natural scientists interpreting what they see when they look through a telescope or a microscope. Since so much of the natural philosophy of the period was the province of theologians, the evidence of empirical science was frequently used to prove (but sometimes to disprove) the existence of design long before man discovered it. In a typical Royal Society stance, Wilkins argued that the microscope reveals tiny, previously unknown details of nature in exactly the same way as God reveals the works of Providence.[103] Microscopes and telescopes enabled men to understand whole designs which 'prove' that 'the Almighty Governour of the Universe' was a providential and benevolent deity.[104] 'So great is the unfathomable Depth of natural Architecture', thought Robert Morris, echoing Shaftesbury, 'that the seeming lowest contemptible Insect, the smallest Mite, or the very Atoms of the Air, is a mysterious Act of Divine Wisdom': we must be brutes indeed not to appreciate 'the immediate Beauties of Nature, and the Hand of a Divine Power alone, in the architectual [sic] Creation of the World, and in all its Works'.[105] And as late as 1793 Edward Harrington would remind the world that 'the African termites bellicosi, a species of ants, is as much superior to [man] in the construction of their buildings, as the Great Architect of the world is to man'.[106]

Such imagery of design in such diverse writing points to a spatial discourse in which numerous writers saw evidence around them of a world that was ordered and harmonized, be that evidence the orbits of the planets, or the proportions of the human body, or the structure of a fly's eye (Hooke's celebrated example). Evidence of disorder could be dismissed easily: that was not disorder in the wider, providential scheme of things, but could be attributed to man's incomplete vision of the whole. One anonymous writer who celebrated harmony without uniformity gave as examples: 'The Firmament, that vast Expanse, [which] is one beautiful Arch, but its Beauties shine by an infinite Variety of Stars', and the five 'inhabitants' of the human head

a malevolent deity. See Hurlbutt, Hume, Newton, and the Design Argument, p. 159. Cf. Martin C. Battestin, The Providence of Wit: Aspects of Form in Augustan Literature and the Arts (Oxford: Clarendon Press, 1974), p. 34, and C. J. Rawson's spirited hostility to Battestin in 'Order and Misrule: Eighteenth-Century Literature in the 1970s', ELH 42 (1975), 471–505.

[103] John Wilkins, A Discourse Concerning the Beauty of Providence, 4th edn (London, 1672), p. 60.

[104] Cheyne, Philosophical Principles, dedication, n.p. On telescopes, microscopes and literature, Marjorie Hope Nicolson is indispensable: 'The Telescope and Imagination', Modern Philology, 32 (1935), 233–60, The Microscope and English Imagination (Northampton, Mass.: Smith College, 1935); both reprinted in Science and Imagination (Ithaca, N.Y.: Great Seal Books, 1956), pp. 1–29, 155–234.

[105] An Essay in Defence of Ancient Architecture, pp. 3–4.

[106] A Schizzo on the Genius of Man (Bath, 1793), p. 71, note.

– the senses – which 'differ and yet triumph in unity', because they 'agree to meet in several distinct Apartments of the same Temple'.[107]

Cosmic order and harmony come from a mind capable of design. The perfect analogue, graspable by even the dullest comprehension, is spatial design, of a house, a city, or even a whole country: as I have mentioned already, the Roman Empire had been imagined as a city, and the whole of Egypt as a house.[108] It would require a writer who sees with the eye of faith to relate the parts to the whole design. This commonplace argument received its most lucid popular expression in the familiar ending of the first part of Pope's *Essay on Man*. Since the architect is a designer, the tautology that he creates order *and* harmony means that the designer delimits space, not time.

An architect's relation to his building could be analogous to a divine designer's relation to the cosmic space he ordered. The poet and the novelist were just as comfortable with the analogue suggesting that they were designers who practically played God. The analogue suggests that a very high value was attached to the organization of space. For most architects the analogue seems to have been taken for granted, exploited far more often in theory than in practice. But for one architect, John Wood the Elder, it was so valuable in practice too that his emphasis on the individual designer is unusually important. Wood exploited the concept of God as architect and, like Burnet, he accepted that Solomon's Temple 'represented the Universe'.[109] Wood meant his own buildings in Bath to be 'Hieroglyphical Representation[s] of the past *History* of the *World*'.[110] Wood therefore answers Bernard Tschumi's question, 'If a space is a representation of an idea or a thought which is signified,, does a space achieve its meaning through its relation to all other spaces in a context, or through all the spaces for which this space has become metaphorical?'[111] Wood's specific context is the whole of human history, so vast that one space acquires its meaning from all other spaces. Participating in the tradition of universe-as-building, Wood created spatial images of an ideology that relied heavily on a progressive view of history. Design meant divinely ordered regularity, not the chance collocation of parts. In an ordered world such as Wood's Bath was supposed to represent, a social hierarchy was maintained, and social spaces – even a whole city – were organized, symmetrical and regular, and so expressed that hierarchy. I will now go on to discuss, in the light of this spatial thinking, Wood's dual roles: as an entrepreneur in the expansion of Bath, and as an interpreter of divine spatial design (and more) in his varied programme of new buildings.

---

[107] *Harmony without Uniformity: Being a Philosophical Defence of Liberty and Charity. Address'd to the Harmonious Tribe of Spirituual Place-Men* ((London, 1740), p. 2.

[108] *On Adam's House in Paradise*, p. 166.

[109] *Origin of Building*, p. 124.

[110] *Ibid.*, p. 90.

[111] Bernard Tschumi, 'Questions of Space: The Pyramid and the Labyrinth (or the Architectural Paradox)', *Studio International*, 190, no. 177 (September/October, 1975), 139, note 11.

PART II

3

The rise of Bath

. . . it is pointless trying to decide whether Zenobia is to be classified among happy cities or among the unhappy. It makes no sense to divide either into these two species, but rather into another two: those that through the years and the changes continue to give their form to desires, and those in which desires either erase the city or are erased by it.

Italo Calvino, *Invisible Cities*

. . . this bathing is profitable for all palsies, apoplexies, caros, epilepsies, stupidity, defluctions, gouts, sciaticaes, contractions, cramps, aches, tumors, itches, scabs, leprosies, cholicks, windyness, whites in women, stopping of their courses, barrenness, abortions, scorbuts, anasarcaes, and generally all cold and phlegmatick diseases, which are needless to reckon up.

Edward Jorden, *A Discourse of Natural Bathes and Mineral Waters* (1632)

In John Wood's day, visitors to Bath used to be reminded that the city's origins were firmly rooted in British myth. Until about 1700 a grotesque statue of the legendary founder of the city, King Bladud, stood over the north gate, only to be replaced by a new, even worse one, that looked 'more like a dressed Puppet, seated in a Ducking Stool, than the Figure of a famous King', but anyone chancing to miss that could always read, on the south wall of the King's Bath, an inscription that commemorated the fantastic achievements of this curious character.[1] The fanciful inscription 'appearing to some of the last [i.e. seventeenth] Century as a legendary Tale . . . was therefore abridged, and, in respect to Time, brought down to the Year 1672', and was then published in Thomas Guidott's *De Thermis Britannicis* in 1691. Particularly well-read visitors might also have known half a dozen different written versions of the Bladud legend.[2]

[1] John Wood, *An Essay Towards a Description of Bath*, 2nd edn (1749), II, p. 324 and I, p 8. The crude statue and the solemn inscription (dated 1699) can still be seen, on the south wall of the King's Bath.

[2] Guidott printed the inscription in Latin (*De Thermis Britannicis* [London, 1691], p. 16). The sources of the legend include: Wace, *Roman de Brut*, 1667–77 and Layamon, *Brut or Chronicle of Britain*, 2,834–95, both known only in manuscript (e.g. British Library, MS Cotton CAL. A.ix.1) until Sir Frederic Madden edited them for publication in 1847; John Higgins, 'Bladud' (*Parts Added to the Mirror for Magistrates*, ed. Lily B. Campbell [Cambridge: Cambridge University Press, 1946], pp. 132–44); John Leland, *Commentarii de Scriptoribus Britannicis* (Oxford, 1709),

Geoffrey of Monmouth, the oldest source of the story, explained that at the time of the prophet Elijah, Bladud built Bath, 'and made the hot Baths in it for the Benefit of the Publick, which he dedicated to the Goddess *Minerva*; in whose Temple he kept Fires that never went out nor consumed to Ashes, but as soon as they began to decay were turned into Balls of Stone'.[3] Furthermore, Bladud was so proficient in necromancy that he learned to fly: but not proficient enough, for 'in one of his flying humours',[4] he 'fell down upon the Temple of *Apollo* in the City of *Trinovantum,* where he was dashed to Pieces'.[5] Geoffrey's source on the strange properties of the undying fires was the third-century writer Solinus, who may have been describing Somerset coal when he wrote that this 'perpetual fire never whitens to ash, but as the flame fades, turns into rocky lumps'.[6] As for Bladud, Geoffrey's account, like most of his 'history', was hardly considered reliable: indeed he was often called the inventor rather than 'translator' of the British history.[7] In a more sober commentary than Geoffrey's, William Camden declared: 'I dare not attribute [the baths'] original to that art [of magic]'; and in another, John Aubrey's friend Dr Guidott considered nature more likely than any 'Art of Magick' to have 'made the Hot Waters in *Bath*'.[8] Stories of magic and perpetual fires Guidott dismissed as 'feigned matters', and the equally sanguine Dr Edward Jorden thought them 'too simple for any wise man to beleeue, or for me to confute'.[9] Daniel Defoe, never guilty of credulity, acknowledged the 'Antiquity of this Place' but refused to 'come in to the Inscription under

pp. 8–11; Spenser, *Faerie Queene*, ii. x. 25–26; *Coryat's Crudities* (London, 1611); William Camden, *Britannia*, ed. Edmund Gibson (London, 1695), cols. 69–70. There were other sources still, such as Aylett Sammes, *Britannia Antiqua Illustrata: or, the Antiquities of Ancient Britain* (London, 1676), which simply repeated Camden or Geoffrey.

3 *The British History*, translated by Aaron Thompson (London, 1718), p. 49.

4 William Burton, *A Commentary on Antoninus his Itinerary* (London, 1658), p. 24; cited by Ernest Jones, *Geoffrey of Monmouth*, University of California Publications in English Vol. 5, No. 3 (Berkeley and Los Angeles: University of California Press, 1944), p. 365.

5 *The British History*, p. 50.

6 Solinus, *Collecteana rerum memorabilium*, quoted by Barry Cunliffe, *Roman Bath Discovered* (London: Routledge & Kegan Paul, 1971, rev. edn 1984), p. 14. See also Samuel Lysons, 'Remains of Two Temples, and other Roman Antiquities discovered at Bath', in *Reliquiae Britannico-Romanae, containing Figures of Roman Antiquities discovered in various parts of England*, I (London: Cadell & Davies, T. Payne, & White, Cochrane, 1813), p. 3. John Jones gave the story currency in his *Bathes of Bathes Ayde* (London, 1572), but Thomas Guidott dismissed it (*A Discourse of Bathe, and the Hot Waters there* [London, 1676], p. 3).

7 E.g. William Lloyd, Bishop of Worcester, declared (around 1703-04) that Geoffrey mingled a few chance truths with his own fictions (see A. Tindal Hart, *William Lloyd 1627–1717: Bishop, Politician, Author and Prophet* [London: SPCK, 1952], p. 229). Cf. Stuart Piggott, 'The Sources of Geoffrey of Monmouth', *Antiquity*, 15 (1941), 269–86, and Ernest Jones, *Geoffrey of Monmouth*, pp. 357–77. For a recent, suprisingly sympathetic view of Geoffrey's history, see Norma Lorre Goodrich, *King Arthur* (New York and Toronto: Franklin Watts, 1986), pp. 41–47.

8 Camden, *Britannia*, col. 70; Guidott, *An Appendix concerning Bathe* (London, 1669), in Edward Jorden, *A Discourse of Natural Bathes, and Mineral Waters*, '4th edn' [actually 5th] (London, 1673), p. 5.

9 *Appendix*, p. 51. Jorden, *Discourse*, 2nd edn (London, 1632), p. 133.

the Figure' which claimed that Bladud 'found out the use of these *Baths*, 300 Years before our Saviour's Time . . . because even the Discovery is ascribed to the Magick of the Day, not their Judgment in the Physical Virtue of *Minerals*, and *Mineral-Waters*'.[10]

In 1802 a guidebook informed tourists that 'till within these fifty years' the inhabitants of Bath had 'maintained their descent from the necromantic Bladud' with an ardour equal to that 'with which the classical states' adopted their deities.[11] That 1750 or so should mark the *end* of such a belief, rather than its renewal, would have dismayed John Wood, who in 1749 had given the Bladud myth its fullest – and most naively charming – expression. Wood told how Bladud had been expelled from the royal court by his father, Lud Hudibras, because 'by some accident or other', he had contracted leprosy. Incognito, he found a job as a swineherd. The pigs too soon became leprous, but were miraculously cured of their disease when they wallowed in the mud above some hot springs in the west of England. Bladud followed their example, was instantly cured, and when he eventually succeeded to the throne of Britain, he set up his court on the site of the hot springs in 483 BC. The city – Bath, of course – was built three years later.[12] In an earlier version of his story, Wood also had Bladud falling to his death on the steeple of Salisbury Cathedral: he later changed this to Trinovantum, which he triumphantly identified as Bath. (Everyone else identified Trinovantum as London.)[13]

Wood ascribed his story of Bladud and the pigs to oral tradition. Although in 1697 respectable Dr Robert Peirce felt certain that 'there is nothing impossible in it, nor very improbable',[14] by the time Wood was writing, Bathonians had long been something of a laughing stock for perpetuating this ludicrous account of their city's origin, even after 'the famous *John* Earl of *Rochester*

---

[10] *A Tour thro' the whole Island of Great Britain*, ed. G. D. H. Cole (London: Peter Davies, 1927), II, p. 432.

[11] *An Historical and Descriptive Account of Bath, and Its Environs* (Bath: R. Cruttwell, 1802), p. 1. Alfred Barbeau, *Life and Letters at Bath in the xviiith Century* (London: Heinemann, and New York: Dodd, Mead, 1904), p. 4, speaks of the Bathonians' pious belief in the legend. The very early commentary by Ranulf Higden accepts that Bladud founded the city, but appeals 'to kendly reason' and a natural cause of the water's heat that 'wassheth of tetres soores and scabbes' (*Policronicon*, 2nd edn [Westminster: Wynkyn de Worde, 1495], fol. xlvi). One hears of Bladud in Bath even today.

[12] Wood, *Essay* (1749), I, pp. 71–76.

[13] *An Essay towards a Description of Bath* (Bath, 1742), I, p. 8. A contemporary MS annotation in the Henry E. Huntington Library's copy exclaims: 'how unguarded Mr. Wood must be to assert this: when there was no Church till 1083 Years after our Saviour.' The Cathedral of Old Sarum was completed in 1258. For Trinovantum as London, see Swift, 'On Poetry. A Rapsody,' 280 (*Poems*, ed. Harold Williams, 2nd edn [Oxford: Clarendon Press, 1958], II, p. 649), and Braun and Hogenberg, *Civitates Orbis Terrarum* (Cologne, 1572–1617; reprinted Cleveland and New York: World Publishing Co., 1966), I, plate 1.

[14] Robert Peirce, *Bath Memoirs: or, Observations in three and forty years practice, at the Bath* (Bristol, 1697), p. 175.

coming to *Bath*, the Story of *Bladud* and his Pigs became a Subject for his Wit, and this proved the Cause of striking it out of the Inscription placed against one of the Walls of the King's Bath'.[15] Then in 1711 Martin Powell ran a puppet show of 'The History of King Bladud, Founder of the Bath', so that, to Wood's chagrin, 'the Tradition is now in a Manner lost at *Bath*'.[16] Actually, it was not lost entirely: in 1736 or so 'a tragedy call'd, the TRANSFORMATION: or the *fall of* BLADUD, as he assum'd the seat of *Jupiter*' was advertised as 'ALMOST ready for the Stage', then about 1760 a standard guide book for tourists retailed Wood's account as if it were fact, and in 1775 an anonymous author was still willing to accept Wood's version of the story, and Samuel Foote's allusion to it in a play cannot have been lost on his audience in 1778.[17] Learning of the story on his way through Bath in 1751, Dr Pococke had observed cautiously, 'There may be some foundation for it in tradition'.[18]

One anonymous joker said that 'a belief of Bladud and his swine made one of the necessary qualifications for an introduction into the body corporate', but whether or not anyone, Wood included, seriously believed the Bladud myth, it was a conspicuous means of advertising the efficacy of the naturally hot spring waters, 'Where Pigs were once, and Princes now are boil'd', as another wit put it.[19] Wood knew, of course, that the enduring reason why Bath attracted so many visitors was the fame of the waters' curative power, 'a Fame', he claimed, exaggerating as usual, 'that stirred up the grand Monarch of *France* to compleat the Works of *Bourbon* [in] 1680'.[20] Appealing to primitive hut theory, Guidott thought that in the distant past 'Sick people in all probability . . . came hither for relief, first making small Cottages for their Conveniences, which were afterwards improved into fairer Buildings. So that now in this particular, there are few places in *England* that exceed it.'[21] Wood, indeed, placed such high value on the waters that he considered it essential 'to expell all private Property to a proper Distance from the Heads of our

---

[15] *Essay* (1749), I, p. 76. I do not know Wood's authority for this anecdote, which, like most Rochester stories, is probably apocryphal but still plausible. Rochester is known to have visited Bath in June 1671 (*The Letters of John Wilmot, Earl of Rochester*, ed. Jeremy Treglown [Oxford: Blackwell, 1980], p. 66).

[16] *Ibid.*, Wood refers to *Spectator*, Nos. 14 (16 March 1711), 31 (5 April 1711), and 40 (16 April 1711). See *The Spectator*, ed. Donald F.Bond (Oxford: Clarendon Press, 1965), I, pp. 130, 172.

[17] *The Transformation* was apparently never printed. See [Thomas Goulding], *The Fortune-Hunter: or, the Gamester Reclaim'd* [Bath, 1736?], p. [102]. [R. Hippesley?], *Bath and It's Environs* (Bath, 1775), canto III; *The Bath and Bristol Guide: or, the Tradesman's and Traveller's Pocket-Companion*, 4th edn (Bath, 1760?), pp. 1–11; in Foote's *Maid of Bath* (London, 1778), p. 6, Sir Christopher Cripple complains: 'I am shunn'd worse than a leper in the days of King Lud.'

[18] Richard Pococke, *Travels through England*, ed. James Joel Cartwright, Camden Society New Series, 42 and 44 (London, 1888–89), I, pp. 4–5.

[19] *An Historical and Descriptive Account*, p. 10; [George Ellis?], *Bath: Its Beauties, and Amusements*, 2nd edn (Bath, 1777), p. 3.

[20] *Essay* (1749), I, p. 219.

[21] Guidott, *Appendix*, p. 12.

Sovereign Fountains, and to enlarge the Bounds of the Baths, to preserve the Springs for the Benefit of Posterity'.[22]

The springs seem to have been in use since the late Mesolithic era (about 5,000 to 4,000 BC), but as Samuel and Nathaniel Buck announced in the caption to their print of Bath, 'not much Credit is given to any Accounts of ye first discoverers of them, notwithstanding ye Inscription . . . of Bladud . . . neither can ye discovery be attributed to ye Romans. But there are Proofs that these last contributed to render them commodious and prevent their mixing with other Waters.'[23] Even before the Romans built their baths there, about AD 60–70, sufferers from 'Palsies, Contractions, Rheums, cold Tumors, affects of the skin, aches, &c.' had sought relief by plunging into the steaming waters, rich with 'Bitumen, with Nitre, and some Sulphur'.[24] Visitors in the sixteenth century, overcoming the exhalation of 'an ill favour proceeding from corrupt water mix'd with earth and brimstone' would find 'an effectual remedy to such bodies as by reason of ill humours are dull and heavy' since the heat of the waters would induce sweating, 'and by that means the career of the humour is curb'd'.[25]

The Bladud myth as retailed by Wood epitomized the experience of thousands of ailing visitors, even those who 'look upon the *Baths* as a Pool of *Bethesda*, that cures by Miracle', as some of 'higher quality', and 'ingenious Education' were wont to do.[26] They could bathe in the spring water, too many at a time for Pepys's comfort,[27] or they could drink it. Although Thomas Guidott 'Arrogates to himself' the happy discovery that the waters could be drunk,[28] two other seventeenth-century doctors – Edward Jorden and John Radcliffe – are usually credited with the discovery that Bath water was equally effective when drunk, provided it was not contaminated by the water in which infected bodies were immersed, a prospect that made Matt Bramble recoil in perfect disgust.[29] In fact, Ranulf Higden's words suggest that the water had been drunk as early as the fourteenth century: 'the water of this bathe be more troubly and hevyer of savour & of smelle than other hote bathes ben yt I have seen'.[30] Drinking the water, said Jorden, should 'heat, dry, mollifie, discusse, glutinate, dissolve, open obstructions, cleanse the kidneys, and blad-

[22] *Essay* (1749), I, p. 228.
[23] Samuel and Nathaniel Buck, *Buck's Perspective Views of Near One Hundred Cities and Chief Towns in England & Wales* (1774). Their view of Bath dates from 1745. See also Barry Cunliffe, 'The Temple of Sulis Minerva at Bath,' *Archaeology*, 36 no. 6 (November-December 1983), 16.
[24] Jorden, *Discourse*, pp. 155, 150.
[25] Camden, *Britannia*, col. 69.
[26] Peirce, *Memoirs*, p. 7.
[27] 13 June 1668; *The Diary of Samuel Pepys*, ed. Robert Latham and William Matthews, IX (Berkeley and Los Angeles: University of California Press, 1976), p. 233.
[28] Peirce, *Memoirs*, p. 259.
[29] Tobias Smollett, *The Expedition of Humphry Clinker*, ed. Lewis M. Knapp, Oxford English Novels (London: Oxford University Press, 1966), p. 45.
[30] *Policronicon*, fol. xlvi. Higden died in 1364.

der, ease cholicks, comfort the matrix, mitigate fits of the mother, help bar-
rennesse proceeding from cold humors, &c'.[31] Despite a high success rate,
such recommendation may seem hard to accept for anyone who has tasted
this sulphurous brown liquid,

that hot, milky, soft, salutiferous Beverage, called *Bath Water*, far beyond any hot
mineral Waters for its Delicacy, and supportable, tho' comfortable Heat [120°F], to
any other such Water hitherto discovered on the habitable Globe, as it possesses that
Milkiness, Detergency, and middling Heat so friendly adapted to weaken'd animal
Constitutions, which all other hot Waters want in due Degree. . .This Water is admirably grateful to the Stomach, striking the Roof of the Mouth with a fine sulphurous
and steely Taste,

or, as Celia Fiennes thought, it 'tastes like the water that boyles eggs, [and]
has such a smell'.[32] What is more, it runs straight through anyone brave
enough to drink it. Sadly, the *coup de grace* was administered in the winter of
1978–79 when the water had to be declared hazardous to public health after
contamination led to a fatal case of amoebic meningitis.[33]

The Bladud legend confirmed the association of Bath with spring waters
and hypochondria. In fact, Fiennes noted, 'the town and all its accommodations is adapted to the batheing and drinking of the waters, and to nothing
else', for as Defoe wrote, Bath 'would have been a very small City, (if at all a
City) were it not for the *Hot Baths* here, which give both Name and Fame to
the Place'.[34] An Anglo-Saxon name for the place, Ackmanchester, meaning
'the City of diseased People', is self-explanatory.[35] The Romans seem to have
used the place only for bathing: they built no fortifications, and probably
established only a small garrison where the Fosse Way crossed the river Avon
at Bathwick, and they apparently knew that the water had curative properties,
since they separated the water supplies.[36]

The Roman name for the city, Aquae Sulis, draws attention to the waters,
of course, but in dedicating their temple the Romans also conflated the names
of Celtic and Roman deities, Sul and Minerva, which the Bladud myth also

[31] Jorden, *Discourse*, p. 151.
[32] *The Journeys of Celia Fiennes*, ed. Christopher Morris (London: Cresset Press, 1949), p. 20.
Defoe, *A Tour thro' the Whole Island of Great Britain*, 3rd edn (London, 1742), II, pp. 257, 261.
This posthumous edition is a revised and expanded version of Defoe. Samuel Richardson
apparently supplied some of the additions, and probably edited the whole. George Cheyne
wrote the section on Bath water, with the purpose of making it 'a very saleable and entertaining
Book to the middling Gentry who want it most and buy most' (to Richardson, 13 December
1740, *Letters of Doctor George Cheyne to Samuel Richardson [1733–1743]*, ed. Charles F. Mullett
[Columbia: University of Missouri Press, 1943], p. 63). To distinguish this edition of the *Tour*
from the one published in Defoe's lifetime, I designate this one 'Richardson, *Tour*.'
[33] Cunliffe, *Roman Bath Discovered*, p. 33.
[34] Fiennes, *Journeys*, p. 21. Defoe, *Tour*, II, p. 432.
[35] Defoe, *Tour*, II, p. 431; James B. Johnston, *The Place-Names of England and Wales* (London:
John Murray, 1915), sub. 'Isle of Man'.
[36] Cunliffe, 'The Temple of Sulis Minerva', p. 16.

exploits. Yet at least as early as the 1590s the name Aquae Sulis, the waters of Sul Minerva, had become corrupted to Aquae Solis, giving rise to a connotation of Bath with Sol, the sun, thus with Apollo and another set of myths and traditions.[37] No Roman buildings were still visible, but Roman remains were found at Bath during the eighteenth century, some by John Wood's own workmen in 1727: with the meticulous care of an archaeologist, Wood recorded exactly what artefacts had been found, and where, and when (to the hour), before handing over the most interesting specimens to the City Corporation.[38] A gilded bronze head – probably depicting Minerva – was the most exciting discovery until the east end of the Roman baths themselves was excavated in August 1755, alas too late for Wood to cherish: he had died fifteen months earlier, on 23 May 1754.[39] The most important discovery of all was the first-century Temple of Sul Minerva itself, in 1790, which confirmed local tradition and gave genuine substance to myth.

Wood had the sense to see that there was a Bath industry waiting to be exploited. With the leisured classes of British society becoming more mobile all the time, lodging houses could prosper. Bath's natural commodity already meant visitors, who were accommodated in quite expensive lodging houses: ten shillings per week for a suite, and five shillings more for a servant's garret. In the season additional charges were levied on visitors: for subscriptions to balls (twice a week at two guineas each) and concerts, and to the library; for walking in the gardens; for newspapers; and five shillings for pen, ink, and paper at a coffee house.[40] Celia Fiennes considered 'the chargeableness of the Bath' to be 'the lodging and firing, the faggotts being very small', but she conceded that 'they give you very good attendance there'.[41] In his vision of a new city, Wood never contemplated reducing the high cost of anyone's stay, but sought to raise the city's income by providing more, and better lodgings for an increased number of visitors. The poor quality of lodging houses was notorious. Queen Elizabeth had condemned Bath as 'dirty of aspect and nasty of smell' (rather like herself), and although Henrietta Maria diplomatically preferred the English spa to the French, she too had hated the primitive conditions at Bath.[42] Something certainly needed to be done, because in 1727, Wood says , the streets were like 'dung-hills, slaughter houses and pig-styes'

[37] See Thomas Gale, *Antonini Iter Britanniarum* (London, 1709), p. 132, who also perpetuates the connection with Minerva. On three maps of Roman Britain and the Roman Empire, Bath was called 'Aque solis' by Abraham Ortelius, *Theatrum Orbis Terrarum* (Antwerp, 1603), the first uniform modern atlas of the world. Lysons thought the corruption of the name was probably a result of a typical error in the Antonine Itinerary ('Remains', p. 9).

[38] *Essay* (1749), I, p. 1.

[39] Cf. Benjamin Boyce, *The Benevolent Man: The Life of Ralph Allen of Bath* (Cambridge, Mass.: Harvard University Press, 1967), p. 218. Cunliffe, *Roman Bath Discovered*, p. 12.

[40] Wood, *Essay* (1749), II, pp. 417–18.

[41] *Journeys*, p. 23.

[42] See James Lees-Milne and David Ford, *Images of Bath* (Richmond-upon-Thames: Saint Helena Press, 1982), pp. 23–24, and Cunliffe, *Roman Bath Discovered*, p. 11.

and 'the Boards of the Dining Rooms and most other Floors were made of a Brown Colour with Soot and small Beer to hide the Dirt, as well as their own Imperfections'.[43] When the Duke of Chandos visited the city in 1726, he was so appalled by his cramped and unsalubrious lodgings that he resolved to build his own, employing Wood as his architect.

Wood did not initiate the improvement and expansion of Bath as a leisure centre, for that desultory process had already begun before he was born, but he planned the city as we now know it. From its 'very small and mean beginning' Bath expanded so fast that by 1791 it had become almost unrecognizable, as Fanny Burney reported when she returned after eleven years' absence to find a 'City of Palaces – a Town of Hills, & a Hill of Towns'.[44] In 1753 the antiquary William Borlase wrote to Sir Thomas Lyttelton: 'Bath, I find, alters & improves every year, and whatever is new built is spatious, airy, and rich in Pediments, Pillars, Porticoes – Their pavements also make walking in their streets, and even riding too, very secure and easy'.[45] All in all, Mrs Pendarves told Swift in 1736, Bath had become 'a more comfortable place to live in than London', which had 'grown to such an enormous size, that above half the day must be spent in the streets in going from one place to another': she liked London 'every year less and less'.[46] Although large tracts of Bath seemed like an endless, noisy, building site, the city had been transformed in about half a century from a rather squalid, cramped provincial town into an elegant and fashionable resort. Whenever anyone commented on this expansion, the name of John Wood was certain to arise: his 'fame, as an *Architect*, will never be forgotten while the name of *Bath* exists'.[47]

As soon as Wood arrived in Bath in 1727, he gravitated towards Ralph Allen, already something of a local celebrity, whose talent was to make the postal system immensely profitable to the government and to himself.[48] Allen also owned a stone quarry at Widcombe. In addition to several minor projects in the city, North Parade, South Parade, and the Royal Mineral Water Hospi-

[43] *Essay* (1749), I, pp. 170, 216. R. E. M. Peach suggested that only the inferior parts of the city were like this (*Historic Houses in Bath and their Associations* [London: Simpkin, Marshall, 1893–4], I, p. i). Not *everyone* was discontented. Tobias Venner had thought Bath 'beautified with very faire and goodly buildings for receipt of strangers' (*The Bathes of Bathe*, in *Via Recta ad Vitam Longam* [London, 1650], p. 345), and in 1687 or earlier, Fiennes was pleased with the lodgings but not with the air (*Journeys*, pp. 17, 236).

[44] Burney to Mrs Phillips and the Lockes of Norbury Park, August 1791 (*The Journals and Letters of Fanny Burney (Madame d'Arblay)*, ed. Joyce Hemlow, with Curtis D. Cecil and Althea Douglas, I (Oxford: Clarendon Press, 1972), p. 35). See also John Collinson, *The History and Antiquities of the County of Somerset* (Bath, 1791), I, p. 28.

[45] British Library, Stowe MS 752, fol. 156, verso.

[46] 22 April 1736. *The Correspondence of Jonathan Swift*, ed. Harold Williams, IV (Oxford: Clarendon Press, 1965), p. 475.

[47] [R. Hippesley?], *Bath and It's Environs* (Bath, 1775), p. 22.

[48] See Boyce, *The Benevolent Man*. Allen said his management of the western postal services had brought the Post Office over £1½ million in forty years (*Ralph Allen's Own Narrative 1720–1761*, ed. Adrian E. Hopkins, n.p.: Postal History Society [1960], appendix 1, pp. 36–38).

tal (as it is now known) all owe their existence to the partnership between the architect and the stone merchant, whose combined efforts continued for a quarter-century until Wood's death.

It is customary to attribute the rise of Bath to Ralph Allen, Richard 'Beau' Nash, and John Wood. Because these three were the most conspicuous of Bath's 'developers', they tend to obscure the less spectacular contributions made by the medical men, Tobias Venner, Edward Jorden, Thomas Guidott, George Cheyne, William Oliver, and Robert Peirce, all of whom – whatever their disagreements – industriously advertised and popularized the healthy qualities of the waters, as their predecessors in the profession had done since the mid sixteenth century.[49] Nor should the architects who succeeded John Wood be overshadowed: his eldest son John, who continued his father's work; Thomas Jelly in the middle years of the century; Thomas Atwood and his successor (and ex-assistant) as city architect, Thomas Baldwin, most active during the 1770s; Baldwin's associate John Eveleigh; Robert Adam, who contributed Pulteney Bridge; Jelly's younger partner John Palmer; and John Pinch; the work of these men continued the expansion of the gracious city into the early nineteenth century.

The landowners who initiated the expansion were mostly speculators who rebuilt on their own land, or bought land with a view to speculation, in contempt of local opposition. But some landowners were cautious about building: Wood recorded how Humphrey Thayer hesitated, after buying the old bowling green and Abbey Orchard 'with a View to improve each Piece of Ground by Building, at the Expiration of the under Tenant's Leases': when in 1730 Wood was trying to get his proposed grand circus approved, 'a Person at that Time in London' prevented the scheme from going ahead, and (to Wood's disgust) Thayer, to his dying day – 9 December 1737 – 'would not enter into the Treaty again with the Zeal of one determined to come to the Point'.[50] Whatever pressure was put on Thayer, the case was clearer for Robert Gay, who, as Member of Parliament for the city, declined to pursue one of Wood's building projects, because (Wood said) he was afraid he might lose votes, even though 'it might have been only intended the better to preserve his Interest among the Electors of the City'.[51] Wood permitted himself only the understatement that Gay's decision was 'a Discouragement',[52] but more aggrieved commentators would point out that the overriding consideration for all these men was personal profit. Even Allen, whose 'Charity is seen farther than his House . . . and brings him more Honour too', was nevertheless accused in later years of vanity, high-handedness, and an

[49] Cf. Peach, *Historic Houses in Bath*, II, p. 111.
[50] *Essay* (1749), I, p. 227, II, p. 245.
[51] *Essay* (1749), II, p. 242.
[52] *Ibid.*

unscrupulous desire for wealth.[53] The city of Bath is a memorial less perhaps to benevolence than to entrepreneurial capitalism.

This expansion of Bath would have been impossible without the Avon Navigation scheme, which finally got under way in the 1720s after fifty years of negotiation, disagreement, and delay. Andrew Yarranton described a proposal which would have connected the Severn and the Thames by way of Bristol and Bath in the 1670s, but 'some foolish Discourse at Coffee-houses laid asleep that design as being a thing impossible and impracticable'.[54] But when the scheme was successfully revived it was Allen who 'did more than anyone else to persuade Henry Duke of Beaufort to pilot through Parliament' the necessary legislation.[55] Wood's part in this project was also considerable: he even refers to digging the canal as something he himself 'had undertaken', and by sending from London 'Labourers, that had been employed on the *Chelsea* Water-Works', he was able to introduce the spade (previously unknown) to Bath workmen, and reduce the cost of earth-removal by one third.[56] Two major advantages of a navigable river between Bath and Bristol were that building materials such as lead could reach Bath more quickly and in larger shipments, and a much greater volume of Bath freestone could be shipped to Bristol, and thence to London, Ireland, and apparently even Lisbon.[57] Wood saw the advantages; it was only when he knew the navigation scheme was certain to go ahead that he began to think seriously of improving Bath.

That Bath freestone was available at all for shipment was due mainly to the entrepreneurial skill of Ralph Allen, whose Widcombe quarry kept the city supplied for over thirty years. Bath is rare among British cities for being almost entirely stone-built, and indeed a significant part of Bath's charm is attributable to the stone's warm golden colour, that 'fine yellow tinct', as Brettingham called it.[58] Bath freestone is soft and prone to crumble before it hardens on contact with air, a fact that even found its way into Richardson's *Clarissa*.[59] These properties make it cheap to quarry, since blasting is unnecessary, but they also make it difficult to work, as London stonemasons found. But those local masons who were accustomed to working with Bath freestone dressed it first, then transported blocks to the building site, where (to Wood's chagrin) rough masons put them directly but carelessly in place.[60]

53 The compliment is from Fielding, *The History of Joseph Andrews*, ed. Martin C. Battestin (Middletown, Conn.: Wesleyan University Press, 1967), p. 235. On Allen's final, troubled years, see Benjamin Boyce, *The Benevolent Man*, pp. 262-98.

54 *England's Improvement by Sea and Land. To out-do the Dutch without Fighting, to Pay Debts without Moneys* (London, 1677–81), I, pp. 64–65, partly quoted by Wood, *Essay* (1749), II, p. 366.

55 Lees-Milne, *Images of Bath*, p. 56.

56 *Essay* (1749), II, p. 241.

57 Richard Graves, *The Triflers* (London: Lackington, Allen, 1806), pp. 63–64.

58 *The Plans, Elevations and Sections, of Holkham in Norfolk*, 2nd edn (London, 1773), p. x.

59 *Clarissa, or the History of a Young Lady*, ed. Angus Ross (Harmondsworth: Penguin, 1985), p. 844.

60 Boyce, *The Benevolent Man*, p. 136.

Allen's stone was transported in wooden wagons which ran two miles down the hill from Widcombe along a railway track to his new stone works on the banks of the Avon where the stone was wrought.[61] By reducing the costs of transport, Allen reduced the price of dressed stone, underbidding his rivals for a contract in Bristol in 1740 by 24 per cent.[62] Allen also succeeded in reducing the unit wages of his workmen, but in return he could at least guarantee them employment.

Most of the businessmen responsible for the expansion of Bath had some sense of public duty. Bath, a 'universal Infirmary', as Cheyne called it,[63] became a centre of charity, too, symbolized by the founding of the General Hospital, which opened in 1740 to receive patients from other parts of the country. To enter that institution, it was a requirement to be poor: the costs of maintaining the patients (110 of them by 1755) were borne mostly by the city, by the thirty-two founders of the hospital, and by various private donors. The hospital's 'chief Benefactor' was Allen, who supplied 'all the Wall-Stone, Free-stone ready wrought, Paving-stone, and Lime used in it' at his own expense.[64] Nash donated £1,000 to the building, and Wood charged no fee for his architectural expertise. All three, aided by Dr Oliver, whom God preserve, of biscuit fame, actively canvassed the wealthy to raise funds for the hospital. Oliver was the hospital's physician and Jerry Peirce its surgeon, from its inauguration in May 1740 until May 1761.[65] In 1749 Gwynn thought the vogue for subscribing to hospitals did not spring truly from charity but from 'real *Interest* and *Pleasure*', an attitude that perhaps lay behind the repeated complaints that the insolent townspeople – 'a sharking People, scum of all the Nation' – displayed 'a very great Narrowness of Spirit' and fleeced 'Your paralytical people, that come down to be parboil'd and pump'd'.[66] In spite of such criticism Bath became almost as famous for its charity as for its new status as the nation's leading resort.

[61] The railway track is pictured in Anthony Walker's well-known engraving of Prior Park (*c.* 1750). The wagons were described by Charles de Labelye, in J. T. Desaguliers, *Course of Experimental Philosophy* (London, 1734), I, pp. 274–79. John Padmore of Bristol devised a simple but ingenious design for brakes that enabled one man to control a stone-laden wagon. See Boyce, *Benevolent Man,* pp. 31–32. The stone works are shown somewhat indistinctly, in Buck's engraving of the city (1745; first published 1774).

[62] City of Bristol Record Office, MS 04285, minutes of the Committee of the Exchange and Market, 1739–68. Wood also publicized this reduction in the price of the stone (*A Plan of the City of Bath* [Bath, 1736]).

[63] *An Essay of Health and Long Life*, 2nd edn (London, 1725), p. 2. The anonymous author of *Diseases of Bath* reported that Cheyne 'Is said for One he cures a Score to kill' (p. 6).

[64] Richardson, *Tour*, II, p. 263.

[65] Our anonymous poet considered Peirce 'humane', and, despite his being a surgeon, 'honest' (*Diseases of Bath*, p. 4).

[66] Gwynn, *An Essay on Design* (London, 1749), p. 78; *Diseases of Bath* (1737), p. 4; Richardson, *Tour* II, p. 263; Foote, *The Maid of Bath,* p. 2. See also [Goulding], *The Fortune-Hunter,* p. 23; and Richard Graves, *The Spiritual Quixote: or, the Summer's Ramble of Mr. Geoffry Wildgoose* (London, 1773), II, p. 2.

Bath's rise as a fashionable social resort was due in large part to the efforts of Beau Nash, self-styled 'King of Bath'. This improbable Welsh adventurer instituted rules for proper behaviour to which all visitors – no matter how lofty their status – were obliged to adhere. Richard Graves simply expressed a commonplace when he said that Nash 'had greatly reformed and regulated the manners and behaviour of his subjects in the public room'.[67] But there was a darker side, too. According to Wood, the Gaming Act of 1739 was passed at the request of the Bath corporation, to rid the city of 'fraudulent, and deceitful' gaming and gamesters, and according to the compilers of the 1742 version of Defoe's *Tour*, 'Gaming used to obtain here, as at all publick Places, to a scandalous Degree; but the Act prohibiting that pernicious Practice, has a good deal checked its Progress', but they cannot have known that Nash was, in Goldsmith's words, 'himself concerned in the gaming-tables, of which he only seemed the conductor'.[68] Scandal would follow later.

Long before the arrival of Nash in 1705, Bath had an undesirable reputation for immorality: back in 1572 another Welshman, John Jones, issued a stern warning to male visitors: 'See that altogither whyle ye be there, and lenger, yee auoyde copulation, that is, the vse of women'.[69] The temptations of Bath were evidently undiminished by time. Delicate sensibilities were offended that mixed bathing was permitted: a crusty colonel in one of Thomas D'Urfey's plays finds naked bathing 'very nauseous' and Pander, a character in another light comedy, claims that the 'Class' of demure prudes 'decreases daily' thanks to 'spreading Libertinism'.[70] Dr Jorden (as quoted by Wood) most certainly was not amused: 'The baths are bear-gardens, where both sexes bathe promiscuously', so perhaps he thought they deserved their unpleasant fate: 'passers-by pelt them with dead dogs, cats and pigs': this was considered such a serious problem that a local law was passed, 'That no Person shall presume to cast or throw any Dog, Bitch, or other live Beast, into any of the said Baths', but the law apparently did not prevent anyone from throwing *dead* animals at the bathers. (The fine was 3s 4d.)[71] Although Nash helped to palliate Bath's notoriety, he never entirely suppressed it.[72] Throughout the century, Bath was said to be full of loose women, cheats (as the Bath scenes in Smollett's *Peregrine Pickle* reveal), procurers and profli-

---

[67] Graves, *The Spiritual Quixote*, I, p. 277.

[68] Wood, *Essay* (1749), II, p. 388; Richardson, *Tour*, II, pp. 255–56; *Collected Works of Oliver Goldsmith*, ed. Arthur Friedman (Oxford: Clarendon Press, 1966), III, p. 317.

[69] *Bathes of Bathes Ayde* (London, 1572), fol. 30, recto.

[70] Thomas D'Urfey, *The Bath, or, the Western Lass* (London, 1701), I, i; Gabriel Odingsells, *The Bath Unmask'd* (London, 1725), p. 6.

[71] Wood, *Essay* (1749), I, p. 217, II, p. 408. Cf. Humphry Clinker, p. 47.

[72] Cf. [Eliza Haywood], *Bath-Intrigues*, with introduction by Simon Varey, Augustan Reprint Society, No. 236 (Los Angeles: Clark Library, 1986); *The Bath, Bristol, Tunbridge and Epsom Miscellany* (London, 1735), especially pp. 11–13; 'Bath Intrigues', an obscene verse, erroneously attributed to Rochester in *The Works of the Earls of Rochester, Roscommon, Dorset, the Duke of Devonshire, &c.* (London, 1732).

gates: a veritable 'sink of profligacy and extortion', in fact.[73] After his brief account of the antiquity of the city, Defoe admitted:

There remains little to add, but what relates to the Modern Customs, the Gallantry and Diversions of that Place, in which I shall be very short; the best Part being but a Barren Subject, and the worst Part meriting rather a Satyr, than a Description . . . now we may say it is the Resort of the Sound, rather than the Sick; the Bathing is more a Sport and Diversion, than a Physical Prescription for Health; and the Town is taken up in Raffling, Gameing, Visiting, and in a Word, all sorts of Gallantry and Levity. The whole Time indeed is a Round of the utmost Diversion.[74]

Those who continued Defoe's *Tour* added puritanically that Bath 'helps the Indolent and the Gay to commit that worst of Murders, that is to say, to kill Time'.[75]

The story of Nash's reign in Bath is too well known to need repeating, but it is important that despite his own hypocrisy he tried to make Bath a decent, urbane place, to give it a reputation for propriety and so make the ambience of the city attractive to visitors.[76] Nash's personality was inimitable, as his colourless successors soon proved, so that within a few years of his death in February 1761, Bath quickly sank again into unmitigated notoriety. In 1745 Bath was reported to have 'every Thing that can render it delightful & Entertaining, agreable for Persons of that high Rank & Elegancy who resort to It',[77] but such social stratification became gradually less rigid, more demo-cratized. By the early nineteenth century, when sea water was preferred to spa water and Brighton was the rage, Bath's Assembly Rooms were held in general contempt, and the famously decorous social behaviour for which Nash had been largely responsible had become just a fond memory for the nostalgic. Pat Rogers sees Nash as 'the ultimate instigator' of the expansion of Bath, 'not just because he helped to make the town prosperous, or brought the Woods' clientele to Bath, but principally because he created the climate in which architecture of such grandiose ambition could stand without absur-dity'.[78] But Nash was only one of the three who made Bath what it was: Allen's commercial enterprise and Wood's imagination built the physical facilities of the city. Together with his son, Wood devised an idiosyncratic Utopia with an astonishingly broad intellectual basis. The Woods were real innovators.

[73] *Peregrine Pickle*, chs. 68–70; *Humphry Clinker*, p. 57. The spa towns were all notorious (see *Mist's Weekly Journal*, 18 September 1725). Bath society provoked a good deal of satire, of which Christopher Anstey's *New Bath Guide*, first published in 1766 and reprinted continually for four decades, was merely the most famous.

[74] Defoe, *Tour*, II, p. 433.

[75] Richardson, *Tour*, II, p. 253.

[76] A point made by one perfunctory verse, 'Upon Mr N....s Leaving Bath' (Clark MS P745 M1, a poetical miscellany/commonplace book). The obvious source on Nash is Goldsmith's 'Life of Richard Nash' in *Collected Works*, III, pp. 285–398, some of which is plagiarized from Wood.

[77] *Buck's Perspective Views*.

[78] Pat Rogers, *The Augustan Vision* (London: Weidenfeld and Nicolson, 1974), p. 56.

Architectural Utopias had, of course, been in vogue for centuries before Wood turned his attention to Bath, but the distinctive feature of Utopias, by definition, was that they never got built. Among the more recent English attempts, Inigo Jones had 'wanted to transform London into an augustan city in which the architecture would be more than a mere setting for royal policy, but would condition and help its implementation'.[79] Neither Jones's scheme for London's improvement, nor Wren's plans to rebuild the city after the Great Fire, nor even Hawksmoor's bizarre scheme for Cambridge, could be realized. Although Bath turned out not to conform exactly to Wood's systematic proposals, it came closer than practice usually does to theory. The creators of modern Bath built a new, unique city, which enveloped and overshadowed the old. London and, later in the century, Edinburgh, expanded rapidly with additions in a similar architectural idiom, but neither could boast Bath's combination of medicinal virtue, social life, and a concentration of monumental public and private buildings.[80]

By the time Wood the elder had finished with Bath, he had trebled the size of the old city. Even though his most private intentions (discussed in the next chapter) remained in obscurity, Wood gave the city what its visitors wanted: comfortable lodgings, elegant squares, wide streets. He said the older housing within the city walls was neither beautiful nor convenient, 'for there is not a Street, Lane, Alley, or Throng, whose Sides are straight, or whose Surface is upon a true depending Line, to give them the least Beauty: Nor is there any principal Way but what lies in Common to Men and Beasts.'[81] As if these horrors were not enough, the streets also had open sewers, and water dripping down on passers-by from roof spouts. But, Wood prophesied, 'All these Defects, however, seem to be upon the point of decreasing', and with his characteristic note of self-righteousness, 'if the Corporation of the City had come into the Scheme I proposed in the Year 1727, most of them had been removed long before now'.[82] Wood was seeking to accommodate only the well-to-do, since they alone gave the city some substantial return in hard cash, and they alone could afford to squander their money on the other pleasures Bath offered. The scale of the public rooms – particularly Baldwin's Pump Room (1791–92; finished by Palmer, 1793–96) and Wood the Younger's

---

[79] Joseph Rykwert, *The First Moderns: The Architects of the Eighteenth Century* (Cambridge, Mass.: MIT Press, 1980), p. 139; Rykwert also notes the fashion for Utopias, exemplified in an earlier era by Tomaso Campanella's *Civitas Solis* (Frankfurt, 1623), and Johann Valentin Andreae, who described an imaginary Rosicrucian community in *Christianopolis* (Strasburg, 1619).

[80] Lavedan cites Edinburgh's Royal Circus, Ainslie Place, and Morey Place (all early 19th Century), as 'le dernier echo de l'art des deux Wood' (*Histoire de l'urbanisme*, II, p. 467). The standard account of 18th-century Edinburgh is A. J. Youngson, *The Making of Classical Edinburgh 1750–1840* (Edinburgh: Edinburgh University Press, 1966), including very brief remarks on Wood the Elder, p. 74.

[81] *Essay* (1749), II, p. 352. On straight lines as the source of beauty, see, for instance, Christopher Wren, *Parentalia* (London, 1750), p. 351.

[82] *Essay* (1749), II, p. 352.

Assembly Rooms (1769–71) – suggests that either the assembly rooms were uncomfortably overcrowded, or relatively few visitors actually attended the public events. Bath may have seemed enormous to Matt Bramble, but the spaces seem very small to me. Although Wood calculated that 12,000 visitors could now be accommodated, his spaces were intended for the use of few people, not for the public at large.

The uniqueness of eighteenth-century Bath consists, in part, in the personal version of Palladianism that John Wood brought to his individual buildings and their disposition. Although he contemplated constructing Assembly Rooms in Bath, 'almost upon the same Footing with the [Earl of Burlington's] Assembly House at *York*', Wood was not quite in the main stream of English Palladianism.[83] Perhaps more than even Burlington's school, Wood realized that the Palladian idiom should be seen to be new and yet remain traditionally British at the same time.[84] The theory behind Wood's architecture is an amalgam of myths and traditions that enabled him to imagine a magnificent city.

Palladio himself recognized one function of architecture as 'ornament' when he praised 'the antients' for building roads 'in such a manner, that also in them might be known the grandeur and magnificence of their minds'.[85] In a much broader conception, Lewis Mumford writes that 'Mind *takes form* in the city; and in turn, urban forms condition mind. For space, no less than time, is artfully reorganized in cities': he adds, 'The city is both a physical utility for collective living and a symbol of those collective purposes and unanimities that arise under such favouring circumstances'.[86] Georgian Bath is a nearly perfect realization of these precepts: the new city was the physical result of the system of financial capitalism that had begun to gather momentum in the last years of the seventeenth century. Bath was built *on* that system's greatest strength, credit; it was built mostly *by* middle-class entrepreneurs and businessmen, who knew how to exploit the network of credit for their own profit.[87] Wood's designs were neither shocking nor controversial, for the spaces of his new city embodied the aesthetic and social ideals of the wealthy and leisured. Although the Palladian revival was not Hanoverian, nor especially Whiggish, Georgian Bath was a good example of Mies van der Rohe's dictum that 'Architecture is the will of an epoch translated into space; living, changing, new.'[88] Yet in an apparent paradox the story of Geor-

---

[83] *Essay* (1749), II, p. 320.

[84] Cf. T. P. Connor, 'The Making of *Vitruvius Britannicus*', *Architectural History*, 20 (1977), 14–30.

[85] *The Four Books of Architecture*, translated by Isaac Ware (London, 1738), p. 57.

[86] *The Culture of Cities* (New York: Harcourt, Brace, 1938, reprinted 1970), p. 5.

[87] For an account of the social and economic development of Bath, see R. S. Neale, *Bath: A Social History, 1680–1850* (London: Routledge & Kegan Paul, 1981).

[88] Rykwert, *On Adam's House in Paradise*, p. 18.

gian Bath is the story of John Wood: unlike any other British city, Bath's architecture reveals the hegemony of one mind.[89]

[89] Wood's dominance in this respect is unusual. Other architects designed buildings in Bath at the same time as Wood, but none rivalled his range or ingenuity. Tradition, at least, ascribed to the Earl of Burlington two houses in Bath: one for himself in the Orange Grove, and one for General Wade in the Abbey Churchyard (see R. E. M. Peach, *The Life and Times of Ralph Allen* [London: D. Nutt, Chas. J. Clark, 1895], p. 66).

4

An architect's imagination: John Wood's Bath

The city, however, does not tell its past, but contains it like the lines of a hand, written in the corners of the streets, the gratings of the windows, the antennae of the lightning rods, the poles of the flags, every segment marked in turn with scratches, indentations, scrolls.

Italo Calvino, *Invisible Cities*

Sparkling with ideas, John Wood arrived in Bath on 16 May 1727, and at once volunteered to plan a comprehensive rebuilding of almost the entire city.[1] His precocious talent was harnessed by individual businessmen and speculators, but not by the city corporation, whose members, he would later complain, 'thought proper to treat [his] Schemes as Chimerical; tho' there were some of the Members of that Body of Citizens that acted otherwise, and as Men capable of being guided by self-evident Principles'.[2] From 1727 until 1781 the two John Woods, father and son, were responsible for the spacious layout and for about one third of the neo-Palladian buildings of Georgian Bath, including the two landmarks of the city: the Circus (or King's Circus as it used to be known), a form introduced into English architecture by the

---

[1] Wood was probably a Bathonian, and not a Yorkshireman, as was once thought. His father was a builder in Bath. An obituary of Wood in the *Bath Journal*, 15 July 1754, said he was fifty when he died on 23 May; a John Wood had been baptized in St James's Church on 26 August 1704, and a John Wood had been a pupil at Bath's Bluecoat School in 1711. For biographical notes, see: Howard Colvin, *A Biographical Dictionary of British Architects 1600–1840*, 2nd edn (London: John Murray, 1978); A. Barbara Coates, 'The Two John Woods, 18th Century Architects of Bath', Dissertation, R.I.B.A. (1946), of which there is also a copy at the Bath Reference Library; and Charles E. Brownell, 'John Wood the Elder and John Wood the Younger: Architects of Bath,' Ph.D. dissertation, Columbia University, 1976.

[2] John Wood the Elder, *An Essay Towards a Description of Bath*, 2nd edn (London, 1749), II, p. 243. For contemporary disapproval of the corporation's rejection of Wood's scheme, see Gwynn, *London and Westmister Improved*, p. 14.

father, and the Royal Crescent, a form invented by the father, but usually credited to the son.[3]

Wood the Elder designed the Circus but died in May 1754, shortly after laying the first stone, so construction was left to his son, then aged twenty-six. The Circus was completed in 1766. Within a year its neighbour, the Royal Crescent, had been started. Only a few years earlier Wood the Younger had built the Liverpool town hall, again to his father's orthodox neo-Palladian design. The Royal Crescent is unique among Wood the Younger's buildings for its monumental classicism. The son's other buildings are considerably more restrained and less daring. Of the buildings he designed without his father's direct influence, Wood the Younger's assembly rooms in Bath are classical, certainly, but hardly monumental, despite his use of an Egyptian hall for the interior, and as we have seen, he turned his attention away from relatively large scale public buildings towards cottages for labourers, which bore little relation even to the model villages his father had designed for Allen's workmen in the 1730s and 1740s.[4] Since the most conspicuously classical buildings that Wood the Younger constructed were not his own designs but his father's, it is conceivable that the classicism of the son's earlier buildings was chiefly owing to his father's work, and that half his career was spent finishing what his father had begun.

Wood the Elder has generally been treated as a brilliant town-planner, but 'merely' a competent, routine neo-Palladian architect. Barbara Coates, for instance, says 'There is no doubt that his real genius lay in the conception of a city as a whole, more than in the actual composition of individual buildings', which, although 'fine', are overshadowed by the achievements of the leading neo-Palladians, Colen Campbell, William Kent, the Earl of Burlington, and Sir John Vanbrugh.[5] R. S. Neale identifies Wood's genius as a planner in

[3] Coates, 'The Two John Woods', p. 95; *Humphry Clinker*, ed Lewis M. Knapp, Oxford English Novels (London: Oxford University Press, 1966), pp. 34–37. Brownell, 'Architects of Bath', pp. 127–29, suspends judgment, as does John Summerson, 'John Wood and the English Town-Planning Tradition', *Heavenly Mansions* (London: Cresset Press, 1949), p. 101. See also William Lowndes, *The Royal Crescent in Bath: A Fragment of English Life* (Bristol: Redcliffe Press, 1982), pp. 10–11. Since Wood the Elder left a manuscript drawing of a crescent, he seems certain to have invented it, and the subsequent argument of this chapter will suggest a context in which a crescent is a product of the father's preoccupations. Walter Ison attributes the Crescent to Wood the Younger's 'personal inspiration' ('A Show-Place of European Fame', *Apollo*, n.s. 98, no. 141 [November 1973], 347). One of Robert Adam's undated drawings was a plan of a crescent for Bath; see Arthur T. Bolton, *The Architecture of Robert and James Adam (1758–1794)* (London: Country Life & George Newnes; New York: Scribner, 1922), vol. 2, index of drawings.

[4] Patrick Gregory and Charlotte Ellis, 'Restoration of Cottages at Prior Park Road, Bath', *Architects Journal*, 177, no. 7 (16 February 1983), 57-66.

[5] Coates, 'The Two John Woods', p. 95. See also Summerson, 'John Wood', and John Fleming, Hugh Honour, and Nikolaus Pevsner, *The Penguin Dictionary of Architecture*, 3rd edn (Harmondsworth: Penguin, 1980), p. 349. For Vanbrugh's 'personal form of neo-Palladianism', see Kerry Downes, *Vanbrugh* (London: Zwemmer, 1977), p. 113, and for a less reverent view of Vanbrugh's fame as 'At Court, Vitruvius the second', Swift, *Poems*, ed. Harold Williams, 2nd edn (Oxford: Clarendon Press, 1958), I, p. 87.

terms of the 'social organisation of space', and helpfully discusses his role in the economic development of Bath.[6] The disposition of Wood's urban buildings certainly is ingenious, and was influential, but it is inseparable from his individual buildings, of which he was justifiably proud. Indicating a different dichotomy in Wood's works, Howard Colvin suggests provocatively that any 'connection there may have been between Wood's antiquarian researches and his architectural projects is a subject that deserves investigation',[7] yet any distinction between the 'antiquarian researches' and the 'architectural projects' is also finally artificial, because Wood's books are central to an understanding of his buildings.[8] It would have been inconceivable to Wood to separate his various spheres of activity.

If we think of Wood as an orthodox neo-Palladian architect, we may 'read' his buildings in terms of Palladian proportions, symmetries, and rhythms, *pace* Wittkower.[9] But Wood actively participated in other intellectual traditions that make his designs more symbolic than they look. Pico della Mirandola's words apply so appropriately to Wood's mind that they are worth quoting at length:

Solent quicunque in aliquam disciplinam se totos ingurgitarunt, omnia ad illam referre quam libentissime, non tam propter ambitionem, ut scire per illam omnia uideantur, quam quod ita illis uidetur, quibus scilicet usu uenit quod per niues iter agentibus, nam caetera quoque illis alba uideri solent, candoris habitu in oculos iam recepto, reliqua in se transformante, sic amantibus, perdite quicquid occurrat amatae, aut faciem, aut omnino aliquid refert sub ditionem unius imaginis, tota imaginaria amantis facultate redacta. Qui Theologus est, nec aliud quam theologus, ad diuinas causas omnia refert, Medicus ad habitum corporis, Phisicus ad naturalia rerum principia, Mathematicus ad figuras & numeros, quod Pithagorici factitabant, hac ratione cum essent ueteres Chaldaeorum in coelestium motibus metiendis & stelllarum [*sic*] cursibus obseruandis iugiter assidui, nec aliud quicquam eorum magis ingenio detinerent, omnia illis erant stellae, hoc est, ad stellas libenter omnia referebant . . .[10]

Those who are accustomed to devote themselves entirely to any discipline refer everything to it with the greatest delight, not so much on account of an ambition to explain everything thereby, as that things seem that way to them. What evidently happens to such people is like what happens to people who are travelling through snow: everything looks white to them, because they are already in the habit of perceiving whiteness, and so they then transform everything else into that, too. So with lovers, whatever confronts one who is desperately in love, he wholly refers anything to one dominant image, reducing all other images to the face of the beloved. He who is a theologian

[6] *Bath: A Social History 1680–1850* (London: Routledge & Kegan Paul, 1981), pp. 173–226.

[7] *Biographical Dictionary*, p. 910.

[8] A point made in different ways by Brownell, 'Architects of Bath', *passim*, and Christine Stevenson, 'Solomon "engothicked": the elder John Wood's restoration of Llandaff Cathedral', *Art History*, 6 (September 1983), 301–14.

[9] Rudolf Wittkower, *Architectural Principles in the Age of Humanism*, 4th edn (London: Academy, 1973), pp. 40–41.

[10] *Disputationes adversus astrologiam divinatricem*, bk 12, ch. 3, in *Opera Omnia* (1557; facsimile reprint, Hildesheim: Georg Olms, 1969), p. 721.

and nothing but a theologian refers everything to divine causes; the doctor to the nature of the body; the physician to the natural principles of things; the mathematician to figures and numbers, as the Pythagoreans were wont to do. In this manner, when the ancient Chaldeans were assiduously measuring the celestial motions and continually observing the courses of the stars, everything to them was stars: that is, they delightedly referred everything to the stars . . .

As it happens, Wood was a Pythagorean who continually returned to 'figures and numbers'. He was also absorbed by his own 'theory': his interpretation of mythical British history, of the Bible, and of Roman Bath.

Although Wood is probably the most famous British provincial architect of the period, and he receives his fair share of attention from historians of architecture, he is scarcely more than a familiar footnote for literary scholars. He appears so infrequently in the recorded lives of Bath's visitors that surprisingly little is known about him. There is very little contemporary gossip, few statements about his personality, only a handful about his writing, and no authenticated portrait.[11] But his correspondence with the Duke of Chandos, ably discussed by C. H. Collins Baker and Muriel I. Baker,[12] reveals the prickly personalities of both men, and from a handful of other surviving documents – mostly business correspondence – it is possible to create a sharper image of John Wood.

Late in the nineteenth century Sir Jerom Murch recorded the tradition that Wood was 'a proud, sensitive man' who hated pretension.[13] Certainly, Wood could be cynical and arrogant. He was obsessive, fiercely competitive and ambitious, yet also deeply religious. He was an ingenious designer and a meticulous draughtsman. He also suffered badly from asthma.[14] In the early 1740s he often declined to travel the fourteen miles from Bath to Bristol, to discuss progress on the Corn Exchange (which he was building) with the Bristol Exchange Committee. The reason he usually gave was ill health, but he twice exasperated the committee by saying that he would not travel because it looked like rain.[15] Wood's effrontery had been more extraordinary when, as a young man, he had built himself a house on the site where he was putting

[11] For contemporary comments on Wood's books, see below, notes 73, 126. A painting attributed to William Hoare shows (allegedly), Wood, Allen, Richard Jones (Allen's clerk of works), and Robert Gay, but the portraits seem stylized (reproduced in Neale, *Bath: A Social History*, fig. 9). Another portrait (also sometimes attributed to Hoare) is said traditionally to be of one of the Woods, but no one knows which: this picture used to hang at Berkley House, Berkley, near Frome. A third portrait is said on uncertain authority to be of Wood: it was given to Bath's Royal Literary and Scientific Institution in 1896 as a portrait of Allen.

[12] *The Life and Circumstances of James Brydges, First Duke of Chandos* (Oxford: Clarendon Press, 1949), ch. 13.

[13] *Biographical Sketches of Bath Celebrities* (London: Isaac Pitman & Sons, and Bath: William Lewis & Son, 1893), p. 180.

[14] City of Bristol Record Office, MS 01152 (62, 66).

[15] *Ibid.*, MS 01152 (15, 37), and Minutes of the Committee of the Exchange and Market, 1739–68, MS 04285, minute of 31 July 1741. According to John Macky, the journey from Bath to Bristol took three hours (*A Journey Through England*, 3rd edn [London, 1732], II, p. 146).

up a new lodging house for the Duke of Chandos. Chandos – himself not a complaisant person – was speechless.[16] Neither Wood nor Chandos ever deviated into acquiescence. Wood's inflexible personality caused continual friction both with his employer and with the craftsmen and labourers working under him, indeed with anyone who crossed his path, such as a surveyor named Killigrew – hired by Chandos – who soon proved 'obnoxious' to Wood. Anne Phillips, tenant landlady at Chandos Buildings, with whom Wood conducted a running war, complained to the Duke about 'an abusive Letter' in which Wood told her to stop meddling with his workmen, but Wood had authorized them to start their noisy work at 4 am. Yet Wood was undeniably provoked, and not only by Mrs Phillips, who was as troublesome as he was; at Chandos Buildings he had to endure a threat of arson, a case of vandalism, wrongful arrest, and a prosecution for unpaid wages to a mason.[17]

Wood never cared for compromise. His designs, which he consistently refused to alter to please anyone else, not only came from his imagination: sometimes they stayed there. An agent for the Bristol Exchange Committee, Edward Foy, complained:

What encourag'd Mr. Wood obstinately to persist in proceeding after such an unpresidented manner I must leave to your notice[.] the Freemason told me Mr Wood never did nor would give any drafts, this press'd me to acquaint you with it, & the many errors committed some that have been alter'd & many still remaining[,] all which being expensive & changing the Idea of the building dos sufficiently demonstrate the absolute necessity I lay under of dischargin my duty.[18]

And Foy contemptuously dismissed Wood's 'exhibiting an impracticable draft of a building and pratling in terms of art of grand performances'.[19]

In a career of twenty-eight years as an active architect, Wood is known to have been responsible for thirty or so substantial architectural projects, mostly in and around Bath.[20] He also read widely, was a Justice of the Peace

---

[16] Baker and Baker, *Life and Circumstances*, pp. 311–12.
[17] City of Bristol Record Office, MS 01152 (24); Henry E. Huntington Library, Stowe MSS, ST 57/29, Chandos to Wood, 21 April 1727 (p. 311); Chandos to Anne Phillips, 1 March 1727 (p. 221); Chandos to Wood, 26 April 1730, ST 57/34, pp. 302–3.
[18] City of Bristol Record Office, MS 01152 (3), letter of 29 January 1742.
[19] *Ibid.*, MS 01152 (30), letter of 27 November 1741.
[20] In addition to the work listed by Colvin, Wood did some repairs (when the 'ingenious' John Padmore's engineering skills had failed) in St Nicholas' Church, Bristol, in 1731 (John Latimer, *The Annals of Bristol in the Eighteenth Century* [n.p.: for the author, 1893], pp. 179–80. The relevant vestry minutes were destroyed during the 1939–45 war). Wood was also 'employ'd in other buildings at the Bath' for Viscount Castlemaine, Chandos' brother (Chandos to the Bishop of Llandaff, 10 October 1730, ST 57/36, p. 48). Tradition also has it that Wood built at least a part of Berkley House.

for Somerset, and wrote five books.[21] Wood's productivity alone is remarkable – he also came up with a design for the Bristol Corn Exchange at one week's notice. When Chandos gave Wood his first contract as an architect at the age of twenty-three, Wood must have been only just out of his apprenticeship.[22] Although Chandos smugly told his agent, 'I was willing to encourage a young Man just coming into the World', he had already tried unsuccessfully to secure the services of Edward Shepherd and then John Strachan, before turning to Wood.[23] Despite his being Chandos' third choice, Wood showed exceptional talent and promise, for he was recommended by Lord Bingley, under whose expert eye he had been 'bred up'.[24] It was while working for Bingley, first as a surveyor at Bramham Park in the West Riding of Yorkshire, then in some unidentified capacity on the Harley-Cavendish estate north of Oxford Street in London, that Wood had made a name for himself by 1726.[25]

From his first commission until his death John Wood worked exclusively in the neo-Palladian idiom. Summerson notes that in English neo-Palladianism

Three main loyalties were involved – loyalty to Vitruvius; to Palladio himself; and to Inigo Jones. Vitruvius stood for the fundamental validity of the antique and the value of archaeological inquiry. From Palladio came the general mode of expression of a modern architecture – principles of planning and proportion and the rich potentialities of rustication. Finally, Jones supplied extensions and variations of Palladio and, in addition, ways of treating ceilings and fireplaces which were wanting in Palladio.[26]

[21] Richard Pococke, *Travels through England*, ed. James Joel Cartwright, Camden Society, New Series 42 and 44 (London, 1888—89), I, pp. 4–5; *The Bath and Bristol Guide: or, the Tradesman's and Traveller's Companion*, 3rd edn (Bath, 1755), p. 13; Jerom Murch, *Biographical Sketches*, p. 180. The two John Woods are often confused, but it does seem that each of them was a Somerset JP: their obituaries in the local papers both said so (*Bath Journal*, 27 May 1754, and *Bath Chronicle*, 28 June 1781). These notices were reprinted in the *Gentleman's Magazine*, 24 (1754), 244, and 51 (1781), 295. Wood the Elder has also been said to have been a Fellow of the Society of Antiquaries, but his name is not in the Society's records (information by courtesy of Mr F. H. Thompson, secretary of the Society).

[22] Most London apprenticeships, including architects, lasted seven years, from 15 to 22 (R. Campbell, *The London Tradesman* [London, 1747], p. 306). See [George Dance the Younger ?], *An Essay on the Qualifications and Duties of an Architect, &c* (London, 1773), pp. 12–16, quoted by Barrington Kaye, *The Development of the Architectural Profession in Britain: A Sociological Study* (London: Allen & Unwin, 1960), p. 49.

[23] 4 April 1728 (ST 57/31, p. 175), and Baker and Baker, *Life and Circumstances*, pp. 300–01. Aged only seventeen, that is if we have his date of birth right, Wood had been leasing properties in his own name in Oxford and Edward Streets in London, presumably with a view to developing them as a builder (British Library, Add. MS 18240, fols. 1–42). He still held leases in Marylebone in 1732.

[24] Chandos to James Theobald (an agent for Chandos in Bath), 4 April 1728 (ST 57/31, p. 175). Bingley had been an active member of the first New Churches Commission, before it atrophied in 1716–17.

[25] For Bramham, see *Vitruvius Britannicus*, II (1717), plates 81–82, and Eric Gee, 'Bramham Park', *York Georgian Society Annual Report* (York, 1976), 15–17. For Wood's work there, see Colvin, *Biographical Dictionary*, p. 910, and Brownell, 'Architects of Bath', p. 15.

[26] *Architecture in Britain 1530–1830*, 7th edn, Pelican History of Art (Harmondsworth: Penguin, 1983), p. 361.

Although Wood was as loyal as other English neo-Palladians to these three presiding geniuses, there is an unorthodox dimension to his loyalty. He trotted out the primitive hut theory and accepted Vitruvian principles, but argued that they were not original.[27] He accepted Palladian proportion, but saw himself as a rival of Palladio.[28] And he admired and occasionally imitated Inigo Jones, but was more interested in Jones's dubious researches into the origin of Stonehenge than in ceilings and fireplaces.[29]

Evidently Wood neglected, to begin with, such trivia as ceilings and fireplaces. His early interiors were carelessly conceived and constructed, though he did improve this side of his work later. At Chandos Buildings he gave the kitchen and pantry the best view, and his wainscotting was 'spoilt' by being installed 'before the House was dry';[30] also, the roof leaked and the chimneys filled the rooms with smoke. He would have similar problems (though not his own fault) when he built Lilliput Castle for Jerry Peirce.[31] Wood's flimsy interior walls fell down every three years or so, and his attempt to install 'water closets' at Chandos Buildings was a fiasco that made the old Duke explode with rage and accuse the young architect of unforgivable incompetence. The problem was that the toilets had wooden pipes, thus accidentally confirming one writer's scornful remark that Bath was a place where 'the Company . . . have scarce Room to converse out of the Smell of their own Excrements'.[32] On 29 August 1730 Chandos fulminated against the dishonesty and 'insufferably ill' work of 'one who pretended to be an Architect', and on 10 October he was telling the Bishop of Llandaff that the outside work was 'very well perform'd, but as for ye inside, it is generally agreed . . . that no work can be worse done', yet Chandos did not 'attribute this either to [Wood's] want of capacity, or understanding his business, or to his want of honesty, but purely to a want, of due care in making his agreement'.[33] These early disasters certainly do reveal a young man's inexperience, but Wood just shrugged off Chandos' fury. Chandos realized that Wood agreed too low a price in his eagerness to secure a contract, and so when the cheeseparing

---

[27] *The Origin of Building: or, the Plagiarism of the Heathens Detected* (Bath, 1741), pp. 4–5, 7–8.

[28] *An Essay Towards a Description of Bath* (Bath, 1742), I, p. 92.

[29] Wood mentions Jones mostly in connection with Stonehenge, but he also considered Jones the probable architect of the Bath Guildhall (1625), though on thin evidence (*Essay* [1742], I, pp. 83–88, and [1749], II, pp. 316–17).

[30] ST 57/31, pp. 68, 111.

[31] *Essay* (1749), II, pp. 236–37. Wood had evidently not read Delorme's *Premier Tome*, bk 8, ch. 7, which described a system for preventing chimneys from letting smoke into houses (fol. 267, verso). Merriman's 'purifying air-stove' had not yet been invented (Loudon, *Observations on Laying out Farms* [London: John Harding, 1812], p. 97, note). Wood's problems with chimneys were common in his day.

[32] Richardson, *Tour thro' the Whole Island of Great Britain*, 2nd edn (London, 1738), II, p. 43 (see ch. 3, n. 32) and Wood, *Essay* (1749), I, pp. 6–7. For an essay and illustrated guide to the history of the toilet, see Lucinda Lambton, *Temples of Convenience* (New York: St Martin's Press, 1978), and expect suspicious glances from librarians or booksellers.

[33] ST 57/35, pp. 228–29, and ST 57/36, p. 47.

millionaire held Wood to his original estimate, Wood cut his costs by buying cheap and inadequate materials. In 1734 Wood evidently paid much more serious attention to interior design at Francis Yerbury's Belcomb Brook Villa, where he created an exquisite octagonal room, and again at Prior Park, where the hall and the gallery drew praise from visitors until alterations after his death made the hall dark and gloomy.[34] However, in all his architecture Wood was generally less interested in interiors than in exteriors, the disposition of ornaments, and the symmetrical rhythms of massive façades. His creative energy went mostly into large, sweeping effects.

Wood's first independent project in Bath was Queen Square, begun in December 1728, and named in honour of Queen Caroline.[35] Thinking Robert Gay's land 'the most eligible to begin Building upon', Wood acquired 99-year leases from Gay and began his scheme in November 1726 'for Building a Street [now Barton Street] of one thousand and twenty five Feet in Length, from South to North, by fifty Feet in Breadth, from East to West, for a Way to the grand Part of the Design'.[36] However, in the early summer of the following year, 'Mr. *Gay* began to discountenance my Scheme for his Land': this was 'such a Discouragement to me, that it made me not only contract my Designs, by shortening *Berton Street* five Hundred Feet; but, at the Instance of some Friends, form a Plan for rebuilding the Town before it should be extended'.[37] Wood therefore 'soon dropt [his] Agency under Mr. *Gay*, and determined instantly to become an absolute Contractor with him for Ground sufficient to compleat the fourth Part of an open Area', which became Queen Square.[38]

In Queen Square, Wood developed an idea that had recently been thwarted by circumstance in London. In the mid-1720s Edward Shepherd wanted to design the whole of the north side of Grosvenor Square to resemble the front of a great Palladian palace, although it would in fact have contained several independent houses.[39] But other builders declined to co-operate with

---

[34] *An Historical and Descriptive Account of Bath, and Its Environs* (Bath, 1802), p. 135. For Belcomb Brook Villa, now called Belcombe Court, see Wood *Essay* (1749), II, pp. 237–39; and *Country Life*, 108 (22 December 1950), 2,146–50.

[35] *Essay* [1749], II, p. 343. For Queen Square, Allen supplied stone but apparently no money ('The Life of Richard Jones', MS transcript in Bath Reference Library, pp. 3–5). Cf. Neale, *Bath*, pp. 151–53.

[36] *Essay* (1749), II, pp. 240–41.

[37] *Ibid.*, II, p. 242.

[38] *Ibid.*, II, p. 243.

[39] For Shepherd, see Colvin; for his scheme, see Summerson, 'John Wood', pp. 90–91. Walter Ison, *The Georgian Buildings of Bath from 1700 to 1830*, rev. edn (Bath: Kingsmead Press, 1980), p. 239, suggests that designs by John Price for the Lawne at Headley, Surrey, and by Colen Campbell for a seven-house terrace on the east side of Grosvenor Square may have influenced Wood. John Simmons began work on the east side in 1725. More recently, Howard Colvin (*Dictionary*, p. 64) and John Harris have drawn attention to the precedent of Henry Aldrich's Peckwater Quadrangle (1707) at Christ Church, Oxford (*The Palladians* [New York: Rizzoli, 1982], p. 16).

Shepherd, who never obtained all the leases and had to be content with a half-finished project. At the time, Wood was working for Bingley on the neighbouring Cavendish estate, and may possibly have been employed for some minor work in Grosvenor Square itself. He took Shepherd's idea to Bath.

Wood designed facades of whole blocks in Queen Square, sub-letting to builders who would agree to conform to his designs. Interiors were arranged according to the wishes of the tenants, himself among them.[40] This simple system became standard practice in Bath, where no two interiors are alike, and the backs of the houses are as jumbled as the fronts are ordered.[41] Wood was not taking a particularly great financial risk in 1727; there was enough potential profit in building private houses, as there would continue to be in providing lodging houses for well-heeled tourists. Later in the century, when competition was fiercer and the financial risk of expansion greater, architects found that the leasing and sub-leasing of property in Wood's manner could prove disastrous; several, including Wood's son, went bankrupt.

Wood's conceptual unit in Queen Square was not the isolated house, but the street, or the block, and the open space it contained. Although he too failed to obtain all the necessary leases for the west side of the square, which had one house in the middle of the range set back from the street with a courtyard before it, the plan was still a success. Viewed from the centre of the south side, the buildings on the north, west, and east were meant to resemble a 500-foot long palace. The buildings themselves do not form an exact square, but the enclosure in the middle of the area does. The layout of the buildings was to have been 350 by 300 feet, the enclosure 200 by 200: as they now stand, the buildings occupy a space of 316 by 306, the enclosure 206 feet square. Queen Square 'is situated . . . on an High, Airy, and Healthy Spot of Ground' in the Upper Town, and it stands on a slope, which made the west and east sides difficult to design in Wood's desired uniform fashion: but the cost of levelling the ground, £4,000, was 'a Sum too large to be risqued in the Infancy of any Scheme, much less in one begun by People of moderate Circumstances'.[42] The final design of the 'stately new Square', the enclosure 'handsomely laid out', quickly met with widespread approval, and has pleased almost everyone since.[43]

Wood did not intend his buildings to be entirely obscured by trees, as they are now. In his day, the 'four Quarters of the Square' were 'inclosed with

---

[40] Cf. Philippa Bishop, 'Interior Decoration in Bath of the Eighteenth Century', *Apollo*, n.s. 98, no. 141 (November 1973), 350–59.

[41] Gwynn was appalled by the 'heap of confused irregular buildings' behind the Circus (*London and Westminster Improved*, p. 13 and note). Cf. Mumford, *The Culture of Cities*, (New York: Harcourt Brace Jovanovich, 1938, reprinted 1970), p. 128, on the even greater contrast, of slums behind elegant façades, of Edinburgh's Charlotte Square.

[42] Essay (1749), II, p. 344.

[43] Richardson, *Tour*, 4th edn (London, 1742), II, p. 258.

Espaliers of Elm and Lime Trees; and those Quarters are planted with flow'r-ing Shrubs'; like his buildings, the vegetation was predominantly horizontal rather than vertical. Wood's Egyptian obelisk, added in 1738–39 in the centre of the enclosure, provided the only vertical lines.[44] The walks were gravel, with grass verges beside hedges. The resulting 'Verdure is always pleasing to the Eye, and very much adds to the Beauty of the Square . . . and the Trees planted in it eclipse a great Part of the Basement of the Building on one Side: But yet I preferred an inclosed Square to an open one, to make this as useful as possible: For the Intention of a Square in a City is for People to assemble together.'[45]

Just off Queen Square Wood constructed, in 1732–34, a proprietary chapel for the use only of the local residents. It was 'the Fashion of the Place, for the Company to go every Day pretty constantly to hear Divine Service at the great Church, and at *St. Mary*'s Chapel in *Queen's-square*, where are Prayers twice a Day'.[46] St Mary's was Doric outside, Ionic inside, its ceiling said to have been decorated by the accomplished Italian-Swiss brothers, Paul and Philip Fran-chini.[47] The whole chapel bore 'testimony to Mr. Wood's architectural taste . . . An ancient temple at Athens is said to have suggested the plan'.[48] The Temple of Minerva at Athens – that is, the Parthenon – has been cited implausibly as Wood's model for St Mary's but, as Brownell points out, the obvious source is Inigo Jones's St Paul's, Covent Garden.[49] As James Lees-Milne puts it, the purpose of the proprietary chapels was 'materialistic, even snobbish . . . To build this first proprietary chapel at a cost of £2,000 Wood formed a syndicate of twelve residents in the square, including himself, to whom he sold pews like freeholds. Thereupon the rich and exclusive pro-prietors chose their own incumbent, having obtained a licence to do so from the Bishop.'[50] These 'People of moderate Circumstances' were evidently not rich enough to afford £4,000 between them to level the sloping ground, but exclusive they were. The purpose behind the central enclosure of Queen Square was the exclusiveness of a new London square: 'the Spot whereon [the residents] meet, ought to be separated from the Ground common to

[44] The obelisk was erected at the behest of Nash (Wood, *Essay* [1749], II, pp. 347–48), who asked Pope for an inscription honouring the visit of the Prince and Princess of Wales in 1738. Pope eventually responded, and the bland text is presumably his. See *Correspondence of Alexander Pope*, ed. George Sherburn (Oxford: Clarendon Press, 1956), IV, pp. 170, 176.

[45] *Essay* (1749), II, p. 345.

[46] Richardson, *Tour*, II, p. 255.

[47] Bishop, 'Interior Decoration', p. 350. Geoffrey Beard rejects the attribution to the Franchinis of the interior work at St Mary's and No. 15, Queen Square. Neglecting Bishop, Beard takes issue with George Newenham Wright's *An Historic Guide to Bath* (Bath: R. E. Peach, 1864). See Beard's *Craftsmen and Interior Decoration in England 1660–1820* (London: Bloomsbury, 1981), p. 260.

[48] *Historical and Descriptive Account*, p. 53.

[49] Brownell, 'Architects of Bath', pp. 31–32.

[50] James Lees-Milne and David Ford, *Images of Bath* (Richmond: St Helena Press, 1982), p. 113.

Men and Beasts, and even to Mankind in general, if Decency and good Order are necessary to be observ'd in such Places of Assembly; of which, I think, there can be no doubt.'[51] The social status of the inhabitants evidently rose, for in 1749 Wood noted that Queen Square was such 'a perfect Sample of a well-regulated Place' that 'most of the Houses are now purchas'd and inhabited by People of Distinction and Fortune'.[52] Provided they reside in fashionable Queen Square, with access to their own private chapel, architects too are therefore not to be ranged with mankind in general. Wood's organization of space expresses his approval of social hierarchies, his emphasis on small, exclusive social groups, which are still placed together in conformity.

Wood's new buildings in Bath catered to the territorial instincts, needs, or desires of the leisured classes. This is equally true of the buildings themselves and of their disposition in the expanding city. The central enclosure of Queen Square, with its social boundaries marked off explicitly by iron railings, is Wood's supreme expression of this territoriality. But the kinds of buildings that Wood chose to design are also significant. Wood imagined and built a series of buildings and urban spaces with rigidly specific functions. Assembly rooms such as Lindsey's, which he built in 1728–30, were designed for a specific range of social activities under the control of Nash's 'laws'.[53] Gardens and enclosures were for walking and conversation. The Circus was for lodging. Each space had a specific function: concerts did not take place in the Abbey, nor games on the green, as they do now. Elaborate entertaining was not (in Wood's view) appropriate in one's lodging, although it had perhaps become a little more common at the end of the century ('we do not profess to give dinners – few people in Bath do', Elizabeth meditates, in *Persuasion*, but she issues an invitation nonetheless).[54] In the Bath of Nash and Wood, there was little opportunity for different kinds of action within a single space. This explains why Wood's *Essay* twice includes Bath's famous rules (drawn up by Nash) for proper behaviour 'to be observed by every Person of Fashion'.[55] These social conventions led Richard Warner to describe Bath as 'The *Temple* of *elegant* Pleasures where the rites of the goddess were better systematised, and her laws more rigidly obeyed than in any other spot within His Majesty's dominions';[56] these words suggest aptly the way in which Bath was a social

---

[51] *Essay* (1742), II, p. 14. Cf. James Ralph, *A Critical Review of the Buildings of London and Westminster* (London, 1734), p. 30, on the similar function of the enclosure in London's Leicester Square.

[52] *Essay* (1749), II, p. 347.

[53] Wood was 'directed' by Humphrey Thayer 'to contrive such an Assembly House for the famous Dame *Lindsey*, as could be turned to other Uses for a small Expence'; he designed the house so that 'it might be turned into Four or Five private Habitations' (*Essay*, [1749], II, pp. 242, 319), which does not mean that the quotidian function of the space could be adapted and re-adapted at will but that the structure itself could be altered.

[54] *Persuasion*, ch. 22, *The Novels of Jane Austen*, ed. R. W. Chapman, 2nd edn (Oxford: Clarendon Press, 1926), V, p. 219.

[55] *Essay* (1749), II, pp. 249, 412–13.

[56] *Literary Recollections* (London, 1830), II, p. 1, quoted by A. J. Turner, I. D. Woodfield, and H.

image of the nation in miniature, a systematically devised machinery for regulating discourse. The conventions reflected the limiting function of the laws of the nation as a whole, such as those that bounded space by defining property and trespass: Wood even speaks of the social rules as conceived 'for the better Government of the Company that frequented the City', and he devotes a whole section of his *Essay* to the city's ancient and modern statutes.[57]

Wood's regulatory designs for open, urban space encourage the illusion that Bath is not overcrowded. The Crescent is certainly expansive, not least because of the long, wide lawn that stretches out before it, but the rest of Bath is not like this. By any standards, the space in Queen Square is not enormous. Partly because the elder Wood's buildings are not high, to Uvedale Price's disappointment, they seem more intimate and less monumental than the Crescent,[58] but they also enclose spaces where action, such as it was, was largely confined to central areas. Since the eye exaggerates movement at the periphery of its field of vision, a public space will seem less crowded if movement occurs, or seems to occur, mostly near its centre. Wood's urban space therefore determined action – in Queen Square, the action of assembly – and social hierarchy. As Edward T. Hall puts it, man's 'perception of space is dynamic because it is related to action – what can be done in a given space – rather than what is seen by passive viewing'.[59] Thus perception of Queen Square and the Circus is determined partly by passive viewing and partly by the action, in the eighteenth century usually just people walking, which occurred in the space enclosed by the buildings. Our perception of these spaces today is necessarily affected by the huge trees that seem to fill them and by the automobiles that circulate remorselessly around them.

The railed central space of Queen Square is just as important for Wood's purposes as the building around it, which delimit and define that space. Richard Sennett says, 'In the great squares of such cities as Paris or Florence, unlike those of London, the arrangement of townhouses around a common space provided a superb mingling ground for the residents. The density of these areas, as portrayed in Arnold [*sic*] Zucker's *Town and Square* was very high, even in modern terms'.[60] But Sennett (and Zucker) must be modified, because so far from being Parisian or Florentine, Queen Square was a London idea, which Wood intended precisely to provide a common 'mingling ground' exclusively for the residents.

The points of entry at the four corners of Queen Square deny spectators a view of the whole square until they are inside it. The last of Wood's projects, the Circus, is a bolder conception, whose three entrances (or, to the eight-

S. Torrens, *Science and Music in Eighteenth Century Bath* (Bath: University of Bath, 1977), p. 15.

[57] *Essay* (1749), II, pp. 248, 353–419.

[58] Uvedale Price, *Essays on the Picturesque*, rev. edn (London: J. Mawman, 1810), II, p. 219.

[59] Hall, *The Hidden Dimension* (1966; Garden City, N.Y.: Anchor, 1969), p. 115.

[60] Sennett, *The Uses of Disorder: Personal Identity and City Life* (New York: Vintage, 1970), p. 159.

eenth century, one entrance and two exits) are so placed that spectators cannot see *out* of the area as they enter it. One of the distinctive features of these two urban designs is their treatment of visual space. Not only do both areas create a frame of private dwellings around a space for public activity: they also exploit the surprise that a visitor experiences on a sudden encounter with an enclosed space. To enter Queen Square or the Circus is analogous to entering a house, so that the nature of the space and its entrances suggests that one must wait on the threshold as a guest unless one is privileged to be a participant in the activity that the space defines as appropriate.

Wood's designs were therefore more social than monumental. Despite its incompleteness on the west side, Queen Square was domesticated monumental architecture, on a small scale, but still more grandiose than anything built in Bath since the Guildhall was finished in 1625.[61] Queen Square contrasted with the medieval buildings and tight, narrow spaces a few streets away. Only one later commentator noted acidly:

> But then that *Square* – within whose center rail'd
> Lies Taste upon an obelisk impal'd;
> Mark, how from servile squeamish order free,
> The different buildings sweetly disagree;
> This boasts a richer, that an humbler grace,
> Like courtiers in, and courtiers out of place.[62]

Residents of the Square and the Circus would never have been such near neighbours if Wood's first plans had been executed, for he originally envisaged the Circus, in 1730, on the other side of the city, on 'the Ground of the Abbey Orchard'.[63] In April 1738 Wood decided to put a forum, not a circus, on the Abbey Orchard, but it is not clear if this was also when he opted for the present site of the Circus. The eventual topography of the Upper Town is remarkably unified, both aesthetically and in accordance with Wood's adaptation of Vitruvianism. Wood's attempt to persuade the local residents to waste their money flattening out the slope is a clue to the geometrical bookishness of his design: good on paper, but not on a hill. Despite the slope, which obstinately curtailed Wood's plans, the nucleus of the Upper Town – square, circus, crescent – is still relentlessly geometrical.[64]

From the north-east corner of Queen Square, Gay Street, which Wood built and named after Robert Gay, runs up the hill into the Circus. Dominating the

[61] *Essay* (1749), II, p. 316.
[62] [George Ellis?], *Bath: Its Beauties and Amusements*, 2nd edn (Bath, 1777), p. 3.
[63] *Essay* (1749), II, p. 247.
[64] A map of classical Rome with Renaissance additions (Braun & Hogenberg, *Civitates Orbis Terrarum*, 6 vols. [Cologne, 1572–1617], reprinted in 3 vols. [Cleveland and New York: World Publishing Co., 1966], II, p. 49) suggests that Wood could just have been imitating the sequence of Forum, Colosseum, and Circus Maximus.

corner is No. 41 Gay Street, where in 1740 Wood built an 'architectural curio' of a house with a remarkable oriel window: according to tradition Wood built this, the only striking house in the street, for himself.[65] The other, rather drab houses that line Gay Street connect two approved Vitruvian shapes, the square and the circle. Wren had thought that 'the square and the circle are the most beautiful' of all 'Geometrical Figures' (a natural beauty),[66] and the orthodox Palladian interpretation of these shapes was that they were natural and harmonious. Robert Morris found that beauty consisted simply in proportion:

The Square in *Geometry*, the Unison or Circle in *Musick*, and the Cube in *Building*, have all an inseparable Proportion; the Parts being equal, and the Sides, and Angles, &c. give the Eye and Ear an agreeable Pleasure; from hence may likewise be deduc'd the Cube and a half, the Double Cube; the Diapason, and Diapente, being founded on the same Principles in *Musick*.[67]

Although Wood would quarrel with nothing in this statement of the nature of proportion, in his commentary on his own architecture in Bath, he generally had very little to say about the cube, cube-and-a-half, and double cube of his designs. In Queen Square and the Circus, Wood's conceptions were for once just as strictly Vitruvian as they were Palladian, but they were also Biblical and Britannic, as we shall see.

Responding to the hint supplied in Smollett's *Humphry Clinker* ('a pretty bauble; contrived for shew, and looks like Vespasian's amphitheatre turned outside in'), Sir John Soane dismissed the Circus as a trivial toy,[68] and the versifier who was dissatisfied with Queen Square was similarly unimpressed by the monotonous 'Three ranks of columns' foisted on the public by men who say 'That massive and majestic are the same'.[69] Summerson, agreeing with Smollett, describes Wood's Circus as 'roughly speaking, a miniature model of a Roman amphitheatre – turned inside out . . . in fact, the Colos-

[65] Emil Kaufmann, *Architecture in the Age of Reason* (Cambridge, Mass.: Harvard University Press, 1955), p. 33. Cf. Brownell, 'Architects of Bath', p. 64, on Wood's 'pictorial' conception of the 'imaginative bow window'. Charles J. Robertson, *Bath: An Architectural Guide* (London: Faber and Faber, 1975), p. 65; he adds that 'No. 41 [Gay Street] is known to have been the town house of the younger Wood'. Tradition has also said that Wood the Elder lived at No. 15 Queen Square, and died at No. 24. Ison, 'Show-Place', 345, says Wood completed No. 15 for Sarah Clayton.

[66] Christopher Wren, *Parentalia: or, Memoirs of the Family of the Wrens* [London, 1750], p. 351. Cf. J. A. Bennett, *The Mathematical Science of Christopher Wren* (Cambridge: Cambridge University Press, 1982), pp. 119–24. Since Alberti's *De Re Aedificatoria* (1485), it had been customary to find evidence of beauty, nature, and God in circles (see Rudolf Wittkower, *Architectural Principles*, ch. 1).

[67] *Lectures on Architecture*, II (London, 1736), p. 174.

[68] Summerson, 'John Wood', pp. 99–100. *Humphry Clinker*, p. 34: the paragraph from which this comes excepts Wood's 'ingenuity and knowledge' from the general condemnation of Bath's architects and their passion for building.

[69] *Bath: Its Beauties and Amusements*, p. 3.

seum'; even though the Circus is circular and the Colosseum ellipsoid, Wood could have been inspired by reading Carlo Fontana's bizarre scheme for building a baroque church inside the ruins of the Roman monument.[70] Certainly, the three layers of classical columns – Doric at street level, Ionic on the first story, Corinthian at the top, in the 'correct' sequence – seem to be borrowed from the Colosseum. And in the central space of the Circus Wood built: nothing. The relatively sparsely vegetated central enclosure in Queen Square was railed off to keep unwanted visitors out of what amounted to a private park. But the central area of the Circus, since about 1790 the site of five huge plane trees that obliterate one-third of the buildings from any given point of view, was originally almost entirely bare of any ornament whatsoever.[71] Thomas Malton's well-known watercolour (c 1784) shows that the vast cobbled area was adorned by a solitary lamp post, which was later replaced by a reservoir. Wood's early plan to erect an equestrian statue of George II in the centre never came to anything. At any rate, Wood rigorously excluded Nature in the form of trees, shrubs, or grass from his plans for the Circus. Wood adhered to the orthodox view that a city was planned rather than 'organic', even though the beauty of the city was the natural one of geometrical proportion.

Although as adopted in other cities, the form of the Circus, like the Crescent that evolved from it, is commonly understood now as a means of linking and blending the possibly disparate buildings on streets adjacent to it, that was not how Wood conceived it.[72] His idea was that the spectator's attention would be held by the impressive sweeping curves, which, by displaying the three orders of columns, contain the history of architecture in a single urban space. So far from being a link between streets, the Circus is a self-contained spatial entity, but because Wood pioneered the form of the Circus in English urban architecture, his achievement is usually interpreted as innovative street planning. Wood described most of his buildings in and around Bath, but he did not mention his plans for the Circus, which of course he did not live to see.

In 1742 Wood brought out his *Essay Towards a Description of Bath*, which he expanded considerably in 1749.[73] In between these, in 1747, he published

---

[70] Summerson, 'John Wood', p. 98. A copy of Carlo Fontana, *L'Anfiteatro Flavio descritto e delineato* (The Hague, 1725), was in the Wood family library.

[71] Lees-Milne and Ford, *Images of Bath*, pp. 71, 311, put the date of planting at 1790; the earliest view of the Circus to show the trees is a sepia drawing dated 1829 by A. Woodroffe, published by Charles Duffield in his *Series of Views in the City of Bath* (Bath, 1828–c 1831), in *Images of Bath*, catalogue no. 512 (p. 312).

[72] Cf. Summerson, 'John Wood', p. 106.

[73] The 1749 edition was reissued in 1765 (and that reissue was reprinted in facsimile in 1969). The antiquary Smart Lethieullier told Charles Lyttelton (brother of Sir George, and President of the Society of Antiquaries), 'there is hardly any book so bad but something may be learnt out of it' and though Wood's *Essay* was 'almost a heap of Absurd Nonsense yett a fact or Two serves to give a hint for farther Enquiry' (20 January 1753: British Library, Stowe MS 752, fol. 80, recto).

Choir Gaure, a treatise on Stonehenge written in September 1740 for Edward Harley, Earl of Oxford.[74] Inigo Jones apart, architects did not usually turn their attention to Stonehenge.[75] The most famous and intriguing of all neo-lithic monuments was subjected to scrutiny by antiquarians, who rarely agreed on its dimensions but generally accepted John Aubrey's modest specu-lation ('with humble subscription to better judgement') that it had been a Druid temple, and of course the legend has stuck, largely owing to William Stukeley's enthusiastic endorsement of the idea.[76] Dissatisfied with so many conflicting measurements, and determined to give his twelve-year-old son 'the strongest Ideas of Accuracy in this his first practical Lesson of Surveying', Wood measured Stonehenge carefully and exactly, and wrote a colourful account of how he did it. He followed John Aubrey and John Toland, but demolished much of Stukeley's new theory by showing it was based on yet more inaccurate measurements and calculations. Wood had no doubt that Stonehenge was 'the Remains of a Druidical Temple; and externally, of the real Monopterick Kind', which he lovingly reconstructed.[77] He avoided Stukeley's mistake of 'proving' that its dimensions were measured in round numbers of cubits, perhaps the most controversial part of all the arguments, since no one had ever determined just how long a cubit was, though there was no shortage of speculations.[78]

Stukeley, whose injured pride was to persuade him in snappish old age that Wood's argument was mad, had suggested that Stonehenge was a Druid temple designed in imitation of 'the glories of *Solomon*'s temple, at least of other temples made artfully in imitation of it; such as those of *Sesostris* in

[74]   *Choir Gaure, vulgarly called Stonehenge, on Salisbury Plain, described, restored, and explained* (Oxford, 1747). British Library, Harleian MSS 7354 and 7355 are the draft of Wood's survey and the earliest version of *Choir Gaure*. The title is derived from *chorea gigantum*, the dance of the giants – an allusion to a popular myth about Stonehenge. Cf. Francis Grose, *The Antiquities of England and Wales*, 2nd edn, VI (London, 1785), p. 40.

[75]   *The Most Notable Antiquity of Great Britain, vulgarly called Stone-Heng* [sic], *on Salisbury Plain, Restored, by Inigo Jones*, 2nd edn (London, 1725). Jones considered Stonehenge a Roman monu-ment, and initiated a debate that drew in his son-in-law, John Webb (who published Jones' findings in 1655), Walter Charleton, who thought the origins were Danish, and John Dryden. Cf. J. Alfred Gotch, *Inigo Jones* (London: Methuen, 1928), pp. 16–17.

[76]   *Choir Gaure*, p. 49; Aubrey, *Monumenta Britannica, or A Miscellany of British Antiquities*, ed. John Fowles and Rodney Legg (Boston: Little, Brown, 1981), p. 24. Joshua Childrey was 'clearly of opinion that they are natural stones, and placed there *ab initio*; Then which I think nothing is plainer' (*Britannia Baconica: or, the natural Rarities of England, Scotland, & Wales* [London, 1661], p. 49). *Stonehenge: A Temple Restor'd to the British Druids* (London, 1740) earned Stukeley the sobriquet of 'Arch-Druid', as Lethieullier called him (British Library, Stowe MS 752, fol. 31, verso). See Stuart Piggott, *William Stukeley: an Eighteenth-Century Antiquarian*, rev. edn ([London]: Thames and Hudson, 1985), esp. pp. 79–109.

[77]   *Choir Gaure*, p. 5.

[78]   Proposed measures – all different – were offered by: Walter Ralegh, D'Aviler, who referred readers to Perrault and Delorme; Stukeley; and Newton and his posthumous editor, Thomas Birch. For the last two, see *Miscellaneous Works of Mr John Greaves* (London, 1737), II, pp. 405–33, which Wood had read (*Essay* [1749], II, p. 348).

Egypt, and others about *Phoenicia*.'[79] Wood was convinced that Stonehenge was a temple 'principally in Honour of the Moon; and that the several Parts of the Work were intended as an Emblematical Representation of the several Parts of the Religion and Learning of the *British* Druids.'[80] He intended to publish one volume of his 'thoughts concerning the *British* Monuments of Bath' and a second on Stonehenge and Stanton Drew, eight miles from Bath, and where the remains of a stone circle still survive.[81] In the end, Wood incorporated his thoughts about everything except Stonehenge in the *Essay*, so that *Choir Gaure* is a companion piece to the *Essay*, although it is rarely seen as one.

The first part of the *Essay* (in both editions) is an account of the origin of Bath – Bladud and all – consonant with the ideas expressed in *Choir Gaure*. Ancient Bath, Wood's imagined Druidic settlement, was a capital city with three centres: one at the site of the hot springs, one at Stanton Drew, eight miles west, and a third fifteen miles south of the springs at Okey, or Wookey Hole. Thus, the area covered was a triangle of 15 by 8 by 10 miles: about the size of Babylon 'when *Cyrus* took it'.[82]

Undeterred by the need for better evidence, Wood convinced himself that Bath had been a Druid city. Without even troubling to dispute points of etymology, he said with disarming candour that Ackmanchester, a Saxon name for Bath, meant the city of 'Oak Men', though everyone else preferred 'city of sick people'.[83] Stanton Drew, he added, was a name meaning 'Oak Mens City'.[84] In both the *Essay* and *Choir Gaure*, Wood said that the Druids had founded the first British university, at Stanton Drew, whose name he conveniently took to be a corruption of Stamford.[85] Consciously echoing Vitruvius, who wrote 'not as a lofty thinker, nor as an eloquent speaker, nor as a scholar practised in the best methods of literary criticism, but as an architect who has a mere tinge of these things', Wood emphasized to the Earl of Oxford that his conjectures were 'the Ideas of an Architect, not of a

---

[79] Stukeley, *Stonehenge*, p. 17. See also Christopher Chippindale, *Stonehenge Complete* (Ithaca, N.Y.: Cornell University Press, 1983), pp. 94–95.

[80] *Choir Gaure*, p. 94.

[81] *Choir Gaure*, p. 24. See Charles William Dymond, *The Ancient Remains at Stanton Drew in the County of Somerset* (Bristol: for the author, 1896), and two books by Aubrey Burl: *The Stone Circles of the British Isles* (New Haven and London: Yale University Press, 1976), pp. 103–06; and *Prehistoric Avebury* (New Haven and London: Yale University Press, 1979), p. 225.

[82] *Essay* (1749), I, p. 41. Wood's settlement may have been the first triangular one since Andreae's Christianopolis (see chapter 1, above). Wookey Hole is a natural cavern in Cheddar Gorge. Wood's information about Babylon probably came from Herodotus, Xenophon, or Strabo.

[83] *Essay* (1749), I, p. 45. Cf. Robert Peirce, *Bath Memoirs: or, Observations in Three and Forty Years Practice, at the Bath* (Bristol, 1697), p. 1: if the city were renamed 'upon the same consideration' of its ancient purpose, 'it might be call'd CRIPPLE–TOWN'.

[84] *Choir Gaure*, p. 7.

[85] It seems to have been Wood's invention that Stanton Drew was a Druid *university*: that it was a Druid settlement was agreed by Aubrey, Toland, Stukeley, and even Pococke. Cf. Camden, *Britannia*, col. 81.

Scholar, of an Historian, or of an Antiquary'.[86] The architect thought that Bath had been the seat of Apollo, he accepted the Bladud myth, as we have seen, and decided that Bladud was one and the same with the Greek Abaris, whose engraved 'portrait' by William Hoare was inserted in the *Essay* and was promoted to frontispiece for *Choir Gaure*. The plate shows 'Bladud, to whom the Grecians gave the Name of Abaris' in suitably ancient British attire, standing on a shallow hill. Huddled together in the background are a rude cottage, a Greek temple, and a Roman rotunda, together representing the historical progress of architecture. Since Wood identified Trinovantum as Bath, and Dr Gale, in his commentary on the Antonine Itinerary, had said 'That the Sun had a Temple in that City',[87] it followed for Wood that Abaris must have been a priest of Apollo: that he was received as such in Greece was attested by Iamblichus and Porphyry. Wood added to this the authority of Diodorus Siculus, who declared that 'the *Britons*, or *Hyperboreans* paid [Abaris] the highest Honours' as such a priest.[88] The gifted Bladud/Abaris, according to Wood, had been a pupil of Pythagoras, and as an Arch-Druid, had first spread the Pythagorean doctrine - including the all-important geometry – in Britain. Eccentric as he may seem, Wood was actually in good company in propagating such a mythology. Eusebius and Scaliger at least had Abaris visiting Pythagoras in 563 BC., and John Toland and William Selden had, between them, identified Abaris the Hyperborean as a Celtic Druid with knowledge of the doctrine of Pythagoras.[89]

In Roman guise, Bath as Wood wanted it would recreate the mythical British history that he was sketching in the late 1730s and early 1740s. *Choir Gaure* emphasizes the crescent moon as the emblem represented by the stones laid out in the centre of the circle at Stonehenge, which suggests a Druidical origin for Bath's Royal Crescent. The Doric frieze of the Circus, designed in the 1740s, is decorated with metopes that can be interpreted in several ways: Britannic, rural, masonic, Druidic, or accidental. On the parapet Wood placed acorns, which Coates and Neale interpret most plausibly as Druidic symbols.[90] The shape of the Circus could not have been modelled on the Colosseum, of course, but might have been suggested by Jules Hardouin-Mansart's circular Place des Victoires (1685) in Paris, and yet Wood was probably too isolated from other European architecture to have been Mansart's imitator. Summerson has suggested the precedent of André le Nôtre's

---

[86] Harleian MS 7354, fol. 3, verso, and Vitruvius, I, i, 18.

[87] *Antonini Iter Britanniarum* (London, 1709), p. 132.

[88] *Essay* (1749), I, pp. 14, 33.

[89] William Lloyd, *A Chronological Account of the Life of Pythagoras and of other famous men his contemporaries* (London, 1699), p. 7. Piggott, *Stukeley*, p.124. William Borlase doubted Toland's 'conjecture' that Abaris was a Druid but accepted that he was a priest of Apollo and thought Druidical tenets did owe something to Pythagorean doctrine (*Antiquities, Historical and Monumental, of the County of Cornwall*, 2nd edn (London, 1769), p. 74).

[90] Coates, 'The Two John Woods', p. 63; Neale, *Bath: A Social History*, p. 199.

favoured circular garden design, but in the light of Wood's singular obsession with British history, Coates is probably right that Wood was most likely 'thinking of the Druid circles at Stonehenge or Stanton Drew, and that he interpreted them in the only way he could, in the Classical style'.[91] Stuart Piggott adds convincingly that the three entrances are placed according to a plan of Stonehenge drawn by Inigo Jones (and published for the second time in 1725), so that the outer circle of the Circus corresponds to the ditch that surrounds the stone remains of Stonehenge.[92] More convincingly still, the measurement of Wood's outer circle matches the circumference of the present chalk wall at Stonehenge.[93] Wood thought that Stonehenge was modelled on the measurements of Cyrus's decree for rebuilding the Solomonic Temple, and he approved in any case of circles, because they imitate God's 'perfect Figures', which 'universally tend to a circular Form', consisting of 'the utmost *Regularity*, the sweetest *Harmony*, and the most delightful *Proportion*'.[94] Wood might even have intended an echo of the holy city itself, since any number of maps showed Jerusalem as a city enclosed by a circular wall.[95] Wood shows influence usually only from books, and in his own copy of Desgodetz' *Edifices Antiques*, which he certainly read, he could gaze on semi-circular amphitheatres and several other circular Roman structures, such as the Temple of Bacchus, the Temple of Faunus, and the Pantheon, which Wood thought 'the most perfect Piece of Architecture *Rome* ever produced'.[96] Unlike Palladio or Burlington, Wood never designed a rotunda, but he chose to draw attention in his *Essay* to the apparently irrelevant information that Lilliput Castle, the small house he built for Jerry Peirce, stood on a site that had once been used for Druid sacrifices.[97] In view of Wood's exploitation of space in the Circus, it is entirely likely that he thought of his urban plan as a combination of temple and theatre, but most likely a Druid temple and a Roman theatre. Neale notes that Wood's Bath, usually said to be Roman, was really Britannic, but the Circus is more of an amalgam than that: it is Roman and Britannic and Biblical.[98]

Summerson's seminal article on Wood's urban planning links his historical imagination with some of his architectural conceptions, and yet Summerson's Wood is a harmless eccentric, who misunderstood what he read but

[91] Summerson, *Architecture in Britain*, 7th edn, p. 391; Coates, 'The Two John Woods', p. 63.

[92] *The Druids* (Harmondsworth: Penguin, 1974), p. 129.

[93] Neale, *Bath: A Social History*, p. 199.

[94] *Origin of Building*, p. 71.

[95] For example, British Library, Additional MS 32343, fol. 15, showing a circular city with five gates (see Walter Cahn, 'Solomonic Elements in Romanesque Art', in *The Temple of Solomon: Archaeological Fact and Medieval Tradition in Christian, Islamic and Jewish Art*, ed. Joseph Gutmann [Missoula: Scholars Press for the American Academy of Religion and The Society of Biblical Literature, 1976], pp. 46–47).

[96] *Choir Gaure*, pp. 43, 48, 57.

[97] *Essay* (1749), II, p. 236.

[98] Neale, *Bath: A Social History*, pp. 187–89.

responded with wrong-headed brilliance.[99] Although there is a good deal of truth in this image of Wood, I think it is ultimately unfair to him. True, in addition to his Bladud/Abaris story, Wood seems to have misapplied the functions of Roman monumental public buildings to eighteenth-century Bath. But in the 1749 *Essay* Wood said

I proposed to make a grand Place of Assembly, to be called the *Royal Forum* of *Bath*; another Place, no less magnificent, for the Exhibition of Sports, to be called the *Grand Circus*; and a third Place, of Estate with either of the former, for the Practice of medicinal Exercises, to be called the *Imperial Gymnasium* of the City, from a Work of that Kind, taking its Rise at first in *Bath*, during the Time of the *Roman* Emperors.[100]

One wonders what Wood had in mind; perhaps a thermal establishment something like the Baths of Diocletian? Anyway a Roman gymnasium in Bath does seem improbable, nor was there any firm archaeological evidence of one, but Summerson's commentary suggests that Wood was practically verging on insanity. In its modern form, Wood's imagined 'gymnasium' was probably intended for invalids who had 'no Place' near the Pump Room 'to retire into, when the Waters begin to operate; or for gentle Exercise, so essential to their inward Use'; his actual scheme to build such a facility above the Pump Room was rejected in 1733, because of private commercial interest, not because anyone thought it a hare-brained whim.[101] And, although irrelevant to contemporary life, Wood's idea of a circus for sports is not as mad as Summerson suggests, for there was one reasonable source. In his *Villas of the Ancients*, Robert Castell included his commentary on Pliny's Tuscum letter: 'Further from the House, beyond the *Ambulatio*, lay this Place of Exercise, to which he chose to give the Form of the *Circus*, because the Exercises that were used in it were like those that were used in those publick Places of Diversion.'[102] Castell made it plain that this 'circus' was not circular, but the typical elongated shape of a Roman hippodrome. Even allowing for the loose use of 'circus', 'cirque', and 'circle', in Wood's day, there is no reason to assume that Wood's original '*Grand Circus*' for sports was meant to be circular, nor that the circular structure now known as the Circus was the idea that Wood originally conceived as a place for 'sports'. He more probably conceived of a place for walking, for parade, and he certainly meant it to be Roman.

The scheme for a 'Forum' had actually started in 1738, when Wood began to build on land leased from the Duke of Kingston in the Abbey Orchard, and decided not to build a circus there.[103] In the 1742 *Essay* Wood insisted that Queen Square

[99] Despite some disagreements, this paragraph is largely indebted to Summerson, 'John Wood'.

[100] *Essay* (1749), I, p. 232.

[101] *Essay* (1749), II, p. 270.

[102] (London, 1728), p. 29.

[103] *Essay* (1749), II, p. 247, and British Library, Egerton MS 3647, fol. 91 (Wood's lease of the land from the Duke of Kingston).

must be looked upon but as the Barton to an open Area, to be surrounded with Buildings, which I purpose to begin in the Spring of next Year, on the South-East Side of the City, and which I hope to make the *Royal Forum*, or *Grand Place of Assembly at* Bath: It shall represent the Forums, or Places among the Antients, where Kings were wont to convene the People; and I will endeavour to give it an Air of Magnificence, equal to any Thing of its Kind.[104]

Queen Square – hardly a *'Grand Place of Assembly'* but a place of assembly all the same – was just the beginning. Wood finally built two more places of assembly: the complex of parades that he fancied was a forum, and the Circus. He was obsessed with spaces for public assembly:

GENERAL Society among People of Rank and Fortune was so far from being established at *Bath* the Beginning of the present Century, that the Nobility would not Associate with the Gentry at any of the Publick Entertainments of the Place: But when proper Walks were made for Exercise, and a House built for Assembling in, Rank began to be laid aside, and all Degrees of People, from the Private Gentleman upwards, were soon united in Society with one another.[105]

Queen Square, the Circus, and North and South Parades all indicate Wood's desire to articulate Roman magnificence, and his equally ardent determination to bring the upper and upper-middle classes together in social and commercial contact. His aim was close to Nash's, as Goldsmith (plagiarizing Wood) described it: to create an environment in which 'General society among people of rank or fortune' could be 'established', so that 'the nobility' might abandon their 'tincture of *Gothic* haughtiness' and deign to 'keep company with the gentry' at some of the 'public entertainments of the place'.[106] By being Palladian, Wood's buildings emphasized Roman tradition and history, so that they ultimately provide a framework for public activity by alluding to the activity that Wood thought appropriate to a forum in a Roman city.

As Wood eventually completed it, the project of a forum in the south-east of the city consists of North Parade, South Parade, and the connecting streets between them, leading up to what is now Grand Parade. The buildings of North and South Parades are not particularly striking to the passive eye. Wood's designs were far from palatial, surely because he was more interested in the social use of the space in front of his buildings. As Robert Adam would say in 1778, 'The parade, the convenience, and social pleasures of life, being better understood, are more strictly attended to in the arrangement and disposition of apartments'.[107] While the disposition of apartments was not

---

[104] *Essay* (1742), II, p. 16.

[105] *Essay* (1749), II, p. 411.

[106] *Collected Works of Oliver Goldsmith*, ed. Arthur Friedman (Oxford: Clarendon Press, 1966), III, p. 300.

[107] Arthur T. Bolton, *The Works in Architecture of Robert and James Adam (1758–1794)* (London: Country Life and George Newnes, and New York: Scribner's, 1922), I, p. 76. Cf. Mumford, *Culture of Cities*, p. 105.

Wood's main concern (because he left that as usual for the occupants to decide), the two Parades were places for parade, intended precisely for the public social demands of Bath's fashionable clientele.[108] The whole area – not Wood's most successful or interesting work – looks nothing like a Roman forum, but it is what Wood wanted, a 'grand Place for publick Assembly'. Wood's architecture, his dream of what he would do to Bath, originates not so much from an incredibly impracticable misunderstanding, but more from a conception of urban space as a social site for 'real and apparent People of Rank and Fortune': in eighteenth-century Bath, this meant providing spaces for promenading, seeing and being seen, for meeting 'in the Baths, Pump Rooms, Coffee Houses, Assembly Houses and other Places of general Resort', going to 'select Parties, or on mutual Visits'; Wood confidently thought everyone could 'imagine all the different Scenes of Life to be Acting in this theatre of the Polite World'.[109] He built Bath, then, on the basis of his personal conception of the city's history, and he fashioned its spaces for the use of the ruling class and for the bourgeoisie.

The disposition of buildings was only one element, but a crucial one, in Wood's conception of architecture. Wood had more theories besides Druidism. He explained his entire system in a remarkable book that sank almost at once without trace: *The Origin of Building: or, the Plagiarism of the Heathens Detected* (Bath, 1741). Here Wood supported the argument 'that the *Jewish* sacred Structures' – Noah's Ark, the Tabernacle, and all the versions of the Solomonic Temple – were constructed earlier than any edifice in Egypt, Persia, Greece, or Rome, and therefore that the architecture of those four empires is all derived from the Hebrew.[110] His proof relies mainly on Archbishop Ussher's chronology of the world, which established virtually beyond dispute 4004 BC as the year of the creation. (Ussher calculated that the process began between 9 and 10 o'clock on the evening of Saturday, 23 October).[111] Wood also adopted some small modifications from Bernard Lamy and Samuel Bochart, from Josephus in the translations by Thomas Lodge, Roger L'Estrange, and William Whiston, and from some few additions supplied by Isaac Newton.[112] In the light of the debate about the chronology that had

---

[108] As Mary Ann Schimmelpenninck noticed; her observation is quoted in *The Original Bath Guide* (Bath: William Lewis & Son, 1919), p. 75, a publication that contains advertisements for a bookshop called the 'Bladud Library', and a bottled mineral water (aerated) known as 'Sulis' (pp. 235, 219).

[109] *Essay* (1749), II, p. 446.

[110] *Origin of Building*, p. 180. Newton's private views of Solomon's Temple were similar to Wood's, but Wood knew neither Newton nor – it seems – Stukeley, who recorded but did not publish Newton's remarks (*Memoirs of Sir Isaac Newton's Life*, ed. A. Hastings White [London: Taylor and Francis, 1936], p. 18).

[111] James Ussher, *The Annals of the World* (London, 1658). Cf. James Barr, 'Why the World was Created in 4004 BC: Archbishop Ussher and Biblical Chronology', *Bulletin of the John Rylands University Library of Manchester*, 67, no. 2 (Spring, 1985), 575–608.

[112] Bernard Lamy, *De Tabernaculo foederis, de sancto civitate Jerusalem, et de Templo ejus* (Paris, 1720);

been going on since the mid-seventeenth century, Wood's was not an eccentric position to adopt.

There was nothing unusual about the claim that the Greeks had developed but not invented the art of architecture, but it was less conventional to claim, as Wood did, that the Greeks, 'being a People naturally inclined to Fiction . . . so dressed up their Story of the Origin of the *Orders*, that the *Romans* very readily have given the Invention of those beautiful Parts to them'.[113] So far from inventing the classical orders, said Wood, the Greeks stole the idea from Solomon's Temple, where all three orders were used for the first time.

The basis of Wood's argument had gained fairly wide currency since its appearance in 1604 in a vast commentary on Ezekiel by a Spanish Jesuit, Juan Bautista Villalpanda, who, Rykwert says, 'set up the dominant image of the temple in the seventeenth and even the eighteenth century'.[114] And Villalpanda is cited as the source of Wood's theory by Colvin and Summerson.[115] At the heart of Villalpanda's argument were two beliefs: that Corinthian columns had first been used in Solomon's Temple – and so Vitruvius was wrong to attribute their invention to the Greek architect Callimachus – and that the geometric proportions of architecture came from God ('Templi Architectus fuit ipse Deus') but simple observation of the universe, rather than divine revelation, furnished these proportions.[116] A much abridged version of Villalpanda's thesis could be found in a less esoteric but less easily accessible source: John Shute's *First and Chief Groundes of Architecture*, the first

Samuel Bochart, *Geographia Sacra* (Frankfurt, 1674); *The Works of Josephus*, translated [from Arnauld D'Andilly's French edition] by Thomas Lodge (London, 1676); *The Genuine Works of Flavius Josephus*, translated by Roger L'Estrange (London, 1702); *The Genuine Works of Flavius Josephus*, translated by William Whiston, 2 vols. (London, 1728); Isaac Newton, *The Chronology of Ancient Kingdoms Amended* (London, 1728). On 24 February 1725 the *Daily Post* advertised 'The Temple of Solomon, a large two Sheet Print . . . taken from the Model erected at Hamborough, and lately brought to Town.' Johann Jakob Erasmus of Hamburg had exhibited, in London and other European cities, a model of Villalpanda's reconstruction of the Temple (Rykwert, *The First Moderns*, p. 157; for an illustration see Rykwert, *On Adam's House*, pp. 132–33). Le Corbusier's version of the Tabernacle is copied directly from Whiston.

113 *Origin of Building*, p. 4.
114 *Apparatus urbis ac templi Hierosolymitani* (Rome, 1604): being vol. 3 of Hieronimo de Prado, *In Ezechielem explanationes* (1596–1604). Rykwert, *The First Moderns*, pp. 156–57, and Rykwert, *On Adam's House*, pp. 121–35.
115 Colvin, *Biographical Dictionary*; Summerson, *Architecture in Britain*, p. 391.
116 For commentary on Villalpanda, see: Aldrich, *Elements*, p. 18; D'Aviler, *Cours*, pp. 6, 298; Bromley, *Philosophical and Critical History*, I, p. 376; Jousse, *Secret*, p. 2; Michel Sanmicheli, *Li Cinque Ordini dell'Architettura Civile* (Verona, 1735), p. 6. Recent studies include: Gregor Martin Lechner, 'Villalpandos Tempelrekonstruktion in Beziehung zu barocker Klosterarchitektur', in *Festschrift Wolfgang Braunfels*, ed. Friedrich Piel and Jorg Trager (Tubingen: Wasmuth, 1977), pp. 223–38; Helen Rosenau, *Vision of the Temple: the Image of the Temple of Jerusalem in Judaism and Christianity* (London: Oresko, 1979); Wolfgang Herrmann, 'Unknown Designs for the "Temple of Jerusalem" by Claude Perrault', in *Essays in the History of Architecture presented to Rudolf Wittkower*, ed. Douglas Fraser, Howard Hibbard, and Milton J. Lewine (London: Phaidon, 1967), pp. 148–49; and René Taylor, 'Architecture and Magic: Considerations on the *Idea* of the Escorial', in *Essays*, ed. Fraser, Hibbard, and Lewine, pp. 90–92, 94–95.

English treatise on architecture. Wood, who seems to have read French but not Latin, and preferred English translations anyway, might have known Villalpanda's argument only through Shute, but, whatever the state of his Latin, he might have struggled through the original, because his family library contained a copy of Villalpanda.[117] In fact the argument was relatively easy to obtain, at least in Latin, since Brian Walton's great Polyglot Bible printed Louis Cappel's detailed Latin commentaries on Villalpanda and on the Temple of Solomon. Cappel noted that Villalpanda's 'reconstructed' Temple was too large to fit on top of Mount Moriah, but if even these judicious essays – themselves illustrated with appropriate engravings – were not obvious enough as a source, Villalpanda's argument could also be found in Fréart's *Parallèle*, or Evelyn's English translation.[118]

The loudest reaction to Villalpanda had always come from theologians, not architects.[119] 'The most learned and laborious Temple student, that ever proceeded into publick light', said Samuel Lee, Villalpanda was really just one more commentator on Ezekiel.[120] Although the basis of his argument was quite widely accepted, the details of his 'imaginary Scheme', as Wren called it, were not.[121] Claude Perrault would have none of it, scornfully rejecting 'the Opinion of *Villalpandus*, who pretends that *God*, by a particular Inspiration, taught all these Proportions to the Architect of *Solomon*'s Temple, and that the *Greeks*, whom we esteem the Inventors, learn'd them only, from these Architects'.[122] Perrault attributed the whole argument to 'superstitious Reverence'. Wood usually acknowledges his sources, yet he does not mention Villalpanda in *The Origin of Building*.[123] An engraved plate of Villalpanda's reconstruction of the Temple had recently appeared in Johann Fischer von Erlach's *Entwurff* (1725), and then in Thomas Lediard's English edition of Fischer (1730), but Wood did not follow Villalpanda's actual reconstruction at all. Like most architectural writers, Wood seems to have recognized Villalpanda's importance but to have treated his individual reconstruction of the Temple with passive indifference. Wood adopted the divine revelation of architectural proportion as fact – the Bible confirmed that – but he persuaded apparently none of his few readers to agree with him. The easiest solution was Ware's: he realized that looking for the origins of architecture took him

---

117 The Wood library was auctioned. See *A Catalogue of . . . the Property of Mr. Wood, Architect* (London, 1795).
118 *Biblia Sacra Polyglotta*, ed. Brian Walton, VI (London, 1657), pp. 1–21, esp. p. 15.
119 See Taylor, 'Architecture and Magic', 90–1, note 99, and Herrmann, 'Unknown Designer', p. 144.
120 Samuel Lee, *Orbis Miraculum, or the Temple of Solomon, portrayed by Scripture-Light* (London, 1659), preface, n.p.
121 *Parentalia*, p. 356.
122 *A Treatise of the Five Orders of Columns in Architecture*, translated by John James (London, 1708), p. xiv.
123 Wood does mention Villalpanda in his *Essay* (1749), I, p. 176.

to ancient Greece, not the Holy Land, so he dismissed speculations such as Villalpanda's or Wood's as unimportant.[124]

The Origin of Building 'is personal', says Summerson, 'and has no particular connexion with Palladianism except that it illustrates in a remarkable way the desire for an absolute sanction, biblical as well as philosophical, for the Vitruvian source of architectural virtue'.[125] The *Origin* is thus set aside as marginally interesting by Summerson, and described summarily as 'curious' by Walter Ison, 'strange' by Howard Colvin, and 'whimsical' by Freeman O'Donohue, all at least more polite than William Warburton, who thought it 'a most ridiculous Book' (and who also said Wood 'was a great fool, and not less a knave').[126] Recently, Charles E. Brownell, Christine Stevenson, and R. S. Neale have begun to treat Wood's fascinating book with the seriousness that Rudolf Wittkower thought it deserved. *The Origin of Building* is not the isolated oddity that even Wittkower said it was: such a 'peculiar' book was rare for an architect to write, but the broad lines of its argument were utterly common in the wider context of theological debate.[127] The *Origin* also casts a revealing light on its author's mind, because it shows us how a self-taught scholar – no mere 'mechanick' – interpreted evidence in his wide reading of architectural writing and history, to create the basis for his own theory of building. All Wood's writings provide us with an insight into the literary and exegetical traditions that lie behind his personal interpretation of the art of architecture.

Wood's creation and disposition of space, as we have seen, had a distinct social function, of the kind I have called 'political' in chapter 1. *The Origin of Building* shows that Wood attempted to give further coherence to his mixture of Palladian style, Roman origin, and British myth and history, by blending all these elements with a divine system of number symbolism that accounts for the proportions of the Jewish buildings. Wood participates in a venerable tradition of sacred geometry that endowed almost all buildings of antiquity with numerological symbolism.[128] In this tradition, the proportions and

---

[124] Ware, *Complete Body of Architecture*, p. 290, and see chapter 1, above. One writer after Wood wrote a similar argument: the Scottish architect George Jameson. See John Archer, *The Literature of British Domestic Architecture 1715–1842* (Cambridge, Mass., and London: MIT Press, 1985), p. 27.

[125] *Architecture in Britain*, 7th edn, p. 366.

[126] Ison, *Georgian Buildings of Bath*, p. 238; Colvin, *Dictionary*; O'Donohue, *D.N.B.*; Boyce, *Benevolent Man*, p. 137. Warburton to Stukeley, 6 August 1763, adding that he 'never saw, nor heard of' Wood's 'book on *Stonehenge*', in *Illustrations of the Literary History of the Eighteenth Century*, ed. John Nichols (London: for the author), II [1817], p. 57.

[127] Wittkower, 'Federico Zuccari and John Wood of Bath', *Journal of the Warburg and Courtauld Institutes*, 6 (1943), 220.

[128] Cf. Nigel Pennick, *Sacred Geometry: Symbolism and Purpose in Religious Structures* (San Francisco: Harper & Row, 1982), p. 60. Andreae's Utopian city was to represent the work of 'that supreme Architect', whose 'numbers and memories' make nothing haphazard (*Christianopolis*, p. 221).

dimensions of ancient buildings were often interpreted to represent divine harmony (or some arcane mystery). Josephus, for instance, held that the 'proportion of the measures of the Tabernacle proved to be an imitation of the system of the World' because the Holy of Holies represented Heaven, and 'the space of the twenty cubits, is, as it were, sea and land, on which men live'.[129] Noting that the Tabernacle was the first building in the history of the world to make use of pillars, Wood then pounces on the emblematic function of the architecture.[130] Although he accepts the convention that the proportions of the classical orders of columns were derived from the proportions of the human body, his theory does not depend on the 'mediation' of Vitruvian man. Wood prefers to consider the direct relation of the universe to a building.

Following Villalpanda, Wood says that the geometric proportions of the Hebrew designs came from God. In this part of his theory Wood is loyal also both to Palladio and to an English version of Vitruvianism first propagated by John Dee's 'Mathematical Preface' to Euclid's *Elements*, and perpetuated by Inigo Jones, John Donne, and Henry Wotton, men 'for whom', Wittkower says, 'Plato's concept of a universal harmony founded on numbers was still an article of belief'.[131] Itself derived from Alberti, Dee's argument was that architecture is an immaterial, imaginative art based not on stones or bricks but on abstract principles of cosmic harmony and proportion, a commonplace that could still be found at the end of the eighteenth century in Boullée's pronouncements that conception must precede production.[132] Wood added that architecture has a mechanical, practical aspect, too, which it would be wise not to overlook.[133] Wood probably knew Dee's 'Mathematical Preface' at first hand, since Euclid's *Elements* was easily obtainable, and had in fact been edited by Whiston, whose work Wood knew, and whom he may have known personally.[134] An abridged version of Dee's concept of the 'Archemaster' appears in John Evelyn's *Account of Architects*, where the word *architect* 'signifies *Fabrum praefectus*, or if you will, *Informator*, which the *President, Superintendent*, or *Surveyor* of the *Works* does fully express'.[135]

[129] *The Genuine Works of Flavius Josephus*, translated by William Whiston (London, 1728), I, p. 77.

[130] *Origin of Building*, pp. 8–9.

[131] *Palladio and Palladianism* (New York: George Braziller, 1974), p. 62. See Catherine Wilkinson, 'Proportion in Practice: Juan de Herrera's Design for the Facade of the Basilica of the Escorial', *Art Bulletin*, 67, no. 2 (June, 1985), pp. 229, 242.

[132] 'Mathematical Preface' to *The Elements of Geometrie of the most auncient Philosopher Euclide of Megara*, translated by H. Billingsley (London, 1570). The 'architectural' part of Dee's preface is also conveniently available in Frances A. Yates, *Theatre of the World* (London: Routledge & Kegan Paul, 1969), appendix A, pp. 190–97. For Boullée, see above, chapter 1.

[133] *Origin of Building*, p. 69.

[134] In London, Bristol, Bath, and Tunbridge Wells between 1726 and 1729, Whiston accompanied his public lectures with scale models of the Tabernacle and Solomon's Temple (*Memoirs of the Life and Writings of Mr. William Whiston* [London, 1749], I, pp. 333–34). I am grateful to James E. Force for drawing this reference to my attention.

[135] Evelyn, *Account of Architects and Architecture* (London, 1706), p. 1.

As interpreted by Palladio and his followers, architecture, like music, sculpture, and painting, is one of Dee's *'Artes Mathematicall'*.[136] All four arts, as Morris said, thus resemble the 'Emanations of the Harmony of Nature' as we perceive harmony in the regular motion of the planets, and they all depend on 'such Rules and Proportions which are the Dictates of Nature, and infallibly please the Imagination; especially in *Architecture'*.[137]

The chronology established by Dee and the other *prisci theologi* of the Renaissance had Plato and Pythagoras learning Egyptian wisdom and Mosaic philosophy. Wood applied this unhistorical assumption to building, and made Moses, skilled in Egyptian astrology, the first architect, which would have to mean that the pyramids at Gizeh are post-Mosaic.[138] Wood even went as far as to say that Vitruvius' principles were pagan only because he had been afraid to present a Jewish theory to Augustus, for everything Vitruvius said, including the twelve 'virtues', had already been worked out by Moses.[139] Wood traced Pythagorean geometry, Palladio's system of proportional relationships, and the middle-eastern places of worship and Druidical stone structures in western Europe, back to Mosaic – and therefore Egyptian – architectural wisdom, in which number was central.

Of the three great precepts of Vitruvian and Palladian architecture, convenience, strength, and beauty, Wood said that the first two were learned by men, but that beauty was revealed by God.[140] Robert Morris, the voice of orthodox English neo-Palladianism, defined this quality of beauty:

> Beauty, in all Objects, spring [*sic*] from the same unerring Law in Nature, which, in *Architecture*, I would call Proportion. The joint Union and Concordance of the Parts, in an exact Symmetry, forms the whole a compleat Harmony, which admits of no Medium; it is agreeably blended through the whole, and diffuses itself to the Imagination by some sympathising Secret to the Soul, which is all Union, all Harmony, and Proportion.[141]

Wood's assertion that beauty was revealed implies that imitating Palladian proportion is the same as imitating Vitruvian proportion, which is in turn the same as imitating the proportions of Solomon's Temple, because all of these proportions are derived from the wisdom of the divine designer, or architect. Any geometric system, whether Vitruvian, Palladian, Euclidean, or Pythagorean, is therefore divine (Wood argues) because proportion is itself divine.[142]

To Wood, not only did number indicate harmony and thus, in a building,

[136] 'Mathematical Preface', sig. d.iii, recto.
[137] Robert Morris, *Lectures on Architecture*, II (London, 1736), pp. 102–3.
[138] *Origin of Building*, pp. 52, 76, 92. Ralph Cudworth had the followers of Moses teaching Jewish philosophy to Pythagoras (*A True Intellectual System of the Universe* [London, 1678], pp. 12–13).
[139] *Origin of Building*, pp. 9–11, 92, 130.
[140] *Ibid.*, p. 39.
[141] *Lectures on Architecture*, I, p. 62.
[142] *Origin of Building*, p. 76.

represent the harmony of the macrocosm: number in Hebrew architecture also symbolized the history of the Jewish people, and through that symbolism number represented God himself.[143] The constituent parts of the Tabernacle, for instance, were (says Wood) 'intended as an Hieroglyphical Representation of the past *History* of the *World*, of the Law of GOD, and of the *Rewards* and *Punishments* attending Vertue and Vice'.[144] He arrived at his conclusion by finding numerical analogies between the dimensions of the building, the number of its pillars, and its ornamentations, and events and periods of time in the history of the Israelites.

Perhaps Wood's most extravagant contrivance is his interpretation of the number symbolism of Solomon's Temple. In the following representative extract, in which he describes the ten bases on which the brass lavers stood, Wood embroiders the biblical description:

> The *Bases*, with the *Lavers* upon them, were made moveable, by four Wheels that were put under every *Base*; and the Superficies of every Side of these *Bases* having been twelve square Cubits, . . . the four Sides of every *Base* amounted to forty-eight square Cubits, so that the Superficies of the Sides of the ten *Bases* together made up the Number of four hundred and eighty square Cubits. Now the cubical Content of the same *Bases* was four hundred and eighty solid Cubits, which makes a Parity of Numbers in their solid, and their superficial Content . . . and this, it's highly probable, was intended to allude to the Number of Years from the *Israelites* coming out of *Egypt*, to *Solomon*'s Beginning the *Temple*, which was just four hundred and eighty.[145]

Although Wood adopted other interpretations from Josephus and his commentators, he rejected Josephus' figure of 520 years between the Exodus and the beginning of the Temple in favour of the Bible's 480. Wood's reason probably had something to do with Bath.

Wood found that, before Walcot parish church in Bath was rebuilt, it 'answered the exact Size and Form of *Moses*'s Tabernacle', then with a reluctance we can only imagine, he corrected his wording by omitting 'exact Size and'.[146] When he measured Bath Abbey, he found that its exterior dimensions were identical with those of Llandaff Cathedral. The comparison is not gratuitous. At Llandaff in the mid-1730s Wood had done some extensive remodelling, thought in the nineteenth century to be barbarous.[147] This cathedral was regarded as the oldest church in Britain, so Wood was overjoyed to find that the east part of the cathedral 'was built to imitate *Solomon*'s *Temple*', while twelfth-century repairs made the nave 'form a Figure similar to that of *Noah*'s

[143] *Ibid.*, pp. 77–82.
[144] *Ibid.*, p. 90.
[145] *Ibid.*, p. 130; cf. 1 Kings 7.
[146] Erratum to *Essay* (1742), II, p. 29.
[147] Wood was recommended by Chandos to the Bishop of Llandaff (10 October 1730, ST 57/36, pp. 47–48). See also Edward A. Freeman, *Remarks on the Architecture of Llandaff Cathedral* (London: W. Pickering, 1850), pp. 85–88, for a vituperative attack on Wood's alterations. The only good account of Wood's work is Christine Stevenson, 'Solomon "engothicked"'.

Ark' and so on.[148] Wood himself attempted to recreate Solomon's Temple at Llandaff by constructing a Corinthian interior inside the ruined Gothic shell of the old church. Inside Bath Abbey, he rapturously announced,

the Nave of the Church, both Ways, answers the Proportions of *Noah*'s Ark.

Again, if we take the West Part of the Nave of the Church, we shall find it to be of the same Proportion with the Inside of *Solomon*'s *Temple*, *viz.* a triple Square; then if we take the Pillars out of it, the clear Area will just answer that of the *Tabernacle*, which was three Squares and a Half in Length: So that this Fabrick contains all the Proportions of the sacred Works of the *Jews*; on which Account it may be looked upon as the most curious Sample of Architecture now remaining; . . . and the few Lines I have to add, shall be to inform the Curious, that the Pillars are so set, as to answer that Manner of Intercolumnation which *Vitruvius* calls Areostylos: A Demonstration that the Founder of the Work was well acquainted with the Profane, as well as Sacred Architecture of the Antients.[149]

Plainly, Wood not only wanted parallels in Bath for the symbolism of Solomon's Temple, but also wanted to show that the oldest British architecture was built on Vitruvian and Biblical principles. Wood's dating of the founding of Bath in 480 BC (hardly controversial by the lights of his time), begins to look like an attempt to match significant numbers, thus making the foundation of Bath numerologically symbolic. As it was, Wood's idea of the Roman camp, the baths, and everything else enclosed within it, was of a set of emblematic designs representing such things as the sun, the moon, the days of the week, and the months.[150] In view of Wood's conviction that ancient architecture was always symbolic, Josephus' awkward figure would have to be rejected: not much of a sacrifice, considering, as Ralegh said, that 'it is a familiar error in *Josephus*, to misreckon times'.[151]

Wood's interpretation of the Temple shows how the past history of the Israelites was represented in architecture. The Temple was also prophetic:

These *Courts* made the middle Part of a large Area, called the great *Court*, which was likewise encompassed with a treble Portico, consisting of three Rows of hew'd Stones, and one of Cedar Beams. On each Side of this *Court* there was a Gate; that on the East was attended by four *Levites*; that on the North by four; that on the South by four; and that on the West by two. Now if we make the Spaces between the Pillars in this great *Court*, the same with those of the inward *Court*, and augment the Number in its Breadth to fifty, then the whole Breadth of this *Court* will be five hundred Cubits on the Outside, the Length will be eight hundred and forty Cubits, and the Number of Pillars will come out at one thousand and eight, answering the Number of Years from *Solomon*'s Beginning the *Temple* itself, to the Birth of Christ.[152]

---

[148] *Origin of Building*, p. 221.
[149] *Essay* (1742), I, pp. 70–71.
[150] *Essay* (1742), I, pp. 68–72.
[151] *History of the World* 11th edn (London, 1736) I, p. 283.
[152] *Origin of Building*, p. 132.

Thus 'this *Divine Piece of Architecture*, was also a *Divine Piece of History*'.[153] It is incredible that Wood should simply determine the number of pillars as he chooses, and then marvel at the magical number that results. Yet he was scarcely more irresponsible than other exegetes.

Nor, certainly, must the prophetic function of the Temple be ascribed to any idiosyncrasy on Wood's part. There was a long, respectable tradition of such interpretation. Samuel Lee, for instance, might disdain particular Pythagorean interpretations, but he was willing to accept without demur that the Temple

prefigured Christ and his Church, was compleatly finished in the three thousandth year of the world, and lasted a whole millenary of years, *viz.* through the whole fourth day of the world [i.e. given that every thousand years of the world's existence correspond to one day of the creation], bating the intercision of a few years, during the Captivity of *Babylon*, which was supplyed by its continuance, about the same quantity of years after our Lords birth, till its dissolution by the Roman armies.[154]

And John Bunyan, using only a Bible and a concordance, saw the Temple as prophetic.[155] Such symbolic interpretation of the Temple had Biblical sanction, of course: Christ had said that the Temple symbolized his body, and, as Stukeley was quick to point out, 'the author of the *Hebrews* largely deduces the necessity of making temples to be the pictures of heavenly things, and particularly of the mediator, *Heb.* iv. 11, 23. which can be done no otherwise than symbolically. And authors that describe the tabernacle and temple, insist upon this largely'.[156] Wood's symbolic interpretations of the Jewish sacred structures enable him to argue that the purpose of architecture is to satisfy the 'principal Function of the Mind': that is, knowledge of God.[157] But the Tabernacle and the Temple are also important because they are both God's houses, and are therefore central to the standard conception of convenience as matching outward appearance to inner temperament or truth.

Like the Hebraic buildings, Wood's own buildings in Bath are 'convenient', but there is also a Vitruvian dimension to Wood's concept of convenience. One purpose of his retelling the anecdotal mythical history of Bladud and his leprous pigs is to show the efficacy of the Bath waters. Wood's *Essay* acknowledges the many

sufficient Testimonies of the bountiful Hand of Nature, in imbibing the Earth with so much Moisture, as is necessary for the Nourishment of the Land, and the Occasion of its Inhabitants.[158]

153 *Ibid.*, p. 128.
154 *Orbis Miraculum*, p. 181. Lee was following Pico della Mirandola.
155 *Solomon's Temple Spiritualiz'd or Gospel-Light fetcht out of the Temple at Jerusalem, to let us more easily into the Glory of New-Testament-Truths* (London, 1688).
156 John 2:19–21. Stukeley, *Abury: A Temple of the British Druids* (London, 1743), p. 8.
157 *Origin of Building*, p. 73.
158 *Essay* (1742), I, pp. 13–15.

Thus supplied with rivers and streams, such 'A Spot of Ground . . . must be Venerable, and convenient to build a City'.[159] He adds triumphantly that Bath 'may be very justly said to be in a SITUATION that RESEMBLES the SPRING; ever Youthful, ever Gay' because it is protected from the unhealthy south, west, or north winds that Hippocrates feared, and because the local soil is perfect, like the situation, 'as tho' both had been made by the Magick of King Bladud'.[160] The low situation of Bath often attracted comment, but none irritated Wood as much as Joseph Glanvill's assertion that Bath stood upon a quagmire, since this would not have squared very well with Vitruvius, who says a marshy area ('palustris vicinitas') should be avoided.[161] Wood therefore justifies Bath in Vitruvian terms as a naturally desirable site: Bath satisfies the Vitruvian requirements of 'convenience' and more than 800 years before Vitruvius wrote, Bladud knew them, because their origin was divine design.

When Wood's *Origin* appeared in print in October 1741, his masterpiece, Prior Park, was about half finished.[162] In 1728 'Opponents' of Bath freestone in London, Colen Campbell among them, 'maliciously compar[ed] it to *Cheshire* Cheese, liable to breed Maggots that would soon devour it', and Allen lost the opportunity of a contract to supply his stone for the Greenwich Hospital.[163] Allen then resolved 'to exhibit his stone in a Seat which he had determined to build for himself near his Works, to much greater Advantage, and in much greater Variety of Uses than it had ever appeared in any other Structure'.[164] It was natural that the principal purveyor of the stone should want his house built with it. Wood's earliest designs for Prior Park were to allow 'the Orders of Architecture . . . to shine forth in all their Glory', but Allen thought such a plan too ostentatious, and the design was apparently modified, leading Wood to make the extraordinary claim that Prior Park as we now see it displays 'an humble Simplicity'.[165] Allen wanted the status symbol of such a house, but ostentation was not his style (neither, exactly, was the

---

159 *Ibid.* Richard Graves' travellers compare Bath to Jerusalem (*The Spiritual Quixote*, I, pp. 264–65).

160 *Essay* (1742), I, pp. 18–19, and (1749), I, pp. 56–57. Hippocrates, 'Airs, Waters, Places', part vi.

161 *Essay* (1749), I, p. 58; Buck's *Perspective Views*; Fiennes, *Journeys*, p. 17; Vitruvius, I, iv, 1.

162 Two manuscript drafts of the *Origin* survive, both dating from the mid-1730s, both significantly different from the printed text. Wood issued a prospectus for the *Origin* in 1739. The earlier MS (dated about 1738 by Brownell, but 1734–7 by Stevenson) is now in Sir John Soane's Museum. The later one, which revises the earlier in places, is in the Bath Reference Library. Both MSS contain a 'Book 5', which was condensed into pp. 220–22 of the published text. See Stevenson, 'Solomon "engothicked"', pp. 305–6 for commentary.

163 In *A Complete Body of Architecture*, p. 43, Ware said that Bath freestone did 'not so well in *London*', where in fact it was seldom used, even after Burlington tried it in 1722 (*Architectural Review*, 91, no. 542 [February 1942], 46).

164 *Essay* (1749), II, pp. 426–27.

165 *Ibid.*, II, p. 427. The east and west ends of the main range would have been broader and more elaborate, if they are what Wood represented in a drawing (no longer reproducible) that survives as Bath Reference Library's MS 728b, fol. 55.

'awkward Shame' that Pope attributed to him): ostentation came from Wood. Since Campbell had been unable to tell the difference in a blind test between Bath stone and Portland stone – to Wood's undisguised delight – Prior Park was in one way Wood's revenge on a rival who had denigrated Bath stone.[166] This explains why the ground plan of Prior Park imitates one of Campbell's designs for Wanstead: Wood wanted to beat Campbell at his own game:

> Mr. *Colen Campbell* having boasted of the Justness of the Hexastyle Porticoe Designed by him before *Wansted* House in *Essex*, it was determined that a juster Hexastyle Porticoe should be executed before this House, and with Columns of a larger Size; and for this End I Designed it with Columns of three Feet one Inch and a half Diameter, which exceeds those at *Wansted* by an Inch and a half; made the Intercolumnations of that Kind which *Vitruvius* calls *Systylos*; and gave two compleat Intercolumnations to the Flank of our Porticoe, instead of the compleat Interval and small Portion of another at *Wansted*.[167]

Work on Prior Park had begun in 1735. The Allens had moved in during May or June 1741, and the final touches were applied in 1748. There is an unlikely story that after a quarrel between Allen and Wood (countered by Wood's role as Allen's agent in Bristol in the mid-1740s), Allen's clerk of works, Richard Jones, finished the work on the east wing when Wood had built the main range and part of the west wing. The only evidence is of the least reliable kind, since it is the assertion of Jones himself, written when he was on the verge of senility (or some other cause of incoherence) and was apparently jealous and disappointed that he had not received more in Allen's will. It was in Jones' interests, therefore, to overstate the extent of his service to Allen.[168]

Even if Jones did finish Prior Park, the whole design was Wood's, whose 'classic taste . . . was never more fitly employed, or more happily exerted, than when thus indulged in all its luxuriance, by the wealth and liberality of Mr Allen', as three seasoned travellers said.[169] The second edition of Wood's *Essay*, published just after the mansion had been completed, described the situation of Prior Park:

> The Comb . . . extends almost to the Summit of that Hill, and terminates itself in the Shape of the Head of a vast Niche, with natural Terrasses rising above one another, like the Stages between the Seats of a *Roman* Theatre; and on one of those Terrasses

166 *Essay* (1749), II, p. 427. Exposure of Campbell's prejudice in front of the governors of Greenwich Hospital did not result in a contract for Bath freestone: purveyors of Portland stone just cut their price by one third.

167 Summerson, *Architecture in Britain*, p. 325. James Lees-Milne sees Prior Park as 'essentially old-fashioned, Palladian and Whig' ('Ralph Allen at Prior Park', *Apollo*, n.s. 98, no. 141 [November 1973], 368). Cf. T. P. Connor's caution ('The Making of *Vitruvius Britannicus*', p. 25). *Essay* (1749), II, p. 432.

168 Boyce, *The Benevolent Man*, pp. 101, 292; City of Bristol Record Office, MS 04285.

169 J. C. Ibbetson, J. Laporte, and J. Hassell, *A Picturesque Guide to Bath, Bristol Hot-Wells, the River Avon, and the Adjacent Country* (London, 1793), p. 144.

Mr *Allen* . . . hath lately built himself a Seat, consisting of a Mansion House in the Center, two Pavilions, and two Wings of Offices: All these are united by low Buildings.[170]

(The two pavilions were not actually built as shown in the *Essay*.) Certainly, the slope and curvature of the combe must have struck Wood as a natural gift: he brilliantly exploited the landscape in designing the three ranges to fit into the 'convenient' space so snugly. Emil Kaufmann sees the inspiration of Prior Park in the 'concept of the most intimate connection of the parts': that is, a connection of house to landscape, so that 'Only by seeing the general arrangement as a whole can one observe the stylistic position of the structure'.[171] But it is just as significant that Wood echoes Vitruvius by likening the combe to the 'natural' terracing of a Roman theatre.[172] This can be partially explained by Wood's seeing things Roman wherever he looked, but he was also alluding to Palladio and to the astrological significance of both the site and the design.[173] The north front of the main range of Prior Park is a Corinthian adaptation of Palladio's Villa Foscari, and the layout of the whole is an orthodox Vitruvian/Palladian shape, three sides of a dodecagon, slightly curved to resemble a crescent.

Before Prior Park was finished, the public were allowed in one day a week to admire it: 'the Perambulation of the Curious was thus Designed':

After viewing the Stables in the Simplicity of the *Dorick* Dress, and coming under a Pavilion, great in its Kind, they were to enter an *Ionick* Gallery which would have had the Effect of a vast long Stage to a Rich Theatre; and this leading them to the Stone Passage that Traverses the Basement Story of the House, from thence they were to ascend, by a Flight of Stone Steps, to a Stone Hall of the *Corinthian* Order, and then pass into the stupendous Porticoe of the same Order.[174]

The steps Wood refers to here were inside the house. The magnificent stone staircase in front of the mansion was not part of Wood's design, but was added in the 1820s by Henry Goodridge. Wood's conception was more austere, and showed off the Palladian rustication to good advantage.

RETURNING from this Pavilion [i.e. portico] into the Hall, and passing through the Dining Room, Dressed with the *Corinthian* Order, a Stair Case, inriched with the same Order, was to amuse them while they were ascending to the Gallery in the Chamber

---

[170] *Essay* (1749), I, p. 96.
[171] Kaufmann, *Architecture in the Age of Reason*, p. 33.
[172] Vitruvius, *De Architectura*, v, iii, 8.
[173] For Wood's interest in architecture's astrological significance see *Origin of Building*, pp. 28–29; also, more generally, René Taylor, 'Architecture and Magic', in *Essays*, ed. Fraser, Hibbard, and Lewine, pp. 81–109, and plate 29 (from Daniele Barbaro's edition of Vitruvius (1557)), and Brownell, p. 50. Smollett associates astrology with Wood's designs (*Humphry Clinker*, p. 36). The Zodiac was quite often invoked in allegorical interpretations of sacred architecture (e.g. by Mersenne, *Traité de l'harmonie universelle*, p. 468).
[174] *Essay* (1749), II, pp. 432–33.

Story proposed to have been finished with all the Elegance and Beauty that could possibly be given to Works in the *Corinthian* Dress, and from this Gallery they were to pass into the Tribunal Seat of the Chapel, where the *Corinthian* Order was to increase in its Magnificence; and by representing Cherubims and Palm Trees, placed alternately, give them an Idea of the manner in which King *Solomon* finished the Inside of his *Temple* at *Jerusalem*.[175]

Wood saw the whole of this Vitruvian/Palladian place as a fit residence not only for Allen, but also for God. In a commonplace but significant departure from Villalpanda, Wood believed Solomon's Temple to have been the first building to display all three authentically classical orders of architecture,[176] and now he incorporated all three at Prior Park, as he would do again later, more spectacularly, in the Circus. Prior Park was to be symmetrical, ordered, ornamented, and proportioned according to the precedent of Solomon's Temple. Prior Park was to be beautiful as the Temple had been beautiful, symbolic as the Temple had been symbolic. The intellectual loyalties of the architect were further confirmed by the 'good use . . . made of the various rills of water which appear to issue from a rock, stricken by the wand of Moses, (a statue of whom is placed above it) and trickling down the precipiece [*sic*]'.[177] Prior Park was therefore a realization of Wood's personal theory of architecture.

Visitors, among them Henry Fielding, were fond of remarking that nature 'seems to triumph' over art on the Prior Park estate. 'Here', said Fielding, 'Nature appears in her richest Attire, and Art dressed with the modestest Simplicity, attends her benignant Mistress. Here Nature indeed pours forth the choicest Treasures which she hath lavished on this World; and here Human Nature presents you with an Object which can be exceeded only in the other.'[178] Another visitor – probably Cheyne – remarked that Allen's 'delightful Gardens' were 'laid out with a Profusion of Fancy, yet with great Oeconomy, as to the Expence: for in short, Mr. *Allen* is contented with the Situation of his House and Gardens, (and indeed well he may, for it is a very fine one) and, instead of forcing Nature by a great Expence to bend to Art, he pursues only what the natural Scite points out to him'.[179] Such remarks are typical. The keynote was moderation: nature was modified and improved,

---

[175] *Ibid.* Fire gutted the central block in 1836, but Wood's chapel escaped damage and still survives, spoiled though it is by its conversion into a library. The whole of Prior Park has been unsymmetrical since 1845, when another chapel was added, on the west wing.

[176] *Origin of Building*, p. 136.

[177] Richard Graves, *The Triflers*, p. 65. See Boyce, *Benevolent Man*, pp. 114–15, and Morris R. Brownell, *Alexander Pope & the Arts of Georgian England* (Oxford: Clarendon Press, 1978), p. 210. The statue was Allen's idea rather than Wood's.

[178] *The History of Tom Jones a Foundling*, ed. Martin C. Battestin and Fredson Bowers, Wesleyan Edition of the Works of Henry Fielding ([Middletown, Conn.]: Wesleyan University Press, 1975), bk 11, ch. 9 (vol. II, p. 613).

[179] Richardson, *Tour*, II, p. 265.

not 'tortur'd'.[180] With plenty of advice from Pope, Allen exploited the natural landscape for his gardens as effectively as Wood did for the house. Together they had learned to 'Consult the Genius of the Place in all'.[181]

One visitor in particular saw something of the symbolism behind the conception of Prior Park, which was 'Large as the Builder's Soul, and as his mind compleat'; this writer goes on to praise the author of all Bath's grandeur, and of the supreme art of the city's monumental architecture. The man responsible for

> ye *Squares, Parades*, and stately *Streets*
> Crescent and Circus, which in ev'ry part
> Surpass ev'n Rome in grandeur, Greece in art

is Allen, not Wood, a point that Stephen Duck made, too.[182] Allen is responsible because he has supplied the stone and dictated the taste which have made Bath the truly great city it is; real greatness is virtue, and Allen's virtue – his famous benevolence – is what Wood's buildings represent.[183] This all accords with Palladio's belief that 'the antient sages' retired to their country houses 'where being oftentimes visited by their virtuous friends and relations, having houses, gardens, fountains, and such like pleasant places, and above all, their virtue, they could easily attain to as much happiness as can be attained here below'.[184]

The Allens' visitors noticed (as who could not?) the happy association of Prior Park and its owner – an important aspect of 'convenience'. Charles Yorke 'soon found those scenes animated by the presence of the master; the tranquillity and harmony of the whole only reflecting back the image of his own temper, an appearance of wealth and plenty with plainness and frugality, and yet no one envying, because all are warmed into friendship and gratitude by the rays of his benevolence'.[185] And William Pitt, who was a frequent guest of the Allens, knew that malicious rumours would have no opportunity to flourish in 'the pure air of Prior Park'.[186] Wood would have recognized an implicit compliment to himself for a design that matched the owner's person-

---

[180] Mary Chandler, *A Description of Bath* (London, 1734), p. 17.

[181] Pope, *Epistle to Burlington*, 57. See Boyce, *Benevolent Man*, pp. 98–140, and Brownell, *Pope & the Arts*, pp. 207–13.

[182] *Bath and It's Environs* (Bath, 1775), p. 31. The idea was borrowed from Mary Chandler, who said in 1734 that Prior Park, once it was built, would be 'Great like thy [Allen's] Soul, in ev'ry Part compleat!' (*Description of Bath*, p. 16). Duck, *Poems on Several Occasions* (London, 1736), pp. 214–15.

[183] *Bath and It's Environs*, p. 36.

[184] Palladio, *The Four Books of Architecture*, p. 46. Cf. Stephen Switzer, *Ichnographia Rustica* (London, 1718), p. 43.

[185] To Warburton, 30 September 1746, quoted by Francis Kilvert, 'Ralph Allen and Prior Park', *Prose Essays*, p. 155, reprinted in *Supplement to the Bath Chronicle*, 18 January 1857 (Bath Reference Library, Broadley Collection, I, p. 211).

[186] I quote from a letter somewhere among the British Library's MSS. Since the reference was stolen and I have not been able to locate the MS again, I beg the reader's indulgence.

ality so well, as Palladio had demanded a house should. Prior Park illustrated Cicero's time-honoured belief that a wealthy man was entitled to a certain display of his wealth, by means of his house. But the house, according to Cicero, was also a reminder of its owner's social responsibility: 'he must keep up the Laws of Hospitality, and entertain Multitudes of all sorts of Persons . . . For a fine and large House that gives Entertainment to no Body, serves but to reproach and upbraid its Owner.'[187] I believe that Wood also designed Prior Park as a symbolic expression of faith in 'those truly Masonic ornaments – BENEVOLENCE and CHARITY', for civil architecture is 'an institution of peace, harmony, and brotherly love'.[188]

According to Wood's *Essay*, 'Bath within these sixteen Years last Past has receiv'd great Improvements' – mostly Wood's own.[189] Charles Lucas was pleased that the 'vitious taste' of the old town 'has been corrected in all the modern buildings in the town: they are layed out in grand streets and elegant squares, with great propriety, true taste and magnificence'.[190] Wood, whose favourite adjective was 'grand', improved the city in the simple sense that he helped to give it wider, more comfortable and properly lighted spaces, where pedestrians need not sink to their ankles in mud. But there was much more to 'improvement' than that:

In the Progress of these Improvements Thatch'd Coverings were exchang'd to such as were Tiled; low and obscure Lights were turn'd into elegant Sash-Windows; the Houses were rais'd to five and more Stories in Height; and every one was lavish in Ornaments to adorn the Outsides of them, even to Profuseness: So that only Order and Proportion was wanted to make Bath, sixteen Years ago, vie with the famous City of *Vicenza*, in *Italy*, when in its highest Pitch of Glory, by the excellent Art of the celebrated *Andrea Palladio*, the *Vicentin* Architect.[191]

What I would call an ideological act of encouraging conformity, Wood called 'improvement'. Wood thought he had improved Bath by creating spaces for the exclusive use of immediately local residents: hence the railed-off central enclosure of Queen Square. He even thought he had helped to improve Bath morally by extending the garden of Allen's town house over the old Bowling Green: he thus put a stop to 'Smock Racing and Pig Racing, playing at Foot-Ball and running with the Feet in Bags in that Green'; it satisfied him further

---

[187] Cicero, *De Officiis*, bk 1, ch. 39. I quote Thomas Cockman's translation, 4th edn (London, 1722), p. 101. Alexandre Laborde noted that the myth of a Golden Age neglected the pleasures of benevolence and hospitality, both relatively modern creations associated with fine architecture (*Description des Nouveaux Jardins de la France et de ses anciens Châteaux* [Paris: Delance, 1808], p. 6).

[188] George Oliver, *The Antiquities of Free-Masonry* (London: G. & W. B. Whittaker, 1823), pp. 73, 118. The possible influence of freemasons on Wood is obscure, and the whole disputed question of any connection between Palladianism and freemasonry is too large to go into here.

[189] *Essay* (1742), I, p. 92.

[190] *An Essay on Waters* (London, 1756), III, p. 232.

[191] *Essay* (1742), I, p. 92.

that 'Grinning, Stareing, Scolding, Eating hot Furmety, Laughing, Whistling and Jiging upon the Stage for Rings, Shirts, Smocks, Hats, &c.' did not 'escape the common Ruin; these Amusements falling likewise'.[192] So in Wood's new city there were places of assembly for the well-heeled, and a hospital for the indigent sick, but nowhere for ordinary people to relax or play, nowhere except the workplace for the cobbler and the chandler.

Wood's idea of improvement is predominantly a question of an affirmation of hierarchy, that is, the political disposition of space, and the uses to which space can be put by those who can afford to pay for it. Knowing that an architect is always limited by the space available, Wood went outside the old city walls of Bath for enough room to realize his schemes for Queen Square and the Circus. The Roman camp at Bath had accommodated, Wood thought, 6,600 men, but modern Bath had twice the population in the same space. But, 'as *Vitruvius* writes, a Camp and a City ought to be founded upon one and the same Plan; and in all my Additions to Bath, I have followed his rule' by giving the new houses twice as much space as the old ones had.[193] Even the old city 'has lately been improv'd in its Buildings; most of the Houses are render'd as commodious as possible, not only for the Entertainment of the Gentry, but for Uses in divers Branches of Business . . . chiefly owing to the Skill and Conduct of the late Mr. Wood, Architect.'[194] Wood believed that the Roman camp at Bath had been designed to imitate the disposition of the twelve tribes of Israel, whose camp had been 'designed' by Moses, the first architect.[195] The layout of Queen Square is evidently based on Wood's interpretation of the plan of the camp of the Israelites.[196] The Circus was based principally on the layout of Stonehenge. Standing on a nearby hill overlooking the city was a house consciously intended to recall Solomon's Temple. John Wood's Bath was an imaginative synthesis derived from the divine, not only a 'Theatre of the Polite World', but a Romano-British-Palladian Jerusalem.[197]

Wood's theories are not obvious to the casual observer who wanders through the streets of Bath. Except possibly Smollett, scarcely anyone then or since has recognized in the Circus, Queen Square, or Prior Park the products of Wood's somewhat esoteric personal intentions. Visitors wrote more about morality and manners than about buildings, but when they did comment on the topography of the city, they described the parades and squares

[192] *Essay* (1749), II, p. 244; and Boyce, *Benevolent Man*, p. 29.
[193] *Essay* (1742), II, p. 102.
[194] *The Bath and Bristol Guide: or, the Tradesman's and Traveller's Pocket-Companion*, 4th edn (Bath, [1760?]), p. 11.
[195] *Origin of Building*, p. 107, and *Essay* (1742), I, p. 102.
[196] See the plan of Queen Square in *Essay* (1749), plate 13, and that of the Roman camp, plates 5, 6. Queen Square might allude to the camp of the Israelites, which Wood took to be a model of the world's first city (*Origin of Building*, plates 29, 30).
[197] *Essay* (1749), II, p. 446.

where the gentry, aristocracy and some bourgeois would stroll and assemble. Visitors noted the social uses of the spacious and elegant streets and walks, handsome facades, order and regularity, not Stonehenge, the Mosaic camp, and Solomon's Temple. Whatever his most private intentions were, Wood, the self-made man, designed a social environment that expresses in spatial form the aspirations of the bourgeoisie of mid eighteenth-century England.

1   Architecture, the Queen of the Arts, from Abraham Bosse, *Des Ordres de Colonnes* (circa 1688).

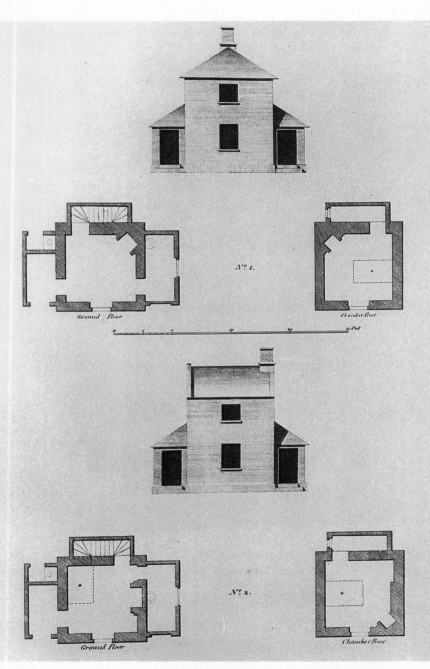

2 Wood the Younger's simple designs for labourers' cottages, 1781.

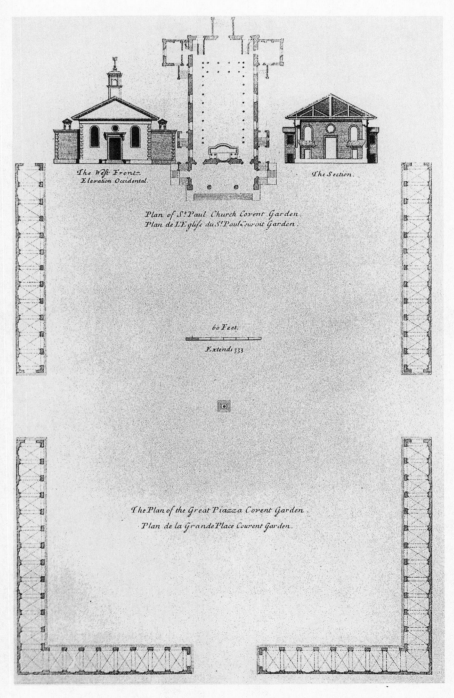

The West Front.
Elevation Occidental.

The Section.

Plan of St Paul Church Covent Garden.
Plan de L'Eglise du St Paul Covent Garden.

60 Feet.

Extends 333

The Plan of the Great Piazza Covent Garden.
Plan de la Grande Place Covent Garden.

3 Covent Garden piazza and St Paul's Church at the beginning of the eighteenth century. The
most noticeable feature is the empty space.

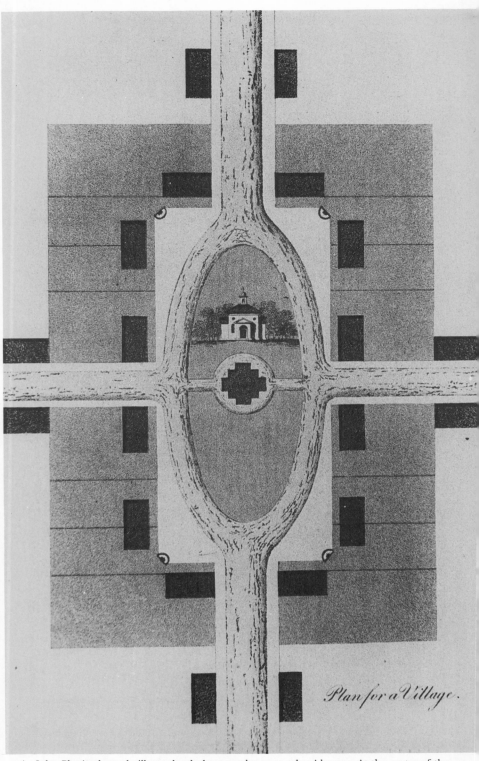

Plan for a Village.

4   John Plaw's planned village: the dark rectangles are workers' houses. At the centre of the village is a chapel.

5   Queen Square, Bath, about 1820. This view shows the north range and, far right, No. 41 Gay Street, with its unusual oriel window.

6 Malton's view of Grosvenor Square in 1792. Wood took the idea for Queen Square's 'palatial' appearance from here.

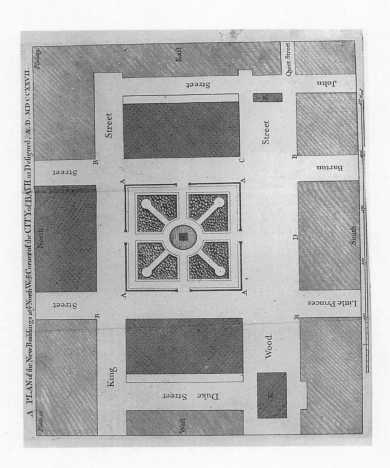

7 Plan of Queen Square, 1727. In the centre is the railed, grassy enclosure.

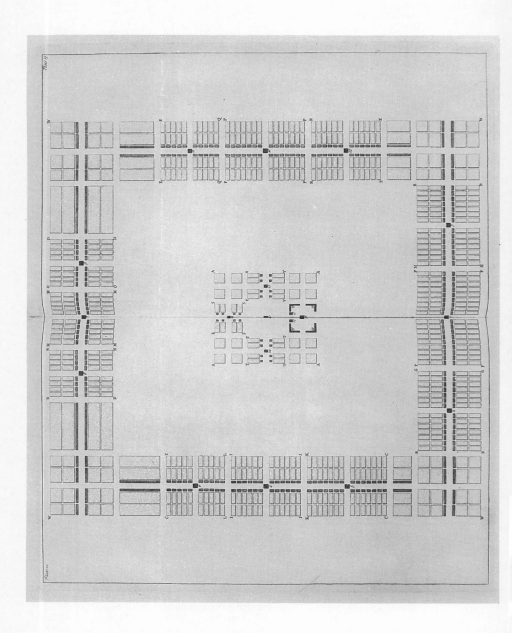

8   Wood's conception of the camp of the Israelites, the likely model for the ground plan of Queen Square.

9 The Circus, photographed in 1922. It is cleaner now, but this photograph at least shows the
buildings without traffic. The columns are Doric at street level, Ionic and then Corinthian, the
whole topped with acorns: a synthesis of Wood's ideas.

10 Thorpe's map of Bath shows, at the bend in the river, Allen's wharf. SE of that, 'Mr Allens way' leads past 'Mr Bennets' to Widcombe, Prior Park ('Mr Allens House') and 'Mr Allens Free Stone Quarry'. Queen Square is visible in the NW corner of the city.

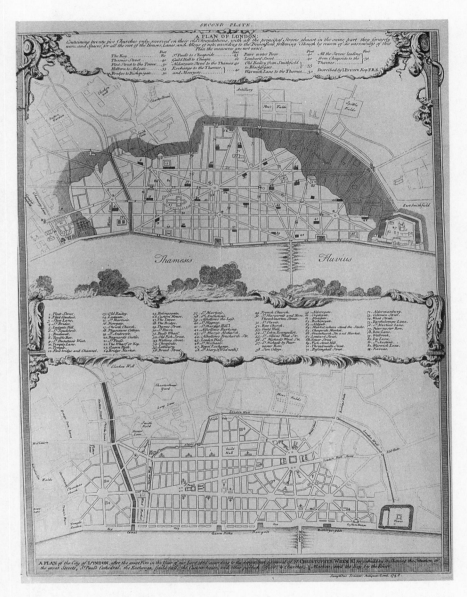

11 Two geometrically immaculate plans for rebuilding London after the Great Fire of 1666: Evelyn (top) and Wren (bottom). Both took too little notice of the needs of the inhabitants.

W.ᵗ Hoare delin.   B. Baron Sculp.ᵗ

BLADUD,
To whom the GRECIANS gave the Name of
ABARIS.

12 The legendary founder of Bath. At bottom left, the evolution of architecture: trees, a hut, a
Greek temple, and a Roman rotunda.

13 Prior Park: the main range and the east wing. Photographed in 1900, it looks no different today. The staircase was added to Wood's more austere design by Henry Goodridge in 1826.

14 Prior Park in 1754, without the staircase. The landscape was never as cultivated as this view
suggests, and the wings show Wood's design, not the completed building. Right: the railway
transporting Allen's stone.

15 A typical architectural title page to a book without any connection with architecture. Every figure in the design occupies a separate compartment, while the columns suggest strength and permanence.

16   Robinson Crusoe's island, showing the major incidents from the novel (vol. 1). Crusoe's barricaded home is in the very centre of the island's space, his country house away in the corner, top right.

PART III

5

Defoe and the politics of space

Hell is a city much like London –
A populous and smoky city.
> Percy Bysshe Shelley, *Peter Bell the Third*, III

LONDON is a World by it self.
> Thomas Brown, *Amusements Serious and Comical* (1700)

Defoe's major prose fiction has a great deal to say about space. Defoe often transports his characters to parts of the world that he himself never visited, whose landscape he knew not at all, and which were sometimes no more than place-names to him. The sense of space in much of Defoe's fiction is therefore frequently vague. Speaking much as her creator might have spoken, Moll Flanders in America admits:

my Husband was a perfect Stranger to the Country, and had not yet so much as a Geographical Knowledge of the Situation of the several Places; and I, that till I wrote this, did not know what the Word Geographical signify'd, had only a general Knowledge from long Conversation with People that came from, or went to several Places; but this I knew, that *Maryland, Pensilvania*, East and West *Jersy, New York*, and *New England*, lay all North of *Virginia* . . .[1]

Since Defoe knew London intimately, as his *Tour* for instance shows, his fiction could be expected to be more specific about the city than it is about American geography, but not so: London is just as vague. Reflecting on Colonel Jack's London, Samuel Holt Monk points out: 'Topographically Defoe is impeccable. But what does he actually show us? Nothing'; but 'We do indeed see scenes and places in the London of the plague year.'[2] Monk is right: yet in *A Journal of the Plague Year* (1722), a brilliantly imagined portrait of London in the crisis of 1665, Defoe does not offer us a literary equivalent of Hogarth's memorably noisy, crowded, bustling 'scenes and places'. For that sort of image in writing, we would have to turn to such a vividly coarse description of the interior of a pub as this one, from Ned Ward's *London Spy*:

[1] *Moll Flanders*, The Shakespeare Head Edition of the Novels and Selected Writings of Daniel Defoe (Oxford: Basil Blackwell, 1927), II, p. 157. References in parentheses in the text are to this edition.
[2] Samuel Holt Monk (ed.), *The History and Remarkable Life of the Truly Honourable Col. Jacque commonly call'd Col Jack*, Oxford English Novels (London: Oxford University Press, 1965), p. xix.

As soon as we came near the Bar, a thing started up all Ribbons, Lace and Feathers, and made such a Noise with her Bell and her Tongue together, that had half a dozen *Paper-Mills* been at work within three Yards of her, they'd have been no more then so many *Lut[e]s* to a *Drum*, or Laidies *Farts* to a Peal of *Ordinance*, which alarm'd Two or Three nimble heeld Fellows aloft, who shot themselves down Stairs with as much Celerity, as a *Mountebanks Mercury* upon a *Rope*, from the Top of a *Church-Steeple*, every one charg'd with a mouthful of *Coming, Coming*.[3]

Ward imagines and defines the space by the activity of the people in it. Defoe imagines his spaces, for all their vagueness, in the same way, but without resorting to Ward's colourful similes and boisterous images of clutter and clatter. Perhaps the closest Defoe comes to such scenes is this account of the exodus of people from Whitechapel, where the plague has not yet reached:

Indeed nothing was to be seen but Waggons and Carts, with Goods, Women, Servants, Children, &c. Coaches fill'd with People of the better Sort, and Horsemen attending them, and all hurrying away; then empty Waggons, and Carts appear'd, and Spare-horses with Servants, who it was apparent were returning or sent from the Countries to fetch more People: Besides innumerable Numbers of Men on Horseback, some alone, others with Servants, and generally speaking, all loaded with Baggage and fitted out for travelling, as any one might perceive by their Appearance.[4]

Here Defoe certainly conveys some sense of busy activity, but he chooses not to emphasize the impact that such a crowd can have on the individual suddenly confronted with it. Ward's London Spy is a countryman plunged into the city and almost overwhelmed by it: Defoe's narrator is a more detached, cool observer, noticing communal activity but not participating in it. The space is generic, as spaces in Defoe's London often are: his is not a city to be described for its own sake by someone who is swept along by its turbulent waves of noisy activity.

We might compare Defoe's calm technique also with Thomas Brown's picture of the busy traffic of a London street, enough to make Covent Garden market in the 1960s seem tranquil:

Make Way there, says a Gouty-Leg'd Chairman, that is carrying a Punk of Quality to a Mornings Exercise: Or a *Bartholomew*-Baby Beau, newly Launch'd out of a Chocolate-House, with his Pockets as empty as his Brains. *Make Room there*, says another Fellow driving a Wheel-Barrow of Nuts, that spoil the Lungs of the City Prentices, and make them Wheeze over their Mistresses, as bad as the Phlegmatick Cuckolds their Masters do, when call'd to Family Duty. One Draws, another Drives. *Stand up there, you Blind Dog*, says a Carman, *Will you have the Cart squeeze your Guts out?* One Tinker Knocks, another Bawls, *Have you Brass Pot, Iron Pot, Kettle, Skillet, or a Frying-Pan to mend:* Whilst another Son of a Whore yells louder than *Homer*'s Stentor, *Two a Groat, and Four for Six Pence Mackarel*. One draws his Mouth up to his Ears, and Howls out, *Buy my Flawn-*

---

[3] *The London Spy*, part I, 3rd edn (London, 1702), p. 4.

[4] *A Journal of the Plague Year*, Shakespeare Head Edition (Oxford: Basil Blackwell, 1928), p. 8. Page numbers in parentheses in the text refer to this edition.

ders, and is followed by an Old Burly Drab, that Screams out the Sale of her *Maids* and her *Sole* at the same Instant.[5]

It is easy to sympathize with Hogarth's Enrag'd Musician, who covers his ears with his hands to fend off an assault on his nerves. In Brown's vision of the teeming city, 'where Repose and Silence dare scarce shew their Heads in the Darkest Night', the observer, parallel to Ward's countryman, is a bewildered Indian visitor. Also, Brown's earthy and athletic prose, like Ward's, is active, full of short, staccato rhythms, but with details ('One draws his Mouth up to his Ears, and Howls out') that would not belong to Defoe's more chaste style.[6] Defoe's characters generally care little for such minute observation of the city or its people, but, caring mostly about themselves, seem to be impressed instead by generalized wholes rather than particular parts. Even though Defoe himself defended St Paul's Cathedral against its detractors by appealing 'to the particular Beauties of every Part separately considered', not to 'the Gross', he preferred to convey a general sense of the scope of London's trade by listing the names and the produce of all the city's markets than to describe how any particular one of them looks, sounds, and smells.[7]

In criticism of Defoe's fiction, Moll Flanders has long been associated almost exclusively with London, and with good reason, because the scenes she describes in London are the most substantial, interesting, and readable, perhaps also because her ignorant neglect of those other British and American landscapes, through which she passes, makes the story of her life in those places less memorable. Defoe encourages most readers, apparently, to think of Moll as a London thief even though she spends much of her life neither living in London nor stealing. In support of the realism of *Moll Flanders*, Dorothy van Ghent enlists Defoe's city: his 'book describes minutely the local scene, London', but Defoe does not describe the city 'minutely' at all, as van Ghent really concedes when she qualifies her assertion, by adding that 'the world of *Moll Flanders* is made up to a large extent of *things*', but scarcely ever appeals to the senses.[8] Here then is one critical judgment that equates 'the world' of this novel with London alone, for the very good reason that Defoe gives us virtually no sense of any other place.

London in *Moll Flanders* is a real, identifiable, familiar place yet, as Max Byrd observes, the city 'remains somehow two-dimensional, an abstract environment, so to speak, without colors or smells or windows and doors'.[9]

---

[5] *Amusements Serious and Comical, calculated for the Meridian of London* (London, 1700), pp. 20–21.

[6] Defoe's style is chaste too in the quite different sense that the novels are coy rather than graphic about sex. Ian A. Bell recommends a comparison with *The English Rogue* and *Fanny Hill* (*Defoe's Fiction* [Totowa, NJ]: Barnes & Noble, 1985], p. 151, note 8).

[7] *A Tour thro' the Whole Island of Great Britain*, ed. G. D. H. Cole (London: Peter Davies, 1927), I, p. 334. For markets, I, pp. 345–48.

[8] *The English Novel: Form and Function* (1953; reprinted, New York: Harper & Row, 1961), pp. 33, 35.

[9] Max Byrd, *London Transform'd: Images of the City in the Eighteenth Century* (New Haven and London:

The reason, I think, is not just that Defoe was not very interested in architecture. Defoe responded to space, as many architectural writers did too, by conceiving it as a political entity, but his London, unlike theirs, is a space that is defined, not by its porticoes and proportions, but by the activity of an individual inhabitant. The city in Defoe's novels is primarily a social artefact, which confirms the dominion of the powerful over the weak. The isolation and alienation of Defoe's principal characters are imagined spatially: in *Moll Flanders* and *Colonel Jack* the spaces of the city are important in spite of their notorious lack of specificity, because they enable a subject in a discourse of power to establish her or his own subjectivity and so overcome the least desirable consequences of their alienation.

Everywhere in Defoe's fiction, including the *Journal of the Plague Year*, the author gives us a location, such as Gray's Inn Lane or Bishopsgate, which is specific only as a map reference, or a much vaguer one like 'a meeting-house', often with no indication even of the typical human activities that occur in those spaces. When one window actually opens in Defoe's fictional London, it provides an opportunity for a pathetic and very striking moment:

Passing thro' *Token-House-Yard* in *Lothbury*, of a sudden a Casement violently opened just over my Head, and a Woman gave three frightful Skreetches, and then cry'd, *Oh! Death, Death, Death!* in a most inimitable Tone, and which struck me with Horror and a Chilness, in my very Blood. There was no Body to be seen in the whole Street, neither did any other Window open; for People had no Curiosity now in any Case; nor could any Body help one another; so I went on to pass into *Bell-Alley*.[10]

As the narrator's matter-of-fact explanation suggests, the woman's shrieking, and the indifference of neighbour and passer-by alike, is typical of London while its inhabitants try to come to terms with the devastation of bubonic plague in 1665. But the activity of this scene is abnormally rare in the everyday life of the city as Defoe and his readers know it in 1722.[11] Elsewhere in Defoe's fictional London windows do not usually open at all, and although his streets are seldom ominously silent like this one, community is suggested not by Brown's vibrant multitude of loud individual voices, nor certainly by palatial facades around railed squares. Community is suggested by simple commercial transactions, the deposit of cash with a banker, the purchase of goods, and the issuing of receipts. The topography of London, the appearance of houses, streets, fields and monuments, does not create the city in Defoe's fiction: nor, it seems, do all the everyday social activities of the mass of normal people who populate the urban spaces. Human activity defines the spaces, but it is individual rather than social activity: Defoe's city is spatially conceived,

Yale University Press, 1978), p. 13.

[10] *Journal of the Plague Year*, p. 99.

[11] Pat Rogers intriguingly links the *Journal* with the South Sea Bubble, in *Eighteenth Century Encounters: Studies in Literature and Society in the Age of Walpole* (Brighton: Harvester; Totowa, N.J.: Barnes & Noble, 1985), pp. 151–67.

by the individual who is alone in it. People are indifferent to others' problems because everyone is isolated. If Crusoe's words could represent Defoe's, we would have a reason for this: 'Man may be properly said to be *alone* in the Midst of the Crowds and Hurry of Men and Business'.[12]

Trying in 1751 to account for London's rapidly rising crime rate, an exasperated Henry Fielding, in his role as a magistrate, concluded that one 'must think' that if the huge irregular mass of buildings, 'Lanes, Alleys, Courts and Bye-places . . . had . . . been intended for the very Purpose of Concealment, they could scarce have been better contrived'.[13] Two years earlier, in *Tom Jones*, Fielding's reformed tearaway, the Man of the Hill, explained how he

hastened . . . back to *London*, the best Retirement of either Grief or Shame, unless for Persons of a very public Character; for here you have the Advantage of Solitude without its Disadvantage, since you may be alone and in Company at the same Time; and while you walk or sit unobserved, Noise, Hurry, and a constant Succession of Objects, entertain the Mind.[14]

Defoe's London too is a place in which people can conceal or lose themselves and so become solitary and anonymous, not usually to hide grief or shame (sentiments which Defoe's characters never experience for long), but to evade their pursuers and enemies. If the noisy London community described by Ned Ward and Tom Brown has any place in Defoe's imagination, it is one with which Moll and Jack engage only reluctantly.

Alone on his island, Robinson Crusoe occasionally feels 'more happy in this forsaken Solitary Condition, than it was probable I should ever have been in any other Particular State in the World', but more often he craves company.[15] Yet in the *Serious Reflections*, Crusoe contrasts his twenty-eight years of 'Confinnement [*sic*] to a desolate Island' with his far greater isolation 'in the Middle of the greatest Collection of Mankind in the World, I mean, at *London*'.[16] Whether or not London was a desirable place to live, the city provided a perfect cover for almost any form of socially deviant subculture, be it sexual, sybaritic, or criminal. In the densely packed, sprawling city, 'that vast Mass of Buildings', whose sheer size awed Defoe, discourse was not easily regulated by coercion.[17] There were several reasons for this: the police force was primi-

---

[12] *Serious Reflections during the Life and Surprising Adventures of Robinson Crusoe* (London, 1720), p. 2. This was the second sequel, the third and final volume in the *Crusoe* series.

[13] *An Enquiry into the Causes of the Late Increase of Robbers* (London, 1751), p. 76.

[14] *The History of Tom Jones a Foundling*, ed. Martin C. Battestin and Fredson Bowers, The Wesleyan Edition of the Works of Henry Fielding ([Middleton, Conn.]: Wesleyan University Press, 1975), I, p. 461.

[15] *Robinson Crusoe*, Shakespeare Head Edition (Oxford: Basil Blackwell, 1927), I, p. 131. References in parentheses in the text are to this edition.

[16] *Serious Reflections*, p. 4. Cf. Anna Howe to Clarissa: 'London, I am persuaded, is the place of all others, to be private in' (*Clarissa*, ed. Angus Ross [Harmondsworth: Penguin, 1985], p. 1,018). For a similar sentiment, *Joseph Andrews*, bk 1, ch. 6.

[17] *Tour*, I, p. 316.

tive, until Fielding and his half-brother John reformed and organized it in the early 1750s; the winding streets and narrow alleys of what Defoe called 'this mighty, I cannot say uniform, Body' were, as Fielding said, conducive to concealment; and in a city whose unplanned topographic and demographic expansion was 'prodigious' ('and how much farther it may spread, who knows?') there was little to encourage any sense of community, and much to encourage an individual's refusal to conform.[18] Despite the architects' endeavours to build 'regular' districts, in some parts of London it was easy to live within spitting distance of neighbours without ever speaking to them. (It is still possible.)

Ward's London Spy is not long without company, but Defoe's urban rogues often describe themselves as friendless (sometimes even when they are not). With a striking reminder of Crusoe, who 'run[s] about like a Mad-man', when his misfortune and his solitude sink into his mind, the death of one of Moll's husbands sets her 'wringing my Hands, and sometimes raving like a distracted Woman', since she now has 'no Assistant, no Friend to comfort and advise me'.[19] Moll responds to her friendless isolation by turning to crime, and only when she needs to dispose of stolen goods does she remember her old acquaintance, the midwife, who becomes her new friend, 'governess', and surrogate mother. The immediate, pragmatic reason for Moll's taking to theft is poverty. Alienation in a hostile city accounts for her decisions. Her subsequent isolated struggle for survival depends, as she explains repeatedly, on her anonymity in public spaces.

Alienation in London explains the anonymity and pseudonymity of Moll and of many other characters in Defoe's fiction. For example, Colonel Jack admits, 'I know little or nothing of myself, nor what my true Name is; but thus I have been call'd ever since I remember; which is my Christian-name, or which my Sir-name, or whether I was ever Christen'd, or not, I cannot tell', because he was never a part of any normalizing social process, remaining an 'outsider' who refuses to conform.[20] Similarly, although Defoe's publishers put Roxana's name on the title page of her narrative, 'the fortunate Mistress' does not refer to her own name at all until she mentions casually, more than half way through her memoirs, the 'foolish Accident' that gave her 'the Name of Roxana . . . all over the Court End of Town, as effectually as if I had been Christen'd Roxana'.[21] Like Moll, she finds it expedient not to expose her identity to a society she perceives (at least initially) as hostile.

Moll almost never tells us the names of other people who cross her path, not even those of three of her five husbands – one of whom gets two different

18 Tour, I, pp. 318, 329, 316.
19 Robinson Crusoe, I, p. 53; Moll Flanders, II, p. 3.
20 Colonel Jack, Shakespeare Head Edition (Oxford: Basil Blackwell, 1927), II, p. 147.
21 Roxana, Shakespeare Head Edition (Oxford: Basil Blackwell, 1927), I, p. 205. Defoe had little or nothing to do with most of the title pages of his novels: see Rodney M. Baine, 'The Evidence from Defoe's Title Pages', Studies in Bibliography, 25 (1972), 185–91, esp. 189, on Roxana.

names and three descriptive epithets, suggesting that names are perhaps arbitrary anyway. 'Moll Flanders' is only a nickname, 'no more of Affinity with my real Name, or with any of the Names I had ever gone by, than black is of Kin to white, except that once, as before I call'd my self Mrs. *Flanders*, when I sheltered my self in the *Mint*', where she 'took Lodgings in a very private Place' (II, 30, I, 63). Moll's 'grand Secret', undivulged to one of her many male admirers, is 'my true Name, who I was, or where to be found' (I, 170). From the very first sentence of her narrative Moll is equally careful not to let fellow criminals – or readers – know her real name, if indeed she herself knows it. Her isolation is protected by pseudonymity, which, as we see here, is associated with her 'very private Place', that is, with her resistance to the threat of political control (even control by criminals) inherent in public spaces.

Again and again, Moll emphasizes this association of her identity and her private space. She may be a common thief, but she does not willingly co-operate with other common thieves. Even when she robs several times together with a young man, she disguises herself as a man so convincingly that, when he is caught, he cannot give evidence against his partner because he cannot identify her.[22] Moll 'often robb'd with these People, yet I never let them know who I was', so that after five years 'the People at *Newgate* did not so much as know me' (II, 29–30). With the exception of her 'governess', Mother Midnight (another generic pseudonym), who lives with Moll, other thieves never know her address, 'nor so much as how to guess at my Quarters, whether they were at the East End of the Town, or the West' (II, 39); they are not close to Moll, in a physical sense that parallels the distance of her 'professional' relationship with the community of thieves, and for that matter the distance of her personal relationships with her husbands and children. Hearing that 'some of those who were gotten fast into *Newgate*, had vowed to Impeach me', Moll 'kept within Doors for a good while' (II, 30). She never lies low: she 'keeps close' (II, 39). Occupying her own 'very private' space, she keeps her distance in all senses, or, to use the expression that bourgeois culture was making current, she keeps herself to herself. Moll reminds us that self-protection lies in other people's ignorance of both her identity and the space she occupies. The safest public place to achieve this private anonymity is populous London: 'mixing with the crowd of people usually passing there [Holborn Bridge], it was not possible to have been found out' (II, 7).

Private and public spaces alike enable Moll to regulate the ways in which others perceive, or fail to perceive, her identity. In the celebrated gold watch episode, where the crowd seizes another pickpocket virtually by mistake, Moll exploits her isolation in a public space to good effect. She camouflages herself effectively, 'for you are to observe, that on these Adventures we always went very well Dress'd, and I had very good Cloths on, and a Gold Watch by my

[22] II, p. 31. On Moll's identity, appearance, and disguises, treated as motifs, see David Blewett, *Defoe's Art of Fiction* (Toronto: University of Toronto Press, 1979), pp. 55–60, 72, 78–80.

Side, as like a Lady as other Folks' (II, 27). She also uses the physical pressure of a London crowd to conceal her actions. The exact location – like the architecture of the building – is unimportant: 'it happen'd in a Crowd, at a Meeting-House'.[23] It matters more that Moll should give her victim 'a great Jostle, as if some body had thrust me against her', only to find that she cannot pull the watch off, that her own watch is being pulled by another thief, and that a third pickpocket is going for yet another watch. Moll calls out, stops 'as it were short', lets the crowd carry her victim forward, and so puts enough distance between herself and her victim that she will not be suspected. All this is no doubt a pickpocket's conventional expertise. There is also a moral – or rather, amoral – dimension to Moll's self-isolating conduct in this scene. To prove that not all luck is good, or, as Ward put it, 'sound Reason and true Experience deny *Shitten Luck to be good Luck*',[24] Moll relates how

At that very instant, a little farther in the Crowd, and very Luckily too, they cried out *a Pick-pocket* again, and really seiz'd a young Fellow in the very Fact. This, tho' unhappy for the Wretch, was very opportunely for my Case . . . and the poor Boy was deliver'd up to the Rage of the Street (II, 27)

which is, however, preferable to Newgate, trial, and transportation or execution. The 'poor' fellow-pickpocket's fate elicits scant sympathy from Moll, since she shares the indifference expressed in Crusoe's question, 'What are the Sorrows of other Men to us?'[25] To Moll, the pickpocket who is caught is as anonymous as she is relieved to be, lost in the crowd. Her concern is with herself, not with other people. The pickpocket does not escape; she does, and she forgets him.

This scene exposes simultaneously Moll's self-consciousness and her alienation from the very people she jostles. Only rarely does Moll's conscience bother her. She is 'tormented' for 'three or four Days' by the thought that she might have stolen someone else's only means of subsistence (II, 6). Soon afterwards she reproaches herself for her cruel inhumanity, but 'The Reflection wore off, and I quickly forgot the Circumstances that attended it' and then the arrest and conviction of a woman with whom she robs 'troubl'd me exceedingly', but she has no more to say about it (II, 22, 40). The discovery that one of her marriages is incestuous fills Moll with horror: she does not care about the crime, but that 'the Action had something in it, shocking to Nature' (I, 91), and so does all she can to put distance between herself and her brother/husband, 'to prevent his touching me' because 'my Heart was alienated from him' (I, 92), although at this point he does not yet know what she knows. Her behaviour makes him threaten to incarcerate her in a

---

[23] II, p. 26; cf. Ian Watt, *The Rise of the Novel* (London: Chatto and Windus, 1957), p. 97: 'a real, particular place', but 'Defoe makes no attempt to describe it in detail'.

[24] *London Spy*, part II, 3rd edn (London, 1701), p. 6.

[25] *Serious Reflections*, p. 2.

madhouse (I, 94, 100), a prospect that frightens Moll and intensifies her alienation: 'I was really alienated from him in the Consequence of these Things . . . I could almost as willingly have embrac'd a Dog' (I, 101), though, as Ian A. Bell points out, Moll's remarks here 'do not seem to fit easily into her otherwise rather blithe personality'.[26] But she expresses her alienation as fear of touch, fear that her personal space will be violated, and then as fear of imprisonment, or enclosure in a space not of her choosing.

Moll's emotional alienation suggests more of her breezy self when she recounts her relief on hearing the 'joyful News' that the young man who could have saved himself by incriminating her, had he known her disguise, 'was Hang'd, which was the Best News to me that I had heard a great while' (II, 36). This callousness is of the same order as her relegating five years of marriage with Robin (but at least he gets a name) to half a paragraph, the other half of which is about her money (I, 57). Similarly, she buries her own dead child in parentheses, and when she worries that she has made 'no Provision' for her five-year-old son, whom she refers to as 'it', she ponders not his financial fate but her own (I, 63, 127).

The climax of Moll's emotional and spatial alienation from the population of London is the scene in which she finally arrives back in Newgate. It is one of the most specific spatial descriptions in all of Defoe's fiction, yet Moll tells us no more about the appearance of the building than she does about the location of the meeting-house:

the hellish Noise, the Roaring, Swearing and Clamour, the Stench and Nastiness, and all the dreadful Afflicting things that I saw there; joyn'd to make the Place seem an Emblem of Hell itself, and a kind of an Entrance into it. (II, 98)

Here, as Byrd notes, Moll 'echoes an eighteenth-century commonplace', by invoking 'the ancient convention of an adventurer's visit to the underworld'.[27] Moll is also invoking the tradition of a *prisoner's* arrival in hell, because prison is hell. When the London Spy and his friend are committed to Poultry Compter for the night, they come 'to a frightful Grate, more terrible than the Scene of Hell in *Circe*, where Oak and Iron were met in Conjunction to Eclipse our Liberty', and where the noxious smells especially are disgusting enough to induce a reader's nausea.[28] Long before Shelley's quip (quoted as an epigraph to this chapter), London was likened to hell, prisons were likened to hell, and London was likened to a prison. Since her birth in Newgate, Moll has been back to the prison once, but only as a visitor who found it depressing. Now, when she comes as a prisoner, the fetid, overcrowded conditions of

---

[26] *Defoe's Fiction*, p. 135.
[27] *London Transform'd*, p. 29.
[28] *London Spy* part IV, (London, 1699), p. 7. Two London prisons were called 'Compters'. The other was in Wood Street. They prompted William Fennor's *The Compters Common Wealth, or a Voiage made to an Infernall Iland* (London, 1617), an early contribution to the motif of prison-as-hell.

Newgate serve as an emblem of the entire city, as indeed they might, for eighteenth-century London was crammed with places of detention. In addition to scores of '*private Houses of Confinement*', which Defoe likened to '*little Purgatories, between Prison and Liberty*', and 119 sponging houses (compared with 135 parish churches) London had 'Twenty-Seven publick Prisons'.[29] Moll's descent into Newgate, the most feared prison of all, also specifically illustrates that she perceives 'that horrid Place', which chills her blood, as a distinctively human institution, defined by the destiny and condition of its unfortunate inhabitants, not by the colour of its stones or the extent of its walls. On arriving in Newgate, Moll says 'I look'd on my self as lost', and for once she does not mean lost agreeably in a crowd that can comfort her with the protection of anonymity (II, 98). She has suddenly been drawn out of her preferred state of isolation and placed in a dismal community of 'harden'd vile Creatures', where she is not isolated any longer, but is more alienated than ever (II, 122). What has eventually befallen her is exactly what she has successfully avoided before. Her arrest has deprived her of the security of her personal space.

Moll has been all along a social being, as her relationship wih her 'governess' shows. Moll can be nothing else but a social being, but what she emphasizes is her uniqueness, rather than society's assimilation of her into any pattern of conformity. In other words, Moll resists the ideological demand for conformity expressed, as I have suggested earlier, by such spaces as Grosvenor Square or Bath's North Parade. 'Society' is not an abstraction that she confronts or that confronts her: Moll is an individual social being, as Marx would say, 'the *totality*, the ideal totality – the subjective existence of thought and experienced society for itself'.[30] Leo Braudy has argued persuasively that Defoe's narrators all flee from 'pressures', some in the form of social institutions – 'family, society, culture, and Providence' – which 'threaten to distort their sense of identity'.[31] Paradoxically, despite her childish desire to become a 'gentlewoman' (I, 5–6), Moll's alienation ultimately implies her bourgeois stance, which ought to suggest her acceptance of the institutions she avoids.

Similar to Moll in some respects, the abandoned 'Son of Shame', Colonel Jack, is 'Wary and Dextrous' at his 'Trade' – theft – but as a youth he is not isolated, since he lives with two other Jacks, the 'major' and the 'captain', and later he is rarely alone.[32] In winter, the boys 'got into the Ash-holes, and Nealing-Arches in the Glass-house, call'd *Dallows*'s Glass-house, near *Rosemary-Lane*, or at another Glass-house in *Ratcliff-Highway*' (I, 9). Early on, he and

[29] *Tour*, I, pp. 356–57. Bell, *Defoe's Fiction*, p. 152, note 32, supplies the corrective that Newgate is a genuine as well as a symbolic threat.

[30] *Economic and Philosophic Manuscripts of 1844*, ed. Dirk J. Struik, translated by Martin Milligan (New York: International Publishers, 1964), p. 138.

[31] 'Defoe and the Anxieties of Autobiography', *Genre*, 6 (1973), 85, 91.

[32] *Colonel Jack*, Shakespeare Head Edition, I, pp. 2, 6. References in parentheses in the text are to this edition.

his 'brothers' fall in with 'a Gang of naked, ragged Rogues like ourselves', seventeen of them altogether, all as 'wicked as the Devil cou'd desire to have them be' (I, 9). Jack is isolated only in the sense that with the 'captain' temporarily gone, the 'major' does not invite the 'colonel' to join in his criminal exploits (I, 18).

Like Moll's alienation, Jack's is expressed spatially when he details his escape route through the streets of London after his latest petty crime, as in this example:

I run like the Wind down the *Cloysters* with it [a stolen bag of money], turn'd on the Left-Hand as soon as I was thro', and cut into *Little-Britain*, so into *Bartholomew-Close*, then cross *Aldersgate-street*, thro' *Paul's Alley* into *Red-cross-street*, and so cross all the Streets, thro' innumerable Allies, and never stopp'd till I got into the second Quarter of *Moorfields*, our old agreed Rendezvous. (I, 66)

This typical Defoean urban landscape is not specific but it is familiar. It is scarcely surprising that Jack should not describe windows and doors, smells or colours, since he is running for his life through a city that he knows intimately. The emphasis is placed, of course, not on his admiration of architecture, but on his flight, and thus on his personal form of exploitation of urban spaces. Descriptions like this, despite amounting to no more than a list of landmarks, may encourage us to think of Jack or Moll as real but pseudonymous individuals who exist in some place besides the imagination of the author. It is a narrative tactic that was not lost on the creator of Leopold Bloom, either. Defoe's minor characters often do not have names, but his London streets nearly always do. However, these streets are no more closely observed or described than the featureless landscapes in which Moll and Jack live in America. What matters most about the spaces of Defoe's fiction is neither topography nor communal activity, but the activity of the isolated human, for as Crusoe says, 'Life in general is, or ought to be, but one universal Act of Solitude'.[33] With a Lockean topographical image Crusoe on his island has an 'innumerable Crowd of Thoughts that whirl'd through that great thorow-fare of the Brain, the Memory'.[34] The image suggests obviously that the city can be perceived in individual rather than social terms. Some critics see Defoe's isolated characters as secularizing the struggle of the lonely Puritan pilgrim, their route a main road through a city (itself often portrayed as a wilderness in Defoe's time), their goal self-preservation in this life.[35] At the same time, isolated in public or private spaces, these characters are all

[33] *Serious Reflections*, p. 2.
[34] *Robinson Crusoe*, I, p. 227.
[35] John Bunyan, *Grace Abounding to the Chief of Sinners and The Pilgrim's Progress*, ed. Roger Sharrock, Oxford Standard Authors (London: Oxford University Press, 1966), p. 160. On Puritan spiritual autobiography, see G. A. Starr, *Defoe & Spiritual Autobiography* (Princeton: Princeton University Press, 1965) and J. Paul Hunter, *The Reluctant Pilgrim: Defoe's Emblematic Method and Quest for Form in 'Robinson Crusoe'* (Baltimore: Johns Hopkins Press, 1966).

engaged in acts that promote self-consciousness as a consequence of alienation.

The isolated human *par excellence*, Robinson Crusoe, has often been discussed, of course, as a myth, as an allegorical representative of Britain's burgeoning middle class, as 'economic man', and as an isolated individual whose self is threatened by 'the mere existence of another person'.[36] Where Moll resists incorporation, Crusoe, deprived of society altogether on his island, acts out a drama in which he achieves the power to incorporate others. Between them, Moll and Crusoe constitute two conflicting aspects of bourgeois ideology: one resists power to maintain her self-consciousness; the other reaches for power to maintain his. The whole fiction of *Robinson Crusoe*[37] obviously depends on Crusoe's isolation and his exploitation of the empty space that he claims for himself. What he does with his space may possibly reveal his adoption of capitalist values, and does reveal his bourgeois ideology.[38]

Exploiting the natural resources of his island with the help of the tools and provisions he salvages, Crusoe becomes eventually self-made and self-sufficient, so that late eighteenth-century political economists, such as David Ricardo and Adam Smith, found in Crusoe the castaway an individual archetype of the builder of capitalism. Marx opposed this position by arguing that labour is social and that, for the majority of his life on the island, Crusoe is isolated from any society at all.[39] Marx also dismissively underestimated Crusoe's religion, his 'original sin' and his prayers, 'since they are a source of pleasure to him, and he looks upon them as so much recreation'.[40] It is hard to treat this last part of Marx's polemic seriously, since Crusoe is at least paying lip service to the role of Puritanism in economic activity, but Marx's equally reductive argument about Crusoe's labour is of more substance. In Marx's perspective Crusoe would have to be mythical because he is cut off from social reality.

People and their relationships are commodities to Crusoe, a point grimly underlined by his sale of Xury into slavery for sixty pieces of eight. Like most

---

[36] Homer O. Brown, 'The Displaced Self in the Novels of Daniel Defoe', *ELH*, 38 (1971), 566. A recent, if perhaps over-ingenious study that emphasizes a political allegory of exile is Michael Seidel, 'Crusoe in Exile', *PMLA*, 96 (1981), 363–74.

[37] That is, of volume one: I am not speaking here of *Farther Adventures* or *Serious Reflections*.

[38] For commentary on Crusoe and economics, see especially Maximillian E. Novak, *Economics and the Fiction of Daniel Defoe* (Berkeley and Los Angeles: University of California Press, 1962), pp. 32–37, 42, 51. Also, Ian Watt, '*Robinson Crusoe* as a Myth', *Essays in Criticism*, 1 (1951), 112; although distinct in part from Watt's commentary on *Crusoe* in *The Rise of the Novel*, this essay was absorbed in his book. Christopher Hill connects Puritanism and capitalism, but somehow makes Defoe more radical than bourgeois, in 'Robinson Crusoe', *History Workshop: a Journal of Socialist Historians*, 10 (Autumn 1980), 7–24.

[39] *Capital: A Critique of Political Economy*, ed. Frederick Engels, translated by Samuel Moore and Edward Aveling, I (1954; reprinted London: Lawrence & Wishart, 1977), p. 50.

[40] *Ibid.*, p. 81.

of Defoe's isolated characters, the only individual who is important to Crusoe is himself. Anyone looking for an archetypal fictional capitalist would find a better example than Crusoe by turning to a merchant hero,

who furnishes every comfort, convenience, and elegance of life; who carries off every redundance, who fills up every want; who ties country to country, and clime to clime, and brings the remotest regions to neighbourhood and converse; who makes man to be literally the lord of creation, and gives him an interest in whatever is done upon earth; who furnishes to each the product of all lands, and the labours of all nations; and thus knits into one family, and weaves into one web, the affinity and brotherhood of all mankind.[41]

Compared with this purveyor of material comforts, Crusoe is not so much a capitalist as a bourgeois (who, admittedly, carries capitalism in his ideological baggage). Despite his isolation from social reality, Crusoe is finally a representative of that 'middle Station of Life' whose self-evident dullness he has rejected, at the beginning of the narrative, in favour of the excitements of travel. Declining to follow his father's reassuring advice to be a comfortable, untroubled bourgeois, Crusoe is at first a would-be traveller, then an eager entrepreneur dealing in slaves, and finally a property-owner of moderate wealth. Crusoe's control of space (as well as money and commodities) defines his fears, his aspirations and his final achievement, which is to maintain possession of the whole island even when he 'gives' parts of it to the inhabitants he leaves behind (II, 104–7). Rising up the economic scale from trader to rentier to property-owner, Crusoe is a mythical representative of the middle class. The fact remains that Crusoe's initial desire to travel indicates a lust not for wealth, but for adventure.[42]

Robinson Crusoe is a tale of romantic adventure, disorientation and reorientation, but not a systematic economic treatise. Yet, the disarmingly styleless prose of Defoe's fiction appropriated the vernacular language of contemporary economic and spatial discourse.[43] To be brief about the economic: Crusoe's efforts as a trader do not turn out to be particularly profitable, but

[41] Henry Brooke, *The Fool of Quality; or, the History of Henry Earl of Moreland* (London, 1764). I quote from the 1776 edition, I, p. 98.

[42] Christopher W. Gray remarks that 'adventure' could, and did, carry the meaning of 'commercial enterprise'. Defoe certainly did use the word in this way, but not in the earliest parts of *Crusoe* that I am discussing here ('Defoe's Literalizing Imagination', *Philological Quarterly*, 57 [1978], 73).

[43] As many have noticed, but with far more emphasis on the economic: see Pat Rogers' convenient summary in *Robinson Crusoe* (London: Allen & Unwin, 1979), pp. 79–82. See too Rogers' 'Crusoe's Home', *Essays in Criticism*, 24 (1974), 375–90. For an entirely different sense of 'space' and 'spatial', see J. Paul Hunter, *The Reluctant Pilgrim*, pp. 93–124. H. Daniel Peck notes the connection between Crusoe's sense of 'place' and his growing 'sense of personal identity' ('*Robinson Crusoe*: the Moral Geography of Limitation', *Journal of Narrative Technique*, 3 [1973], 20–31), and Elizabeth R. Napier suggests that Crusoe's organizing tendency parallels his larger awareness of design, particularly providential design ('Objects and Order in *Robinson Crusoe*', *South Atlantic Quarterly*, 80 [1981], 84–94).

his 'investment' in the Brazilian slave plantation sets him up for life.[44] On the island his economic activity does not imitate the process of capital accumulation, because his capital is initially the gift of chance, he has no consumer society, and he never attempts to create and reinvest a surplus, but resolves 'to sow just the same Quantity [of rice and barley] every Year, that I sow'd the last' (I, 143). Deciding 'That all the good Things of this World, are no farther good to us, than they are for our Use', he keeps only provisions 'to supply my Wants, and, what was all the rest to me?' and so has very little in reserve to share with his first visitor.[45] Although capital accumulation is not Crusoe's priority, he defines himself by what he possesses, and what he possesses, first and foremost, is space.

In one issue of a surprisingly influential (though now entirely obscure) periodical, an anonymous author, probably Charles Povey, wrote on Monday, 8 January 1711, 'A Man is not look'd upon for what Excellency is lodg'd in his Mind, but is valued according to the Wealth he enjoys: Instances of this kind are as common as the Rising of the Sun.'[46] When Gulliver's Lilliputian captors want to know the identity of their gigantic visitor, they empty his pockets and make an inventory of the contents, because his possessions will show them who he is. Like Gulliver, or Pamela writing a list of her clothes, Crusoe defines himself by what he is 'worth', by what he possesses, whether slaves, land, or the tools, clothes, and so on that he salvages from the shipwreck.[47] With an incongruous reminder of Caliban, Crusoe's possessions include the whole island, a claim that is justified by contemporary natural law, as Novak points out.[48] Whether or not Crusoe – or Defoe – has ever read Grotius on this subject, Crusoe quickly decides that occupation of the island gives him the right of ownership, and he never gives up possession. Defoe had an authoritative Puritan precedent; Bunyan's God, after all, was the 'owner', as well as 'Lord' and 'Governour', of Heaven, a place that even Pliable hoped Christian would 'possess'.[49]

What Crusoe does with his island's space is political. In his isolation 'the mind' enjoys 'infinitely more Room to withdraw from the World, than when at best it must wander for its daily Food, tho' it were but the Product of the Field'.[50] When Lord Bolingbroke conceded in 1735 that 'the power of money,

---

[44] True, Crusoe's profit on his first voyage is eight times his outlay: but this is small compared to his Brazilian profits (on an investment managed for him in his absence).

[45] *Crusoe*, I, p. 149, and Novak, *Economics*, pp. 39–40 and 163, note 29.

[46] *Visions of Sir Heister Ryley*, no. 61.

[47] Swift might well have been echoing Defoe. Cf. Maximillian E. Novak, 'Swift and Defoe: Or, How Contempt Breeds Familiarity and a Degree of Influence', *Proceedings of The First Munster Symposium on Jonathan Swift*, ed. Hermann J. Real and Heinz J. Vinken (Munich: Wilhelm Fink, 1985), pp. 157–73.

[48] Maximillian E. Novak, *Defoe and the Nature of Man* (London: Oxford University Press, 1963), p. 51.

[49] *Pilgrim's Progress*, pp. 150–51.

[50] *Serious Reflections*, p. 13. It is notable that the mind, not the body, goes in search of food.

as the world is now constituted, is real power',[51] he was reluctantly registering the transfer of political power, from hereditary landowners to moneyed men, that had occurred in Britain since 1688.[52] The new network of credit and paper money, whose complexities Defoe himself was commissioned in 1710 to justify, gave people engaged in commerce a greater opportunity to accumulate wealth without land, and so to acquire a share of political power. Nonetheless, many people – particularly merchants, bankers, insurers, or rentiers like Crusoe – used their money to buy their way into land, to find 'Room to withdraw from the World', but more importantly to buy power.[53] Although Crusoe clearly does not have to buy any land on his island, he does what the richer moneyed men had been doing in England since 1688; he builds himself a 'Country-House', as he likes to call it (I, 117). Always with security on his troubled mind, Crusoe stakes out an equivalent of the country estate: what is lacking in his version is the complex economy of such an estate, because no one else lives there.

Until Friday arrives, Crusoe is a master with no servants, a point he makes with dry irony when he reflects 'how like a King I din'd too all alone, attended by my servants', that is, his dog, two cats, and a parrot (I, 171). But his kingdom is far from safe, as fear dominates him. There is no barrier preventing cannibals (or anyone else) from landing on the island. Crusoe considers the island as his property, but he has no means of making its boundary, the shore, inviolable: it is a boundary that he recognizes, but unless he can police it, which he alone cannot, no cannibal is likely to respect his property or his person. Crusoe's fear of invasion is rational enough. His other constant fear is an attack by wild animals: 'and yet I could not perceive that there was any living Thing to fear, the biggest Creature that I had yet seen upon the Island being a Goat', but even so his fear is still not entirely irrational.[54] His fear expresses the desire for fixed, recognized boundaries, the division of space into individual units, contiguous but not continuous. So for his country residence, Crusoe constructs 'a little kind of a Bower, and surrounded it at a Distance with a strong Fence, being a double Hedge, as high as I could reach, well stak'd, and fill'd between with *Brushwood*' (I, 117). His thoughts continually turn to enclosure. When he finishes his ladder, his first house has become 'a compleat Enclosure to me; for within I had Room enough, and nothing could come at me from without, unless it could first mount my Wall' (I, 91).[55] Were he to live in his second house, he would 'enclose my self among the Hills and Woods, in the Center of the Island', with the risk of not knowing

---

[51] *The Works of Lord Bolingbroke* (1844; reprinted London: Frank Cass, 1967), II, p. 6.
[52] Cf. Harry T. Dickinson, *Liberty and Property: Political Ideology in Eighteenth-Century Britain* (London: Weidenfeld & Nicolson, 1977).
[53] Cf. Defoe's *Essay upon Publick Credit* (London, 1710), p. 6.
[54] I, pp. 118–19. Cf. Novak, *Defoe and the Nature of Man*, p. 28.
[55] Neo-Palladian spaces separate privileged social groups from 'Mankind in general' (John Wood's phrase). Cf. Pat Rogers, *The Augustan Vision* (London: Weidenfeld & Nicolson, 1974), p. 61.

of chance visitors who might help him escape from his isolation. To enclose himself in this way would be 'to anticipate my Bondage' (I, 116). Yet, like Moll in London, enclosure is exactly what Crusoe desires for his security when he makes another entrance to his cave: 'I was not perfectly easy at lying so open; for as I had manag'd my self before, I was in a perfect Enclosure, whereas now I thought I lay expos'd, and open for any Thing to come in upon me' (I, 118). Crusoe thinks he needs enclosure for his security and shelter, as it shuts out potential enemies, but it shuts out potential friends too; at the same time it shuts him in, which he finds desirable for his safety but frightful for its implications of imprisonment. Enclosure is therefore as ambiguous for Crusoe as it was in the spatial discourse that I have outlined in chapter 1.

At the moment when he discovers the footprint, Crusoe flees in panic to enclose himself in his 'Castle, for so I think I call'd it ever after this', so that his home has come to symbolize his higher status as a member of a propertied class at the same time as it represents the constant fear that dominates his temperament.[56] But this scene also shows that his house is whatever he says it is: if he calls it a castle, then a castle it is. In his desire to enclose himself, Crusoe reveals the customary political habit of assigning definitive functions to spaces. A cave behind his tent serves him 'like a Cellar to my House', and his new cave he elects to call his kitchen (I, 68–69). He creates spaces for particular purposes and names them accordingly. The island itself is his home when he is hopeful of rescue, but 'certainly a Prison' when he loses hope, and reflects 'how I was a Prisoner, lock'd up with the Eternal Bars and Bolts of the Ocean'.[57] The naming of spaces and the assigning of functions are in his power to determine, since he is the owner of the property.

Crusoe's practical reasons for choosing the site for his first 'house' are determined by orthodox Vitruvianism. (Even his unlaunched boat is made from a cedar so large that he wonders 'much whether *Solomon* ever had such a One for the Building of the Temple at *Jerusalem*' [I, 146].) Immediately after his decision to take the useless money from the shipwreck, Crusoe realizes that his most fundamental need is shelter because, like Poor Tom in *King Lear*, he is 'unaccommodated man'. With impeccable devotion to Vitruvian principles, Crusoe becomes a civilized analogue of primitive man as he starts to re-enact the early history of architecture.

Primitive men, according to Vitruvius, 'began, some to make shelters of leaves, some to dig caves under the hills, some to make of mud and wattles places for shelter, imitating the nests of swallows and their methods of building . . . When in winter-time the roofs could not withstand the rains, they

---

[56] I, p. 178. See Benjamin Boyce, 'The Question of Emotion in Defoe', *Studies in Philology*, 50 (1953), 45–58, and Braudy, 'Daniel Defoe and the Anxieties of Autobiography'.

[57] I, pp. 111, 114, 130. Cf. David Blewett, *Defoe's Art of Fiction*, pp. 48–50, and Seidel, 'Crusoe in Exile', *PMLA*, 96 (1981), 363.

made ridges, and smearing clay down the sloping roofs, they drew off the rain-water.'[58] After spending his first night in a tree, in imitation of a bird (if not necessarily a swallow), Crusoe gets on with construction. His first consideration is, as it always will be on the island, security:

My Thoughts were now wholly employ'd about securing my self against either Savages, if any should appear, or wild Beasts, if any were in the Island; and I had many Thoughts of the Method how to do this, and what kind of Dwelling to make, whether I should make me a Cave in the Earth, or a Tent upon the Earth: And, in short, I resolv'd upon both . . . (I, 65)

Vitruvius recommended building on a healthy site with adequate supplies of fresh water and air, sunlight and shade, and specifically advised against building near a marsh. Crusoe realizes quickly that his temporary 'home' is not suitable 'for my Settlement, particularly because it was upon a low moorish [i.e. swampy] Ground near the Sea, and I believ'd would not be wholesome, and more particularly because there was no fresh Water near it, so I resolv'd to find a more healthy and more convenient Spot of Ground' (I, 65–66). He goes on to list his priorities: health, fresh water, shade, security, and (less Vitruvian, but pragmatic in the circumstances) a view of the sea, so that he might see any potential rescuer coming. As time goes by, he thinks rescue less and less probable, and so abandons this last consideration in favour of hiding himself from sight.

Crusoe reminds us continually that his first house is the focal space of all his activities: it is here that he keeps his supplies, his animals, his garden. As the frontispiece to the *Serious Reflections* demonstrates, Crusoe's home is imaginatively the centre of the island, and the spatial centre of the novel, since it is the place to which he returns after each of his excursions. But he does not show much of his once adventurous spirit when, for the first ten months, he is too terrified of the unknown to venture far enough from his enclosure to explore the island, and he has barricaded himself so effectively that he builds a house with neither doors nor windows, 'that there might be no Sign in the Out-side of my Habitation' (I, 112, 91). He creates individual, not social space.

The effects of Crusoe's imperfect roofing, of an earthquake and of a violent rainstorm, may be Defoe's practical way of reminding house owners that maintenance is a constant problem, and they do recall Vitruvian primitives, but they are also hints that even within 'his' island, Crusoe's personal space is this house: he does not even feel particularly comfortable in his country house and, rather uneasily, wants to go back to his first house, 'for as I was fix'd in my Habitation, it became natural to me, and I seem'd all the while I was here, to be as it were upon a Journey, and from Home' (I, 127), which reverses the sentiment that persuaded him to leave his home in England in

[58] *De Architectura*, II, i. 2–3.

the first place. As Crusoe decides to extend the boundaries of his living quarters, storage areas, and pens for his livestock, he begins to resemble either an early eighteenth-century English country squire or else, like Pope's Indian, one who inhabits 'Some safer world in depth of woods embrac'd',[59] like a man in an ancient era living in the primitive situation that eventually evolves into a village. It is hard to say which Crusoe is, until he reflects

> My Island was now peopled, and I thought my self very rich in Subjects; and it was a merry Reflection which I frequently made, How like a King I look'd. First of all, the whole Country was my own meer Property; so that I had an undoubted Right of Dominion. 2*dly*, My People were perfectly subjected: I was absolute Lord and Lawgiver . . . (II, 30–31)

At this moment Crusoe has become the ruler of a colony, and one who 'allow'd Liberty of Conscience', to a Protestant, a pagan, and a Papist, 'But this is by the Way' (II, 31). His role as governor of this outpost of modern British civilization is made wittily emphatic when he and the captain invent a governor for the island to intimidate the mutineers with an illusion of power (II, 61–62). Defoe's myth is the rise of the self-made man, the bourgeois who by dint of hard work and resourcefulness earns himself a position of power.

Once Crusoe 'get[s] a Savage into [his] Possession', he establishes the hierarchical society that his building activity has emblematized all along (I, 231). A man who has been self-sufficient for a quarter of a century can hardly be said to need a servant, but Crusoe does not demur when Friday conveniently volunteers to serve him. Crusoe then promptly teaches Friday his first three words of English: 'master', 'yes', and 'no', and so binds Friday to his will (I, 239). As several readers have pointed out, Crusoe does not even try to discover the poor grateful fellow's real name and gives him a new name of his own choosing,[60] as an English aristocrat might have renamed a servant. The space that is the island, which Crusoe has regulated as much as possible, is bound by his will, and so are his first visitors. Even when he is daydreaming about the conveyance of his property, Crusoe still reminds himself that he is 'King and Lord of all this Country indefeasibly', and enjoys 'a Right of Possession' (I, 114), as well as a right to kill animals and birds for his food, and later a right to kill the cannibals before they kill him. Ownership of the island, he decides, gives him political power. He dreads 'the Thoughts of shedding Humane Blood for my Deliverance', but 'the eager prevailing Desire of Deliverance', as usual, overcomes his Christian scruples (I, 231–32). When eventually he has more people to contend with, who may not be as docile as Friday, Crusoe exercises his assumed right by passing laws that will bind them to his will:

---

[59] *An Essay on Man*, ed. Maynard Mack, Twickenham Edition, vol. 3, part 1 (London: Methuen, 1950), epistle I, l. 105.

[60] E.g., Watt, *Rise of the Novel*, p. 69, and Bell, *Defoe's Fictions*, p. 104. Also, in passing, Hans W. Hausermann, 'Aspects of Life and Thought in *Robinson Crusoe*', part 2, *Review of English Studies*, 11 (1935), 449.

1. That while you stay on this Island with me, you will not pretend to any Authority here; and if I put Arms into your Hands, you will upon all Occasions give them up to me, and do no Prejudice to me or mine, upon this Island, and in the mean time be govern'd by my Orders.

2. That if the Ship is, or may be recover'd, you will carry me and my Man to *England* Passage free. (II, 47)

As Crusoe acquires 'subjects', other than cats, dogs, goats, and parrots, his domain becomes an analogue of a political society growing in sophistication. Crusoe may have used primitive methods, but in his determination of boundaries he is modern, civilized man. However crude and improvised his methods of building seem, the results are sophisticated enough to impress his visitors, whom he entertains hospitably: the captain 'admir'd' Crusoe's 'Fortification' of his 'Castle', now 'perfectly . . . conceal'd' by a thick 'Grove of Trees', but Crusoe is quick to inform the captain that in addition to this 'Retreat' he has 'a Seat in the Country, as most Princes have' (II, 50). Like a provincial capital, Crusoe's castle has become the focal point of the island's new social and judicial system, as it has been since its construction the focal point of Crusoe's isolated existence. The man who has regulated the space of the island has put himself in a strong bargaining position to determine his political future, because he has control of the island's political economy. Crusoe's regulation of space is thus the regulation of discourse.

I am suggesting that Crusoe's possession and exploitation of the island's spaces and resources do not make him a financial or proto-industrial capitalist in practice, but they do represent the colonizing efforts of an 'organic' capitalist, to adapt a term from Gramsci.[61] It is almost impossible to separate financial capitalism from bourgeois ideology's emphasis on the desirability of owning property. Crusoe, like Defoe sometimes, is an organic capitalist in a sense other than Gramsci's in that as a representative bourgeois he participates in the discourse of a capitalist society in the making, without necessarily defending it consciously or explicitly. Crusoe is living out a fictional existence in a discourse that also creates the spatial disposition of a city square, because, as rentier or merchant or colonizer, he expresses the aspiration of the Whiggish middle class to possess and control a space, so raising his status and giving him a measure of political power.

---

[61] Gramsci terms 'organic' those intellectuals who are members of a growing social class rather than of the class it replaces. See *Selections from the Prison Notebooks of Antonio Gramsci*, edited and translated by Quentin Hoare and Geoffrey Nowell-Smith (New York: International Publishers, 1971), pp. 452–53.

6

Fielding and the convenience of design

And though that nature with a beauteous wall
Doth oft close in pollution, yet of thee
I will believe thou hast a mind that suits
With this thy fair and outward character.

Shakespeare, *Twelfth Night*

What a thousand Pities, said I, is it that so Noble a
Palace, which appears so Magnificent and Venerable,
should not have the old Hospitality continued within-
side, answerable to its outward Grandure.

Ned Ward, *The London Spy*

Convenience and design, so important in establishing the spatial discourse
of eighteenth-century Britain, as my early chapters have shown, give shape
to Henry Fielding's fiction. In arguing a 'providential' reading of *Tom Jones*,
Martin Battestin has stressed the importance of design, in the sense that
the design argument employed, as an organizing metaphor.[1] On the few
occasions when Fielding wrote specifically about architecture, he usually
employed the concept of convenience, not in the sense of amenity, but in the
established political sense of an exterior that should express the purpose of
a building and the social status of its inhabitant. In writing that has nothing
to do with architecture at all, Fielding still uses the concept of convenience,
particularly in his portrayal of character. This chapter discusses these two
spatial elements, design and convenience, in Fielding's major fiction. To indicate the nature of Fielding's spatial thinking, I preface the discussion with a
brief survey of his writing about real and imaginary buildings.

In *The Vernoniad* (1741), Fielding describes the Palace of Aeolus, a satire
on Walpole's new Palladian mansion on his Houghton estate in Norfolk:

A hollow pile, whose marble front displays
To Sol its whiteness, and reflects his rays;
Within all dark, impervious to the sight,
The mimick windows ne'er admitting light.[2]

---

[1] *The Providence of Wit: Aspects of Form in Augustan Literature and the Arts* (Oxford: Clarendon Press,
1974), pp. 141–63.

[2] Fielding had also satirized Walpole with a verse epistle written in 1730 but published in 1743
in *Miscellanies*, vol. 1 (Wesleyan Edition, ed. Henry Knight Miller [Middletown, Conn.: Wesleyan
University Press, 1972], pp. 56–58). This verse was followed by another, written and published

The fictional palace displays a facade that conceals. Instead of matching the house's interior, the exterior creates an entirely false impression: there is therefore no harmony: 'convenience' has been inverted. Since the disjunction of white outside, black inside, can only deceive the observer, the house itself suggests hypocrisy. In this case, Walpole's notorious bribery and corruption are represented by the building in which they flourish; the architecture is symbolically allied to moral ideas.

Fielding's penchant for symbolic buildings appears elsewhere, notably in the unfinished *Journey from This World to the Next* (1743), whose narrator has just died when the book begins, but he manages to escape from his body, even though 'the mouth or door . . . and the windows, vulgarly called the eyes', are shut.[3] An invisible coach takes him and his fellow-travellers on their journey through space and time, to symbolic destinations, such as the City of Diseases, 'a very dull, dark, and melancholy place', whose suburbs, unlike those of any other city, 'were infinitely pleasanter than the city itself' (ch. 2). Here, the lady Maladie Alamode has a beautiful 'house, or rather palace', but she herself turns out to be disreputable (ch. 3), as her name (contemporary slang for veneral disease) suggests. The next stage of the journey takes the travellers past a 'most noble building', the Palace of Death, whose 'outside, indeed, appeared extremely magnificent', and whose surroundings are 'inconceivably solemn' and forbidding. Yet the narrator is surprised, as he often is on his way out of this world, to find that 'this palace, so awful and tremendous without, is all gay and sprightly within' (ch. 4): again there is a simple adverse relation between the external appearance and the interior. True convenience is nowhere in evidence.

When the travellers in the *Journey* learn the difference between two main roads – the hazardous one leading of course to virtue, the delightful one to vice – they learn too that the road to vice is lined with 'several noble palaces', but 'the other had little inviting more than the beauty of the way, scarce a handsome building, save one greatly resembling a certain house by the Bath, to be seen during that whole journey' (ch. 5). This compliment to Prior Park associates Ralph Allen's house with rare and conspicuous virtue, as does every one of Fielding's allusions to Allen. Allen's house is therefore associated with the purpose of the *Journey* as a whole: to recommend 'goodness and virtue' as the means to obtain 'the greatest and truest happiness which this world affords' (introduction).

Henry and Sarah Fielding included essays on architecture in *Familiar Letters*

---

in 1743. See Hugh Amory, 'Henry Fielding's *Epistles to Walpole*: A Reexamination', *Philological Quarterly*, 46 (1967), 236–47.

[3] *A Journey from This World to the Next*, introduction by Claude Rawson, Everyman's Library (London: J. M. Dent, 1973), ch. 1. References to chapters in this edition appear in parentheses after quotations.

between the Principal Characters in David Simple (1747),[4] the comparatively little-known quasi-sequel to Sarah's *Adventures of David Simple* (1744). Most of the volume, to which Henry contributed the preface and five letters (nos. 40–44), consists of epistolary fiction vaguely in the genial style popularized by the *Spectator* and its imitators, and although most of the book is not exactly compelling, it does have its moments. Appended to the letters is one of Sarah's most interesting essays, 'A Vision', which describes a visit to four 'moral' palaces, the most attractive being the Palace of Benevolence. In a variation of the fiction of the choice of two roads, the author and various fellow-travellers pass through gates leading to wealth, power, pleasure and virtue; all except the author are so deluded by outward appearance that they mistake avarice for wealth, and so make morally wrong choices. Only the resolute ever survive the difficulties and resist the temptations encountered on the way, and so arrive at the Palace of Benevolence. The material building is unimportant: it remains entirely secondary to the moral qualities associated with it – compassion, tenderness, and 'The Goddess of the Place, who is called *Benevolence*, or *real Love*'.[5] In Sarah Fielding's 'Vision' architecture is an orthodox endorsement of moral values.

One of Henry Fielding's contributions to this collection of letters is also his most extended discussion of architecture. A fictional Frenchman describes a journey up and down the Thames in London. He records several whimsical and ironic observations on popular etymologies, the characters of watermen, the notorious trade of insults known as 'water-language', inns, mobs, and so on, but the first half of the letter is given over mainly to a visitor's perception of some of the principal buildings visible from the river.

Starting from the New Bridge,[6] 'which must be greatly admired by all who have not seen the *Pontneuf*', our French visitor declares his modern taste at once when he notices on the south bank 'a Row of Buildings, not very remarkable for their Elegance, being chiefly built of Wood, and irregular', but he is too far away to make out the order of the pillars.[7] Then to Lambeth Palace – 'a vast Pile of Building, not very beautiful indeed in its Structure, but wonderfully well calculated, as well to signify, as to answer the Use for which it was, I suppose, originally intended; containing a great Number of little Apart-

---

[4] For the connoisseur: a Mrs Wadman and a Reverend Doctor Primrose subscribed to this volume before becoming characters in the fictions of Sterne and Goldsmith.

[5] *Familiar Letters*, II, pp. 389–90. See also Wilbur L. Cross, *The History of Henry Fielding* (New Haven: Yale University Press, 1918), II, pp. 46–51. As the present book went to press, the argument about authorship of 'A Vision' was revived, by Sheridan Baker, 'Did Fielding [i.e. Henry] write "A Vision"?' *Eighteenth-Century Studies*, 22 (1989), 548–51, and J. F. Burrows, ' "A Vision" as a Revision', *Eighteenth-Century Studies*, 22 (1989), 551–65.

[6] Westminster Bridge, begun in 1738 by Charles Labelye, condemned by Batty Langley as an 'INSOLVENT, IGNORANT, ARROGATING *Swiss*,' not only because one of the bridge's piers sank but also because he had pirated Langley's 'rules' for designing the piers (*A Survey of Westminster Bridge, as 'tis now Sinking into Ruin* [London, 1748], pp. iii, vii). Cf. Colvin, p. 498.

[7] II, p. 307. Wood was considered a primitive material and, after the Great Fire, also dangerous.

ments for the Reception of travelling and distressed *Christians*'.[8] The importance of Lambeth Palace is its convenience: its presumed purpose is indicated
in its appearance.

Passing by Marble Hall, 'a most august Edifice, built all of a rich Marble,
which reflecting the Sun-Beams, creates an Object too dazzling for the Sight',
the Frenchman then reaches

a most superb Piece of Architecture of white, or rather yellow Brick. This belongs to
one of the *Bourgeois*, as do indeed most of the Villas which border on both sides this
River, and they tend to give as magnificent an Idea of the Riches which flow in to these
People by Trade, as the Shipping doth, which is to be seen below the Bridge of *London*.[9]

In the manner of Defoe, Fielding gives no more detail of the architecture:
nothing of its idiom, nor of its structure. He ventures only the conventional
observation, of the kind that Henry Aldrich made in his discussion of convenience, that the merchants' houses signify wealth.

Descriptions of buildings on the Middlesex side – Paradise Row, Chelsea
Hospital, Ranelagh Gardens, the undistinguished and indistinguishable 'Sen-
ate-Houses' on Millbank – pay just as little attention to architectural idiom.
Either the buildings are summarily treated, as 'magnificent' and the like, or
they are 'chiefly remarkable' for some social reason. Past New Bridge, on the
Middlesex side,

we saw the Palace of a Nobleman, who hath the Honour to be a Duke of *France* as well
as of *England*, and the Happiness to be greatly esteemed in both Countries.

Near this Palace stands that of another Duke, who, among other great and good
Qualities, is reputed the most benevolent Man in the World.

A little further we saw the Palace of an Earl, of a very high Character likewise among
his Countrymen; and who, in Times of Corruption, hath maintained the Integrity of
an old *Roman*.

The Palaces of these three Noblemen, who do a real Honour to their high Rank,
and who are greatly beloved and respected by their Country, are extremely elegant in
their Buildings, as well as delightful in their Situation; and, to be sincere, are the only
Edifices that discover any true Taste, which we saw in all our Voyage.[10]

These palaces are old Montagu House, old Richmond House, and Pembroke
House. They all stood in or near the Privy Gardens, Whitehall, at the west
end of that extraordinary line of rich men's palaces between the site of the
old Whitehall Palace (where these three stood) and the Fleet Ditch.[11] Old

---

[8] *Familiar Letters*, II, p. 307–8. See Francis Grose, *Antiquities of England and Wales*, 2nd edn, V
(London, 1786), plate facing p. 106. Always the residence of Archbishops of Canterbury since
the 13th Century, Lambeth Palace was certainly no hostel, but it was notable for its large number
of small apartments.

[9] II, pp. 308–9.

[10] II, pp. 317–18.

[11] Most of Whitehall Palace itself was destroyed by fire in 1698. A Dutch engraving of a view of
the old palace is reproduced in Bernard Adams, *London Illustrated 1604–1851* (Phoenix, Ariz.:
Oryx Press, 1983), plate 8. For brief comments on Montagu, Pembroke and Richmond houses,

Montagu House had been built in 1733 for the second Duke of Montagu. The earlier Richmond House was built about 1660, was then used as an office from 1701, and was finally given to Charles Lennox, the second Duke of Richmond, in 1738. The new Richmond House, adjacent to it, had been built in 1710 by Burlington for the first Duke. The third palace, Pembroke House, had been built in 1717–18 for the Earl of Pembroke. The three palaces mentioned by Fielding (as well as new Richmond House) were designed in fashionable neo-Palladian style.[12]

Pembroke House and its recent neighbours were described by Fielding's former associate on the *Champion*, James Ralph, who found something to complain about in all three of them in 1734.[13] Whereas Ralph's purely descriptive *Critical Review* of London's buildings shows a spectator's interest in outward appearances and architectural idiom only, Fielding's main concern is with an important aspect of 'convenience'. The whole of Fielding's essay, and the four quoted short paragraphs in particular, show that Fielding's visitor does not look for structure or architectural ornament, and that he cares little for the cult of the classical orders. Instead, he relates the buildings to the moral qualities of the people who own or occupy them: he associates the three palaces with, respectively, a high personal reputation, benevolence, and political integrity in the face of corruption. It is consistent with his attitude as a whole that the three noblemen's palaces should be the only examples of 'true Taste' on the journey, and that he should tell his readers absolutely nothing else about the outward appearance of these buildings. Despite the omission of architectural details, all these examples of Fielding's writing about architecture share the orthodoxy of the attitudes of Fussell's Augustan humanists who see architecture as an expression of moral ideas, but unlike their vocabulary, Fielding's is not rich here in 'fabricks' and 'frames'.

Fielding's scattered comments about buildings are indebted fundamentally to Locke and Shaftesbury, and more distantly to Bacon. Locke's architectural images posit individual human beings who are analogous to isolated houses: as Fussell interprets him, 'Houses and buildings may touch each other, but they never interpenetrate',[14] an attitude that suggests an unexpected affinity with Defoe. Fielding's fictional Frenchman does not conceive the city as a living entity at all, but as a linear sequence of individual buildings, whose

and illustrations of the first two, see Christopher Simon Sykes, *Private Palaces: Life in the Great London Houses* (New York: Viking Penguin, 1986), pp. 59, 78 and 86.

[12] Cf. *The London Encyclopaedia*, ed. Ben Weinreb and Christopher Hibbert (London: Macmillan, 1983), p. 648. Fielding had dedicated his play *The Miser* to Richmond in 1733, and made him the subject of the poem 'Of Good Nature', which was first published in *Miscellanies* (1743), and in the *Enquiry concerning . . . Robbers* (1751) he echoed the common praise of Richmond's generous nature.

[13] Ralph, *A Critical Review of the Publick Buildings, Statues and Ornaments in, and about London and Westminster* (London, 1734), p. 45.

[14] Fussell, *Rhetorical World of Augustan Humanism* (Oxford: Oxford University Press, 1965), p. 177.

interest for him, as for Shaftesbury, is how their exteriors represent their owners or occupiers. As in the *Journal of a Voyage to Lisbon*, where Fielding describes the architecture of Greenwich Hospital with rather tired epithets ('delightful' and 'doth much honour at once to its builder and the nation'), there is no sense of common purpose or community, no culture of the city.[15] Later in the *Journal* Fielding asks what 'is the best idea which the prospect of a number of huts can furnish to the mind, but of a number of men forming themselves into a society, before the art of building more substantial houses was known?'[16] This seems to suggest that community is actually dispersed by the 'art' of building, but that is where any similarity to Defoe must surely stop, because most of Fielding's characters are not isolated individuals in search of identity, but members of very small self-contained communities.

In *Joseph Andrews* (1742), *Jonathan Wild* (1743), or *Tom Jones* (1749) small social groups, whether criminal gamesters or the 'Family of Love', convey Fielding's characteristic conception of social space. The fact that space is social, that its use is determined by its occupants, matters more than its dimensions or the fabric of construction. One reason why 'cities, courts, gaols and such places'[17] are syntactically indistinguishable is that they enclose the same patterns of behaviour: their political relationships are identical, so that the generalized spaces in all tend towards the social. Of all Fielding's novels *Tom Jones* makes the most of these and other conceptions of space: it is Fielding's most significant contribution to spatial discourse as well as to British fiction. One major aspect of *Tom Jones* that rarely fails to attract attention is its design. No one can miss it, because the narrator continually talks about it.

Early in the eighteenth and final book of *Tom Jones*, the narrator directs his reader to turn back nearly 800 pages to the sixth chapter of book 9.[18] The complicated scene described there, in the mathematical centre of the novel, is pivotal. Alone among the participants in this scene at an inn at Upton-on-Severn, Jenny Jones knows who the parents of Tom Jones really were, although she has always been thought to be his mother. She is travelling by the name of Mrs Waters, and therefore, when some time later Tom discovers that the woman he slept with at Upton was not Mrs Waters but Mrs Jones, he thinks he has committed the dreadful sin of incest. For the truth about any of these complications to have a chance of coming out at Upton, Mrs Waters would have to be identified as Jenny Jones. Only one character

---

[15] *Journal of a Voyage to Lisbon*, 2nd edn (London, 1755), p. 71.

[16] *Ibid.*, p. 161.

[17] *Jonathan Wild*, ed. David Nokes (Harmondsworth: Penguin, 1982), I, p. 8.

[18] That is, 800 pages in the first edition (1749), but merely 600 or so in the standard modern edition, from which all quotations in this chapter are taken: *The History of Tom Jones, A Foundling*, ed. Martin C. Battestin and Fredson Bowers, The Wesleyan Edition of the Works of Henry Fielding, 2 vols. ([Middletown, Conn.]: Wesleyan University Press, 1975). References to book and chapter are given in parentheses in the text.

present at Upton could recognize her, and so identify her: Partridge, but he never even sees her there. Nine books later, we are told:

If the Reader will please refresh his Memory, by turning to the Scene at Upton in the Ninth Book, he will be apt to admire the many strange Accidents which unfortunately prevented any Interview between Partridge and Mrs Waters, when she spent a whole Day there with Mr Jones. Instances of this Kind we may frequently observe in Life, where the greatest Events are produced by a nice Train of little Circumstances; and more than one Example of this may be discovered by the accurate Eye in this our History. (Bk 18, ch. 2)

Because *Tom Jones* displays a conspicuously detailed, complicated, and admirably organized narrative structure, which this example advertises, the novel has attracted comparison with architecture. Although the comparisons cannot always be exact, they are apposite because Fielding's narrator glories so much in his ability as a designer. The earliest reader to perceive the 'architectural' quality of *Tom Jones* seems to have been Edward Gibbon, who wrote in one of the six versions of his autobiography:

The successors of Charles the fifth may disdain their brethren of England but the Romance of Tom Jones, that exquisite picture of human manners will outlive the palace of the Escurial and the Imperial Eagle of the house of Austria.[19]

It is curious that the Escorial should have been intended by its principal designer, Juan de Herrera, to imitate the proportions of Solomon's Temple. The ground plan incorporated an image of Vitruvian man and the theory of Villalpanda, whose commentary was published shortly after the palace's completion towards the end of the 16th century.[20] It seems improbable that either Gibbon or Fielding intended any conscious echo of this piece of arcana, but Gibbon's choice of an architectural image draws attention to the vaunted design of *Tom Jones*.[21]

Many scholars and critics have followed Gibbon, consciously or not, in their commentaries on *Tom Jones*. Frederic T. Blanchard, for instance, who did cite Gibbon, also wrote of the novel's 'immense architectural plan', quoted Sir Walter Raleigh on its 'plot-architecture', and referred to the Victorian architect, better known for his novels, Thomas Hardy, who said *Tom Jones*

---

[19] *Memoirs of My Life*, ed. Georges A. Bonnard (London: Thomas Nelson, 1966), p. 5. Gibbon chose the analogy because he accepted the canard that Fielding's family was descended from the Hapsburgs. See Cross, *The History of Henry Fielding*, I, pp. 1–3.

[20] The official architect was not Herrera, who, however, took over from Juan Bautisto de Toledo. Francesco Pacciotto da Urbino also had a hand in the design. The demarcation of these men's roles remains a vexed question. See chapter 4, above.

[21] Others (besides the narrator) who celebrate the 'design' include: the anonymous author of *The History of Charlotte Summers, the Fortunate Parish Girl*, 2nd edn (London, 1750), II, p. 2; Jerry C. Beasley, *Novels of the 1740s* (Athens: University of Georgia Press, 1982), ch. 7; and Robert Alter, *Fielding and the Nature of the Novel* (Cambridge: Harvard University Press, 1968), p. 30.

'most nearly fulfill[s] the conditions of artistic building'.[22] Among others, Dorothy van Ghent likens *Tom Jones* to 'a complex architectural figure, a Palladian palace perhaps: immensely variegated', and with a dome on top. In his own brilliant study of the intricacies of Fielding's 'constructive art', R. S. Crane cites Oliver Elton's phrase on Fielding's 'ever-to-be praised skill as an architect of plot'. Martin Battestin, extending Crane's argument much further, shows that the 'frame and architecture' of the whole novel are structured as an emblem of the design argument, where nothing is the result of chance, however much appearances may suggest otherwise; Battestin also uses some of the architectural sources that I have discussed in earlier chapters. Finally, in an extraordinary, convincing article, Frederick W. Hilles makes the deceptively tentative suggestion that the plot of *Tom Jones* is structured in deliberate accordance with the ground plan of Prior Park.[23] The plot structure of *Tom Jones* displays symmetry, balance, and a degree of mathematical exactness, all of which suggest to these commentators that architecture is an appropriate analogue.[24]

It was traditional wisdom, as Bacon, Montaigne, Swift and many others had shown, that a book could be an expression of self.[25] It was similarly traditional that a book could be an expression of a space (particularly an architectural space),[26] and now *Tom Jones* exploits space to express not just narrative organization, but also the qualities of people: their good- or ill-nature, motives, and temperaments. The novel's self-conscious designer is a 'moral artist', who determines the 'Boundarys of the Passions' in a whole that he has himself created. This terminology comes from Shaftesbury's definition of a true poet, who is 'a real Master, or Architect in the kind . . . Like that Sovereign Artist or universal Plastick Nature, he forms a *Whole*, coherent and

---

[22] Frederic T. Blanchard, *Fielding the Novelist: A Study in Historical Criticism* (New Haven: Yale University Press, 1926), pp. 498, 503, 513, 560–61.

[23] Dorothy van Ghent, *The English Novel: Form and Function* (1953; New York: Harper & Row, 1961), p. 80; R. S. Crane, 'The Plot of *Tom Jones*', *Journal of General Education*, 4 (1950), 112–30, reprinted in *Twentieth-Century Interpretations of 'Tom Jones'*, ed. Martin C. Battestin (Englewood Cliffs, NJ: Prentice Hall, 1968), pp. 68–93; Martin C. Battestin, *The Providence of Wit*, p. 151; Frederick W. Hilles, 'Art and Artifice in *Tom Jones*', in *Imagined Worlds: Essays on some English Novels and Novelists in Honour of John Butt*, ed. Maynard Mack and Ian Gregor (London: Methuen, 1968), pp. 91–110.

[24] The first three books of *Tom Jones* contain 13, 9, and 10 chapters. The last three contain 10, 9, and 13. Douglas Brooks thinks there is more evidence of numerical structures than this, but I find it hard to agree with him (*Number and Pattern in the Eighteenth-Century Novel* [London: Routledge & Kegan Paul, 1973], pp. 92–122).

[25] 'Myself am matter of my book', said Montaigne. For useful commentary on Montaigne and Swift, see Everett Zimmerman, *Swift's Narrative Satires: Author and Authority* (Ithaca and London: Cornell University Press, 1983), pp. 52–60.

[26] Cf. Thomas Browne's celebrated figure of the Book of Nature as 'that universall and publik Manuscript' (*Religio Medici*, I, section 16, in *Religio Medici and Other Works*, ed. L. C. Martin [Oxford: Clarendon Press, 1964], p. 15). See also Rykwert, *On Adam's House*, p. 190, and Warren H. Smith, 'Architectural Design on English Title-Pages', *Library*, 4th series 14 (1933–34), 289–98. Many authors, including Locke and Swift, referred to their books as buildings.

proportion'd in itself, with due Subjection and Subordinacy of constituent Parts.'[27]

Comic-epic-poem-in-prose or not, *Tom Jones* is a universal novel in the sense that its designer views his characters as figures in a panorama, and on several occasions he treats individual incidents as examples illustrating universal truths. We might call *Tom Jones* an essay in Shaftesburean 'moral architecture' set against a background of usually unspecific yet vivid space. It is tempting to see in *Tom Jones* what Fielding himself saw in *Don Quixote*: 'the History of the World in general, at least that Part which is polished by Laws, Arts and Sciences; and of that from the time it was first polished to this day; nay and forwards, as long as it shall so remain'.[28] This is both an orthodox statement about the relevance of a universal work of literature, and an expression, typical of its time, of the monumental quality of an enduring book: it is also parallel to John Wood's concept of the Tabernacle as 'an Hieroglyphical Representation of the History of the World'.[29]

In both *Joseph Andrews* and *Tom Jones* the principal characters (except perhaps Parson Adams) are something close to hieroglyphical representations: suggestive examples rather than realistic, complex people. As the narrator's comments in Book 18, chapter 2 of *Tom Jones* also suggest, Fielding's emphasis generally is on example, and his comic technique encourages his readers to treat each character as a vehicle for moral example, each incident as typical. Fielding commonly broadens the appeal of the specific example by noting its relation to a broader truth. The relation between the specific and the general is well illustrated by this little discourse on marriage in *Tom Jones*:

The Love of Girls is uncertain, capricious, and so foolish that we cannot always discover what the young Lady would be at; nay, it may also be doubted, whether she always knows this herself.

Now we are never at a Loss to discern this in Women about Forty; for as such grave, serious and experienced Ladies well know their own Meaning, so it is always very easy for a Man of the least Sagacity to discover it with the utmost Certainty.

Miss *Bridget* is an Example of all these Observations. (Bk 1, ch.11)

The importance of these remarks is not what the narrator tells us about Bridget Allworthy herself, but that her behaviour is typical for a woman of her age. In such ways as this *Tom Jones* is representative of life, without seriously pretending to be like life. By making his characters exemplary, Fielding can also deepen and broaden the world they live in, and therefore the human experiences they represent. Spaces are generalized in both *Tom Jones* and *Joseph Andrews*, whose characters take to the road and meet a cross-section of England's rural population on their journeys. Not strictly picar-

---

[27] *Characteristicks of Men, Manners, Opinions, Times*, 5th edn (London, 1732), I, p. 207.

[28] *Joseph Andrews*, ed. Martin C. Battestin, Wesleyan Edition (Middletown, Conn.: Wesleyan University Press, 1967), Bk 3, ch. 1.

[29] Wood, *Origin of Building* (Bath, 1741), p. 90.

esque, Fielding's technique still demands space in which his characters can move. Only on a journey through several small country communities, not just one, can such a cross-section be encountered, because a single village would not be sufficiently complex or demographically diverse. Generalized space suggests both the variety of experience, and the wide applicability of the moral examples. Moving through real but unspecific land- and cityscapes, Fielding's casts of exemplary characters act out sequences of little dramas that also often depend on the politics of space. The delimiting space of the physical world is frequently replaced by the generalized, infinite space of the moral world: when that happens, we are left with essences rather than entities, abstractions rather than concrete social realities. Thus the narrator of *Tom Jones* promises to record only the history of 'those notable Æras when the greatest Scenes have been transacted on the human Stage' (Bk 2, ch. 1), but a stage much larger than one found in, say, Drury Lane. With words so suggestive of a broad sweep Fielding creates a sense of wide space even though the majority of the action occurs in spaces that we would know to be restricted if we could perceive them. The tendency of *Tom Jones* towards generalization and universals – usually moral – indicates wider spaces than those enclosed by the walls of a man's house. In a parallel conception Thomas Whately (thinking of lakes in gardens) said that 'the mind, always pleased to expand itself on great ideas, delights even in its vastness'.[30] If perception is somehow disappointed or disrupted, the imagination may be confined: Whately's routine aesthetics apply as appropriately to fiction as to gardens.

Once on the road, Jones's aimless wanderings take him and other characters to real enough places, including inns, such as the Bell at Gloucester, or the Hercules Pillars at Hyde Park Corner, both familiar to travellers in the mid eighteenth century. Stepping in and out of the narrative are also troops on their way to resist the Jacobite rebellion of 1745, and various friends and patrons of Fielding's, whose intrusions in person, Ian Watt concludes, 'break the spell of the imaginary world'.[31] Fielding reminds his readers, as Defoe did, that his fiction has some relation to issues that take place in a wider, and real, world. Similarly, the participants in the great battle in the churchyard (Bk 4, ch. 8) are just a '*Somersetshire* Mob', but Fielding's mock-heroic narrative takes his readers through a skilful burlesque of a battle between the Greeks and the Trojans. He removes the narrative briefly – and absurdly – from an individual churchyard to a generalized literary version of traditional English rural life. In much the same way, as Hilles points out, Fielding exploits an extended simile to describe '*A dreadful Alarm in the Inn*' where Sophia and Mrs

---

[30] Whately, *Observations on Modern Gardening and Laying out pleasure-grounds, parks, farms, ridings, &c.*, new [i.e. 6th] edn (London: West & Hughes, 1801), pp. 37–39.

[31] Watt, *Rise of the Novel*, p. 285. On the barely conceivable identification of Jones as the Young Pretender, see Ronald Paulson, 'Fielding in *Tom Jones*: the Historian, the Poet, and the Mythologist', in *Augustan Worlds: Essays in Honour of A. R. Humphreys*, ed. J. C. Hilson, M. M. B. Jones, and J. R. Watson (Leicester: Leicester University Press, 1978), pp. 175–88.

Fitzpatrick are lodging (Bk 11, ch. 8): 'Sophia and Harriet may be cooped up in a country inn on the Watling Street, some ninety miles from London; we the readers are not only there but in London itself as well as near the groves and by the streams of ancient Greece.'[32] These are examples of Fielding's studied range of literary allusion working to create a wider horizon than the confines of a room at an inn would allow.[33]

In fact, when Sophia is confined by her father to just such a room at the Hercules Pillars, the narrator simply leaves her there, 'with no other Company than what attend the closest State Prisoner, namely, Fire and Candle' (Bk 16, ch. 2). Although the narrator is silent about the specific room, about the actual space in this scene, as he is about most other scenes set in 'a room' or the like, there is evidence that *Tom Jones* is conceived spatially, as the opening chapter suggests:

An Author ought to consider himself, not as a Gentleman who gives a private or eleemosynary Treat, but rather as one who keeps a public Ordinary, at which all Persons are welcome for their Money . . . it hath been usual, with the honest and well-meaning Host, to provide a Bill of Fare, which all Persons may peruse at their first Entrance into the House; and, having thence acquainted themselves with the Entertainment which they may expect, may either stay and regale with what is provided for them, or may depart to some other Ordinary better accommodated to their Taste. . . . The Provision then which we have here made is no other than HUMAN NATURE. (Bk 1, ch. 1)

The imagery of eating, which fills the rest of the chapter, has received its due share of critical attention, ever since the author of *The History of Charlotte Summers* promised to complement Fielding's feast with supplies of drink, but no one has remarked, to my knowledge, that Fielding here presents his novel as a *place*, specifically a 'public Ordinary', or restaurant, which his readers enter.[34] Although not an analogue or identification that Fielding develops explicitly, the book-as-building announces at the start that we readers are invited to enter the house of fiction and so to engage in a fundamentally social act. Later, he changes the terms of the metaphor in a variation of *theatrum mundi*. His 'theatre of the world' chapter tells members of the 'audience', sitting in different parts of the theatre, how their reactions to a single event (Black George's theft of Tom's £500) will differ according to the social class to which they belong (Bk 7, ch. 1). Thinking of the narrator's 'initial chapters', George Eliot evidently considered *Tom Jones* Fielding's theatrical but informal entertainment, a view Fielding encourages with several theatri-

---

[32]   Hilles, 'Art and Artifice', p. 99.

[33]   See my *Henry Fielding* (Cambridge: Cambridge University Press, 1986), pp. 79, 81.

[34]   *Charlotte Summers*, pp. 4–5. And see Michael Bliss, 'Fielding's Bill of Fare in *Tom Jones*', *ELH*, 30 (1963), 236–43. For a different sense of feast (as a cognate of 'festival'), see Andrew Wright, *Henry Fielding: Mask and Feast* (Berkeley and Los Angeles: University of California Press, 1965).

cal metaphors.[35] But if his use of *theatrum mundi* is associated with the physical theatre of his own day, then this spatial analogy is primarily a model of hierarchy determined by social rank. In any case, as John Preston has pointed out, the narrator is at this point more interested in the audience than he is in the 'play' that they watch.[36] Finally, when the narrator takes leave of his sagacious reader, in the last of the introductory chapters, the relationship between him and his reader has nothing to do with buildings, but everything to do with space and motion:

> We are now, Reader, arrived at the last Stage of our long Journey. As we have therefore travelled together through so many Pages, let us behave to one another like Fellow-Travellers in a Stage-Coach, who have passed several Days in the Company of each other . . . (Bk 18, ch.1)

This metaphor reminds us that reading is a temporal occupation, and that it is a journey through space. Yet reading, no less than writing, is a social, not a private act. This novel starts as a restaurant, then becomes a theatre, and finally becomes a journey on a stage coach. Accompanied by the sociable author, readers have undertaken a journey through pages that resembles that of Tom and Sophia through space.[37]

Fielding's social narrative technique in *Tom Jones* has been subjected to continual critical analysis, and its important role in the structure of the novel carefully evaluated. I do not need to rehearse the well-known arguments.[38] Oscillating between arrogance and playfulness, stern moral lecturing and light chatter, the narrator's assured tone presupposes an audience that is willing to play along with him, to share his values as well as his jokes.[39] The imagined audience is therefore socially close to Fielding himself, and less diverse than the one he postulates sitting in the theatre. But just as the owners of Georgian houses kept their distance from the passers-by, and let their buildings express that distance, Fielding's narrator keeps himself in reserve too, always with the added precaution of irony. Although never aloof, he keeps his readers at arm's length even at some moments when he appears to be jolly and conversational, such as the moment when Sophia falls from her

---

[35] *Middlemarch*, ch. 15: 'he seems to bring his arm-chair to the proscenium and chat with us in all the lusty ease of his fine English'.

[36] John Preston, *The Created Self: the Reader's Role in Eighteenth-Century Fiction* (London: Heinemann, 1970), pp. 119–20.

[37] See also F. Kaplan, 'Fielding's Novel about Novels: the "Prefaces" and the "Plot" of *Tom Jones*', *Studies in English Literature 1500–1900*, 13 (1973), 549.

[38] See: Watt, *Rise of the Novel*, p. 285; Preston, *The Created Self*; and Kaplan, 'Fielding's Novel'. Also, the *locus classicus*, Wayne Booth, *The Rhetoric of Fiction* (Chicago: University of Chicago Press, 1961), pp. 215–18, and Henry Knight Miller, 'The Voices of Henry Fielding: Style in *Tom Jones*', in *The Augustan Milieu: Essays Presented to Louis A. Landa*, ed. Henry Knight Miller, Eric Rothstein, and G. S. Rousseau (Oxford: Clarendon Press, 1970), pp. 262–88.

[39] See, for example, his formulaic expression, 'with Shame I write it, with Sorrow will it be read' (e.g. *Tom Jones*, Bk 5, ch. 5), and my commentary on it in *Henry Fielding*, pp. 92–93.

horse in an inn yard, and the narrator tells us smartly that we are not to laugh (Bk 11, ch. 2).[40] Despite the transparent irony of the very intrusion there, the narrator never quite lets himself go, since the intimacy which that might imply would destroy the sense of his control. More importantly, it would destroy the decorum of the social conventions on which the narrative technique depends: people from eighteenth-century polite society may come close, but not too close, in a public place, and they certainly may not be 'intimate' in as public a place as this novel, where readers are cast as witnesses, or even, as Preston maintains, active participants.[41]

Until the narrative takes Jones on the road, and so to London, the location of almost all that occurs in the first six books of the novel is Paradise Hall. One of the most specific spaces in the novel, Paradise Hall has elicited plenty of commentary, mostly on account of its architectural idiom and the real buildings which probably served as models for it:

The *Gothick* Stile of Building could produce nothing nobler than Mr. *Allworthy*'s House. There was an Air of Grandeur in it, that struck you with Awe, and rival'd the Beauties of the best *Grecian* Architecture; and it was as commodious within, as venerable without. (Bk 1, ch. 4)

Martin Battestin's note describes Allworthy's house as 'an imaginative synthesis of details associated with' Fielding's birthplace, Sharpham Park, Lord Lyttelton's Hagley Park, and Ralph Allen's Prior Park.[42] Everyone who has ever commented on the architecture of Paradise Hall agrees that it is Gothic. Although this is the obvious reading of the passage, there is a lingering ambiguity here. The first sentence does not say necessarily that the house is Gothic: only that the Gothic never produced anything nobler. True, grandeur and awe are, and were then, associated rather with the Gothic than with the neoclassical (which would usually be Roman rather than '*Grecian*'): however, the 'Air of Grandeur' rivalled the beauties not just of Grecian, but of the *best* Grecian architecture. Finally, 'commodious' is an adjective used as a synonym for 'convenient' in one of its many shades of meaning in neo-Palladian writing (and in Johnson's *Dictionary*). 'Commodious' is associated

---

[40] Cf. C. J. Rawson, *Henry Fielding and the Augustan Idea under Stress: 'Nature's Dance of Death' and Other Studies* (London: Routledge & Kegan Paul, 1972), p. 245. Rawson also comments, on *Tom Jones*, Bk 6, ch. 1, that the narrator explicitly challenges any reader who dares disagree with him (*Ibid.*, p. 87). Andrew Wright, *Mask and Feast*, p. 36, recognizes a smile behind such authorial admonitions.

[41] Preston, *The Created Self*, p. 121.

[42] *Tom Jones*, p. 42, note. But cf. Michael McCarthy, 'The Building of Hagley Hall, Worcestershire', *Burlington Magazine*, 118, no. 877 (April 1976), 214–25. Sanderson Miller's Palladian design for Hagley was not even begun until 1751 (Summerson, *Architecture in Britain*, p. 401). There was already a Gothic rotunda at Hagley, and Lyttelton's taste leaned towards the Gothic rather than the Palladian, but the house that Miller replaced – the one Fielding knew when he wrote *Tom Jones* – was, as Horace Walpole said dismissively, 'immeasurably bad and old' (*Correspondence*, ed. W. S. Lewis, 35 [1973], p. 147, cited by McCarthy).

much more strongly with the disposition of space in a neo-Palladian building than in a Gothic one, while 'venerable' naturally suggests an older edifice. This apparently impossible confusion suggests that the house is as much a synthesis of architectural idioms as it is of three identifiable buildings.[43] Significantly, Paradise Hall is commodious *within* and venerable *without*, a contrast that suggests a blend of the new and the old, or modern comforts in an older shell. This is a double meaning of 'convenience' that points to the most common of Fielding's allusions to architecture.

Paradise Hall cannot be separated from its landscaped estate, which resembles the grounds at Prior Park, Hagley and Sharpham, with more exact details borrowed from Prior Park (where Fielding said, 'art' made less impact than usual on 'nature')[44] than from the other two. As Paradise Hall is an analogue of an imaginably real country house, so its owner is an analogue of an imaginably real country squire. Allworthy's generosity and hospitality are conspicuous throughout *Tom Jones*: Allworthy is 'a human Being replete with Benevolence' (Bk 4, ch. 1), his hospitality extended to a wide range of people, even the undeserving (Bk 4, ch. 10). The narrator underlines Allworthy's goodness and hospitality with such descriptive tags, but does not attach any comparable comment to Allworthy's extremely suspect judgment.[45] Because of this emphasis on his benevolence, but not on his shortcomings, Allworthy has always been thought to be a fictional portrait of Allen, or Lyttelton (to whom the novel is dedicated), or both, although such identifications are really not exact enough to be certain. Still, Allworthy resembles Allen more closely than Lyttelton, and does not at all resemble Fielding himself, so there might just be a case for seeing Allen's as the dominant estate in Fielding's conception, rather than Hagley or Sharpham. The whole picture is complicated further because Fielding introduces Allen and Prior Park in the fiction and singles them out for special praise. Yet Allworthy most likely resembles a generic ideal of a country squire and his estate any country estate. For that matter, much the same could be said of Western as a figure of a boorish Jacobite squire.[46] Allworthy is certainly a literary type of a country gentleman,

---

[43] Francis Grose noted later that most writers classed as 'Gothic' all old buildings that were 'not exactly conformable to some one of the five orders of architecture', *Antiquities of England and Wales*, I (London, 1773), p. 63. In *A Philosophical and Critical History of the Fine Arts*, II, p. 301, R. A. Bromley cited Evelyn, *Account of Architects*, p. 9 and Wren, *Parentalia*, p. 305 in support of his own contention that in Gothic architecture 'the idea of a whole is lost'.

[44] Quoted above, chapter 4. Fielding makes the same observation of Paradise Hall; the compliment, as Battestin rightly says, 'would apply equally well to the estates of both Fielding's patrons' (*Tom Jones*, p. 43, note).

[45] Compare *The Created Self*, pp. 123–28.

[46] A search for any possible model for Western has not occupied scholars since R. E. M. Peach dismissed a tradition that Western's prototype was one Baldwin (whom Peach also calls Bennet), who owned Widcombe House, still visible from Prior Park (*Historic Houses in Bath, and their Associations* [London: Simpkin, Marshall, and Bath: R. E. Peach, 1883–84], I, p. xii and II, pp. 33–34, 37 note).

'who understands the Station in which Heaven and Nature have plac'd him. He is Father to his Tenants, and Patron to his Neighbours, and is more superior to those of lower Fortune by his Benevolence than his Possessions.'[47]

Although Allen and Prior Park will not quite go away, the most important fact about Squire Allworthy and Paradise Hall revealed in this chapter of *Tom Jones* is not a pair of specific identifications, but three perfect spatial harmonies: between the outside and inside of the house, between the house and its immediate environs, and between the house and its owner.

The architectural designs of Hagley and Prior Park were often associated with the owners, but this was in any case part of the broader orthodoxy applied to scores of houses. In the case of Prior Park, says Morris Brownell, 'the identification of the house with the virtue of its owner, the reputation of Prior Park as a place "where true taste with grandeur meets", . . . was largely owing to Pope'.[48] Using the identification that Pope had established, Fielding in *Tom Jones* described Ralph Allen's (not Allworthy's) almost superhuman virtues: Allen spent one part of his fortune

discovering a Taste superior to most . . . and another part in displaying a Degree of Goodness superior to all Men, by Acts of Charity . . . he was most industrious in searching after Merit in Distress, most eager to relieve it, and then as careful (perhaps too careful) to conceal what he had done . . . his House, his Furniture, his Gardens, his Table, his private Hospitality, and his public Beneficence all denoted the Mind from which they flowed, and were all intrinsically rich and noble, without Tinsel, or external Ostentation. (Bk 8, ch. 1)

Although Pope was responsible for first publicizing this identification, and Fielding for continuing it, the idea that Prior Park in some way represented Allen's mind was intrinsic to the design of the place: it was exactly what John Wood had set out to achieve along with his other, more esoteric aims. If Hilles is right, and the structure of *Tom Jones* resembles the layout of Prior Park, then there is much more to Fielding's praise than the platitude that Allen's taste dictates the style of the place he lives in. Allen's house and gardens are not distinguished semantically from his famed generosity: all are listed together without distinction. They all 'discover', or manifest 'the Mind', and so does the book in which we read about them.

Paradise Hall is an analogue of Paradise itself, complete with a Satanic figure in Blifil, but, like Prior Park, it is also a palace of benevolence. Further, the narrative itself begins with a gesture of hospitality from the narrator, who, as I have pointed out, tells us that his novel is a place, albeit one with a specific function. The first paragraph opens with a careful distinction:

An Author ought to consider himself, not as a Gentleman who gives a private or eleemosynary Treat, but rather as one who keeps a public Ordinary. (Bk 1, ch. 1)

---

[47] *Tatler*, no. 169, 9 May 1710.
[48] *Alexander Pope and the Arts of Georgian England* (Oxford: Clarendon Press, 1978), p. 213.

That conspicuous adjective 'eleemosynary' recurs in a description of Allworthy's hospitality: his demands on his guests are few,

For indeed, such Solicitations from Superiors always savour very strongly of Com-
mands. But all here were free from such Impertinence, not only those whose Company
is in all other Places esteemed a Favour from their Equality of Fortune, but even those
whose indigent Circumstances make such an eleemosynary Abode convenient to them,
and who are therefore less welcome to a great Man's Table because they stand in need
of it. (Bk 1, ch. 10)

Because an eleemosynary treat or abode smacks of patronizing behaviour,
both the narrator and Allworthy reject eleemosynary attitudes, and display
instead a concern not to be charitable in any sense that implies social superiority or demands gratitude, but simply to be generous and hospitable without
requiring anything in return. They are benevolent.

Benevolence and space have a unique relationship, best known probably
through the architectural symbolism of freemasonry, but equally accessible
elsewhere (see chapter 1). Wood's design for Prior Park was, as we have
seen, based on three things: analogy with sacred buildings, spatial order
as expressed through classical symmetries, and proportion with its various
implications of 'convenience'. These fundamentals enabled Wood to give
spatial form to the mind of the benevolent owner, as Allen's visitors noted,
and it is Wood's achievement that Fielding picks up in his paragraph in
praise of Allen. Fielding's own benevolence and good humour were explicitly
appreciated by the anonymous author of *The History of Charlotte Summers*, who
simultaneously imitated Fielding's spatial conception of a novel by inviting
readers 'out of the open Air, to a handsome Apartment within Doors', and
then introducing them to 'the hospitable Owner' of a 'venerable Mansion'; the
truly generous and benevolent owner is Lady Bountiful, created originally by
Farquhar, but now making her bow in the English novel.[49] As a house can
represent the benevolence of its owner, so can a book represent the benevolence of its author. Given the association of such hospitality with places, *Tom
Jones* is an analogue of benevolence; the novel itself is a palace of benevolence,
too.

Fielding's social, indeed benevolent, act of narration may have started
something for English prose fiction, but in other kinds of writing his own
predecessors included Bacon, who had argued that *philanthropia*, the greatest
'of all the virtues and dignities of the mind . . . answers to the theological
virtue Charity, and admits no excess, but error'. People without such goodness are like 'knee timber', which is 'good for ships . . . but not for building
houses, that shall stand firm'.[50] For Bacon 'the theological virtue Charity',

[49] *Charlotte Summers*, pp. 8, 12–13. This author evidently identified (as most in 1750 would) the
      narrator of *Tom Jones* as Henry Fielding himself.
[50] 'Of Goodness and Goodness of Nature', *The Works of Francis Bacon*, ed. James Spedding, Robert
      Leslie Ellis, and Douglas Denon Heath, VI (London: Longman *et al.*, 1861), pp. 403, 405.

or benevolence, is an expression of God's goodness. In George Cheyne's latitudinarian philosophy, charity is an expression of the love of God, as it is for Allworthy, for 'all Objects ought to be loved in proportion to their Degree of *Beauty, Symmetry* or *Perfection*'.[51]

In *Tom Jones* Sophia, though not absolutely perfect, comes near enough to '*Beauty, Symmetry* or *Perfection*' to command not merely 'the Veneration of our Reader' (Bk 4, ch. 1), but the love of the author himself (Bk 3, ch. 10). When Fielding introduces her with all the mock pomp that he can muster, he dwells on her perfections, in those terms that Cheyne uses to account for charity, beauty, and the love of God. Terms that recur also in architectural writing, these words are distinctly spatial:

Such was the Outside of *Sophia*; nor was this beautiful Frame disgraced by an Inhabitant unworthy of it. Her Mind was every way equal to her Person; nay, the latter borrowed some Charms from the former: For when she smiled, the Sweetness of her Temper diffused that Glory in her Countenance, which no Regularity of Features can give. But as there are no Perfections of the Mind which do not discover themselves, in that perfect Intimacy, to which we intend to introduce our Reader, with this charming young Creature; so it is needless to mention them here . . . (Bk 4, ch. 2)

Since the geometrical proportions of architecture were derived from the proportions of the human body, it is perhaps no surprise that Fielding's language is architectural and geometrical: Sophia's 'Shape was not only exact, but extremely delicate; and the nice Proportion of her Arms promised the truest Symmetry in her Limbs' (Bk 4, ch. 2). Since Sophia's body is a 'Frame' occupied by an inhabitant, the relation between exterior and interior is precisely the concept of 'convenience' applied to an individual.[52] What is more, her beauty is a product of her 'Perfections of the Mind'. Fielding's Shaftesburean concept of 'moral architecture' is further confirmed when of all people, Square is caught in a most humiliating and embarrassing posture, which ought to be enough to demolish his reputation for ever. Crouching naked in Molly Seagrim's bedroom, Square solemnly tells Tom Jones that 'Good Fame is a Species of the KALON and it is by no Means fitting to neglect it' (Bk 5, ch. 5). As Battestin's note reveals, Square alludes to Berkeley's *Alciphron* (1732): 'Doubtless there is a beauty of the mind, a charm in virtue, a symmetry and proportion in the moral world. This moral beauty was known to the ancients by the name of *honestum*, or τὸ καλόν'.[53] Further, Fielding remarks that the pursuit of truth requires 'the searching, rummaging, and examining into a nasty Place; indeed . . . into the nastiest of all Places, A BAD MIND' (Bk 6, ch.

[51] Cheyne, *An Essay of Health and Long Life*, 2nd edn (London, 1725), pp. 2, 7–8, and *Tom Jones*, p. 605, note.
[52] Cf. Bk 4, ch. 6, where Fielding says conscience 'inhabit[s] some human Breasts', even if this looks only like a tired metaphor.
[53] *Tom Jones*, p. 233, note 1.

1), as Locke had perceived it before, and Richardson did too.[54] The relation
of the mind to the body is therefore spatial: a relation of inhabitant to place,
and of place to place. Even 'Virtue herself' will not 'look beautiful, unless she
be bedecked with the outward Ornaments of Decency and Decorum. And
this Precept, my worthy Disciples, if you read with due Attention, you will, I
hope, find sufficiently enforced by Examples in the following Pages' (Bk 3,
ch. 7).

Fielding's other major characters in *Tom Jones* are similarly conceived, in
terms of outer appearance and inner space. In Sophia's case, the outside is
in perfect harmony with the inside. But one of Fielding's favourite themes is
the discrepancy between an attractive appearance and the sordid reality
behind the facade. The discrepancy Fielding uses to describe the Palace of
Aeolus (in the *Vernoniad*) recurs just as effectively in his presentation of
character. To cite just one example, the prudent Blifil gives the outward
impression of being 'sober, discreet, and pious' (Bk 3, ch. 2). As Blifil, he of
'the grave and sober Disposition'

did not, however, outwardly express any such Disgust, it would be an ill Office in us
to pay a Visit to the inmost Recesses of his Mind, as some scandalous People search
into the most secret Affairs of their Friends, and often pry into their Closets and
Cupboards, only to discover their Poverty and Meanness to the World. (Bk 4, ch. 3)

Blifil's mind, like Square's, is a space into which the narrator will not pry, his
selfishness the reason why Sophia 'scorns' him with 'no little Aversion': she
alone passionately announces her hatred of his very name, since it connotes
'whatever is base and treacherous', let appearances suggest what they may to
the contrary (Bk 5, ch. 4). The orthodoxy of such conceptions of character in
spatial discourse is all the more obvious in comparison with Thomas Whately's
commentary on landscape and gardening later in the century:

But though the interior of buildings should not be disregarded, it is by their exterior
that they become *objects*; and sometimes by the one, sometimes by the other, and
sometimes by both, they are intitled to be considered *characters*.[55]

Characterization in *Tom Jones* is a part of spatial discourse because, like the
concept of architectural character, it depends on 'convenience'.[56] Reviewing
the history of the idea of architectural character in 1933, Ernest Pickering
argued that 'Proper character' did not necessarily ensure 'good composition':

A factory may display all the correct graces of classical architecture but may look like
a public library. On the other hand a church may be recognised as a church on account

---

[54] See above, chapter 2.
[55] Whately, *Observations*, p. 66.
[56] Critics concentrating on Fielding's characterization have not discussed the spatial aspect. It has
     been more common to scrutinize the characters' moral psychology, their dramatic or exemplary
     functions, or Fielding's treatment of his own idea of 'conservation of character'.

of the associated elements – the spire and stained glass windows – but be entirely lacking in the principles of good design. Proper character and principles of composition are not synonymous; they appear together only by a conscious effort of the designer.[57]

Although the concept of character in architecture was applied extensively only later in the eighteenth century, it originated earlier with Shaftesbury and was actually put into practice by Robert Morris. The spatial concept of character, of the outward and inward in harmony or disharmony, equates convenience in architecture with ethos in moral architecture. Like the designer of a building, the designer of *Tom Jones* is also an analogue of the designer of the universe, but with the important difference that as few architects ever claimed that their buildings were somehow likenesses of heaven on earth, so Fielding's narrator, given to irony as he is, does not actually claim to be God.[58]

Unlike Sophia, most of Fielding's obviously virtuous characters continually make the mistake of trusting Blifil's or Square's appearance, until at length they acquire the suspicion – or, as the narrator terms it, prudence – necessary for their own survival. Until they learn to be suspicious, they trustingly assume that the outside matches the inside. The most important factor in establishing Jones's reputation, and indeed his fortune, is the exposure of Blifil's hypocrisy, that is, the exposure of the difference between the 'interior' and the 'exterior'. The exposure provides proof to Allworthy and Jones that appearances must not be trusted. A portrayal of hypocrisy always demands some such distinction between external and internal: in Fielding's novels this distinction is continually expressed in the language of 'convenience'.

As Pat Rogers has pointed out, the idea that externals control internals is a central concept in eighteenth-century culture, and is expressed summarily in Fielding's 'Essay on Conversation':

The Art of pleasing or doing Good to one another is . . . the Art of Conversation. It is this Habit which gives it all its Value . . . [and] we can fail in attaining this truly desirable End from Ignorance only in the Means; and how general this Ignorance is, may be, with some Probability, inferred from our want of even a Word to express this Art by: that which comes nearest to it . . . is *Good Breeding*; a Word, I apprehend, not at first confined to Externals, much less to any particular Dress or Attitude of the

---

[57] Pickering, *Architectural Design* (New York: J. Wiley & Sons; London: Chapman & Hall, 1933), quoted and discussed by Colin Rowe, *The Mathematics of the Ideal Villa and Other Essays* (Cambridge, Mass.: MIT Press, 1976), pp. 62–67.

[58] Critics who think of the narrator as an analogue of God, and of the well-ordered plot as a confident affirmation of a well-ordered universe: Ian Watt, Martin Battestin, Aubrey Williams, Henry Knight Miller. Critics who see the plot as an artificial irony that induces more scepticism than confidence: Sheridan Baker, John Preston, Leo Braudy, and David Goldknopf. There is much to be said for William Park's diplomatic solution: double irony and double readers: 'Ironist and Moralist: the Two Readers of *Tom Jones*', *Studies in Eighteenth-Century Culture*, vol. 8, ed. Roseann Runte (Madison: University of Wisconsin Press, 1979), 233–42.

Body: nor were the Qualifications expressed by it to be furnished by a Milliner, a Taylor, or Perriwig-maker; no, nor even by a Dancing-Master himself . . . even Good-Nature itself, the very Habit of Mind most essential to furnish us with true Good Breeding, the latter so nearly resembling the former, that it hath been called, and with the Appearance at least of Propriety, artificial *Good Nature*.[59]

Externals give shape and form to internals, whether in clothing or in architecture. The same concept, with some of the same vocabulary, recurs in *Tom Jones*:

And to say the Truth, there is in all Points, great Difference between the reasonable Passion which Women at this Age [forty] conceive towards Men, and the idle and childish Liking of a Girl to a Boy, which is often fixed on the Outside only, and on Things of little Value and no Duration; as on Cherry Cheeks, small Lily-white Hands, slow-black Eyes, flowing Locks, downy Chins, dapper Shapes, nay sometimes on Charms more worthless than these, and less the Party's own; such are the outward Ornaments of the Person, for which Men are beholden to the Taylor, the Laceman, the Perriwigmaker, the Hatter, and the Milliner, and not to Nature. (Bk 1, ch. 11)

The point will be brought out again, with different emphasis, at the end of *Tom Jones*, where, in a familiar Augustan formulation, Fielding lets his virtuous characters turn their backs on the culture of the city, and return to a pastoral paradise. Having changed his religion so he can marry a rich Methodist, Blifil, meanwhile, will be associated with the city despite residing 'in one of the northern Counties, about 200 Miles distant from *London*', since he plans to buy himself into Parliament. *Tom Jones* shows that when externals genuinely match internals, thus when the 'mismatched' Blifil has been expelled to a remote corner of the novel's moral world, men and women can enjoy their natural status as social creatures. In the 'Essay' Fielding explains that the art of pleasing – fundamentally a social art – springs from man's 'natural Desire or Tendency' to be a social animal:[60] *Tom Jones* ends with a flurry of examples of 'the most agreeable intercourse' between Jones and Sophia, Allworthy, Western, Nightingale and his wife, Mrs Miller and her daughter, Partridge (about to marry Molly Seagrim) and, no less predictably, between the worthy couple and all their neighbours, tenants, and servants (Bk 18, ch. 13).

Such social harmony is possible in a place where true convenience has been realized; the movement of the action of the novel from Paradise Hall to the English country roads and on to London, where Jones reaches his moral nadir with Lady Bellaston, has taken Fielding's characters through obviously differing moral and social worlds. This action culminates in the summarily treated return to Paradise Hall. So far from building an equivalent of New

[59] *The Augustan Vision* (London: Methuen, 1974), p. 51; Fielding, *Miscellanies*, vol. 1, ed. Henry Knight Miller, Wesleyan Edition (Middletown, Conn.: Wesleyan University Press, 1972), pp. 123–25.
[60] *Miscellanies*, I, p. 123.

Jerusalem, Jones and Sophia prefer to return to their version of Eden, now rid of its Blifil, 'that wicked Viper which [Allworthy had] so long nourished in [his] Bosom' (Bk 18, ch. 8). The idyllic retreat, replete with connotations of a stable, ordered, and hierarchical society, is a social paradise where 'Whatever in the Nature of *Jones* had a Tendency to Vice, has been corrected by continual Conversation with this good Man [Allworthy], and by his Union wth the lovely and virtuous *Sophia*' (Bk 18, ch. 13). Life at Paradise Hall is socially harmonious at the conclusion of *Tom Jones*, when the family of love is firmly ensconced in its limited social cosiness. A limited community, the family of love is thus rewarded with property in *Tom Jones*. Jones is, after all, 'rewarded' with an estate by Western. The neighbouring estates, Allworthy's and Western's, are merged, but the outer boundaries of the new, larger estate are as exclusive as ever.

Although 'convenient' characterization together with space as property occur frequently in Fielding's fiction, nowhere else but in *Tom Jones* does Fielding exploit space as an element of narrative organization. *Joseph Andrews*, for instance, makes use of space and place in much less conspicuous ways, such as the arrogant young squire's destruction of other people's hedges, crops, and gardens, or Lady Booby's wielding her authority as director of the parish by trying to remove Fanny from it physically, or her keeping parson Adams waiting below stairs to remind him that she treats him as a domestic (Bk 1, ch. 3; Bk 3, ch. 4; Bk 4, ch. 2). More palpably than *Joseph Andrews*, *Tom Jones* is constructed and directed by a designer who warns us 'not too hastily to condemn any of the Incidents in this our History, as impertinent and foreign to our main Design, because thou dost not immediately conceive in what Manner such Incident may conduce to that Design' (Bk 10, ch. 1) and who constantly draws his readers' attention to his ingenious construction.[61] History, the narrator of *Tom Jones* announces memorably, is like this:

> In reality, there are many little Circumstances too often omitted by injudicious Historians, from which Events of the utmost Importance arise. The World may indeed be considered as a vast Machine, in which the great Wheels are originally set in Motion by those which are very minute, and almost imperceptible to any but the strongest Eyes. (Bk 5, ch. 4)[62]

With what sounds at first like a similar proposition, Fielding invites readers of his last novel, *Amelia* (published two years after *Tom Jones*), to contemplate 'great Incidents' (often only ironically 'great'), which 'are no more to be considered as mere Accidents, than the several Members of a fine Statue, or a noble Poem' (Bk 1, ch. 1). The statement asserts the organic spatial relation

---

[61] It is now generally accepted that *Joseph Andrews* is carefully 'designed': see Douglas Brooks, *Number and Pattern*, pp. 65–91; and Arthur Sherbo, *Studies in the Eighteenth-Century English Novel* (East Lansing: Michigan State University Press, 1969), p. 104.

[62] One of Fielding's admirers and fellow-visitors to Prior Park, Richard Graves, almost repeated Fielding's commonplace words (*Spiritual Quixote*, I, p. 7).

of parts to a whole. In spite of Fielding's implication that *Amelia* conforms to some design to which all incidents and details are important contributions, *Amelia* in fact offers its readers very few signs that direct attention to the whole. The narrative of *Amelia* unfolds in a seemingly inconsequential way, as incident follows incident without much apparent sense of purpose, climax, or pattern, and with a less intrusive but still sociable guide imposing only a loose narrative shape on it all. Generally without the authoritative voice of the narrator of *Tom Jones*, *Amelia*'s narrator concentrates on small incidents, apparently on the parts rather than the whole. *Amelia* turns out not to be narrated by one who glories in his structural marvel, 'considered as a great Creation of our own' (*Tom Jones*, Bk 10, ch. 1), but by one who is sometimes as baffled by occurrences as his readers must be.[63] In *Tom Jones* all will be revealed by the designer of the novel; in *Amelia* revelations are casual, coming upon readers in much the same circumstantial and contradictory ways as they occur in the fictional lives of the characters. *Amelia* is not a narrative that lacks control or design, but after *Tom Jones* Fielding no longer commits himself to conspicuous display of his organizing technique.

A 'convenient' conception of place and character can also be found in *Amelia*, but the action of this novel is located neither in country houses nor on the road nor in West End boudoirs, but almost entirely in the seediest neighbourhood of inner London. Fielding comes closest to delimiting space in Defoe's way in *Amelia*, which expresses a more definite sense of place, of claustrophobic oppressiveness and restricted space, than any other of Fielding's novels.[64] Fielding again names real enough places: Ranelagh and Vauxhall Gardens, St James's Church, Hyde Park and the Mall, or the Opera House in the Haymarket. It may well be possible to identify real buildings behind Bondum's sponging-house and Thrasher's courtroom, too,[65] but the sense of place is created less by physical description of buildings, and more by the characters' attitudes to space – in particular, to restriction and confinement.

Although the first quarter of *Amelia* takes place inside a prison, not named but actually Newgate, Fielding's only concessions to the physical presence of the place are a symbolic bolt (which is so 'very slight' that the cell door eventually flies open without offering even token resistance [Bk 2, ch. 9]), and the turn of a key that locks Booth and Fanny Mathews in her cell for their first adulterous night together (Bk 4, ch. 1). There were no barbs on the prison

---

[63] See Anthony J. Hassall, 'Fielding's *Amelia*: Dramatic and Authorial Narration', *Novel*, 5 (1972), 225–33, and Robert Folkenflik, 'Purpose and Narration in Fielding's *Amelia*', *Novel*, 7 (1974), 168–74. Cf. Eric Rothstein, *Systems of Order and Inquiry in Later Eighteenth-Century Fiction* (Berkeley: University of California Press, 1975), pp. 154–207.

[64] Most critics apparently find *Amelia* oppressive in some way. See, for example, Pat Rogers, *Henry Fielding* (New York: Scribner's, 1979), p. 193.

[65] See Battestin's introduction to the Wesleyan *Amelia* (Oxford: Clarendon Press, 1983), pp. xxx–xxxi. All quotations from *Amelia* are taken from this edition.

walls in *Amelia* until George Cruikshank put some there when he illustrated the novel in 1832.

Fielding draws a distinction between what one might expect a prison to be and what it actually is. Although this prison is evidently not Moll Flanders' terrifying spectre, it is similarly full of inmates, such as Blear-Eyed Moll, who are neither gloomy nor despondent, who do not miserably contemplate their fate, but whose activities and attitudes define the nature of the confined space that is the prison:

Could [Booth's] own Thoughts indeed have suffered him a Moment to forget where he was, the Dispositions of the other Prisoners might have induced him to believe that he had been in a happier Place: For much the greater part of his Fellow-Sufferers, instead of wailing and repining at their Condition, were laughing, singing and diverting themselves with various kinds of Sports and Gambols. (Bk 1, ch. 3)

In some respects, though, the prison will come to be an analogue, like Defoe's Newgate, of the city from whose activity Booth has been unjustly removed: both are dominated in the same way by greed, hypocrisy, injustice, and petty crime. It is outside the prison walls, in the limited freedom of London, that Booth really suffers: from guilt, shame, disquiet, and of course debt. There is also more suffering (told in the form of hard-luck stories) among supposedly free people like Bob Bound, who move about in the streets, than there is among those in jail.

Booth's reaction to imprisonment, which in this novel is emphatically a political instrument at the disposal of the rich and powerful, is fear: not fear of isolation, nor Moll Flanders' fear of the loss of her cherished isolation, but fear of separation from Amelia. At one point they can both forget momentarily 'the dreadful Situation of their Affairs', but when Amelia remembers 'that tho'' she had the Liberty of leaving that House when she pleased, she could not take her beloved Husband with her', she too is 'stung . . . to the Quick' (Bk 12, ch. 2). When Booth fears arrest (as he does for most of the novel), he resolves, like Moll Flanders, to stay out of sight, 'to remain a close Prisoner in his own Lodgings' (Bk 4, ch. 9): once 'delivered from his Fears', he takes a morning walk, but 'Mrs. *Ellison*'s Friend had . . . purchased Mr. *Booth*'s Liberty' only 'so far' that he 'could walk again abroad within the Verge' (the Verge of the Court, where he lodges) without being arrested (Bk 5, ch. 5). His liberty is scarcely greater then than it is when he has 'the Liberty' of the sponging house (Bk 8, ch. 2). The loss and regaining of liberty, the cycle of confinement and release, form a major theme of *Amelia*. Personal freedom is reduced to the spatial restriction of physical movement. Booth dares to 'venture without the Verge' only on a Sunday, the one day of the week when the law did not permit the arrest of debtors.[66] Even outside Newgate, Booth's movements are restricted by an effect of the law. The restriction of his move-

---

[66] *Amelia*, p. 170 and note 2, p. 150, note, and p. 194 and note.

ments limits his freedom in the city just as effectively as when he is under lock and key in Newgate, as is suggested by the scene in which the bailiff lures Booth out of the 'freedom' of his lodgings and into the sponging house where he is confined again (Bk 8, ch. 1).

When Booth is threatened with arrest, he tries to stay within the verge, but he knows that the bailiff's men will carry him off by force if he resists:

> At length he arrived at the Bailiff's Mansion, and was ushered into a Room; in which were several Persons. *Booth* desired to be alone, upon which the Bailiff waited on him up Stairs, into an Apartment, the Windows of which were well fortified with Iron Bars; but the Walls had not the least Outwork raised before them; they were, indeed, what is generally called naked, the Bricks having been only covered with a thin Plaister, which in many Places was mouldered away. (Bk 8, ch. 1)

Such physical descriptions of buildings are rare in Fielding's fiction, yet this passage is typical of the technique of *Amelia*, because the decay of the place itself matches the corruption of the system that supports it and exploits its victims: convenience again. The sponging house is a place of detention, certainly, but its paraphernalia of confinement are more symbolic than practical. By whatever means he may be brought there, the sufferer will usually be kept in there by other forces, such as corruption, rather than by effective physical restraint. Wherever he is, sponging house or lodging house, the debtor is confined, constricted and, above all, exploited.

The main reason why Booth is continually confined is that he and Amelia make judgments about people which they base on outward appearance. Their judgments are nearly always wrong. In Newgate Booth mistakes Fanny Mathews' intentions, at first, until he finds himself not unwillingly seduced, and later he is perpetually at a loss to understand the swift changes of demeanour in Colonel James and his wife. It is predictable that Booth will be deceived by such artful, theatrical control of appearance as Miss Mathews displays (Bk 1, ch. 6), because although he has been exposed before to misleading appearances, he has not yet learned his lesson, for Amelia's sister, who 'had always appeared to be [his] Friend' (Bk 2, ch. 8) has already turned out to be the opposite. To a degree, *Amelia* is the story of Booth and Amelia (but especially Booth) being confronted with people who seem pleasant, reasonable, or generous, but who have sinister and selfish motives behind their facades. Examples of this kind of 'inconvenient' character abound elsewhere in Fielding's writing, but in *Amelia*, it seems, nearly everyone is like this, like Blifil, and with the exception of the eccentric and grotesque Colonel Bath, they are hardly caricatured. There is nothing particularly exaggerated or implausible about the appearance or behaviour of Miss Mathews, or Colonel James, or the nameless lord. Amelia and Booth fail to penetrate these appearances, because they lack suspicion.

With their inability to perceive the 'inconvenience' of character, Booth and

Amelia place themselves constantly under threat. The pattern of seduction is simple; knowing that Booth is not a lone outsider, but a socialite who cannot resist a convivial gathering, Amelia's seducers seek to lend him money on some false or flattering pretence of generosity, or lend him gambling money which he promptly loses: they then call in the loan, and have him imprisoned because he cannot pay it. Booth never learns.[67] Such misinterpretation of motives belongs to Fielding's larger scheme, in which trust, for all that it is an attractive quality, is impossibly impractical without street-sense, or prudence. For, says the narrator, 'It is a good Maxim to trust a Person entirely or not at all' (Bk 7, ch. 8), and it is unwise to trust anyone on the basis of appearance alone.

The suffocating sense of constriction and restriction of space in *Amelia* is achieved by a pattern of assumption, incident and, finally, disappointment or danger when people turn out not to be what they seem. By continually playing off outward appearance against inward character, that is by exploiting convenience, Fielding creates an air of menace that is characteristic of *Amelia*. Being suspicious of one's fellow men is not attractive, but it is necessary. The 'Art of Life', as the narrator of *Amelia* rather portentously calls it, is the art of survival, which readers learn 'by observing minutely the several Incidents which tend to the Catastrophe or Completion of the whole, and the minute Causes whence those Incidents are produced' (Bk 1, ch. 1), words that recall Ware's advice to the aspiring architect as well as *Tom Jones'* remarks on the little incidents that make up history. Only by understanding Shaftesbury's 'moral Architecture' can a reader, as well as a character, penetrate intentionally misleading appearances to discover true motives.

[67] See, for example, Bk 10, ch. 5, Bk 11, ch. 3, Bk 11, ch. 4.

7

Richardson and the violation of space

> Nay, take my life and all; pardon not that:
> You take my house when you do take the prop
> That doth sustain my house; you take my life
> When you do take the means whereby I live.
>
> Shakespeare, *The Merchant of Venice*

Convenience and design, so prominent in Fielding's fiction, do little to shape Richardson's. Although Richardson does occasionally use the outward/ inward contrast, to show for example that Lovelace 'can put on the appearance of an angel of light; but has a black, a very black heart', characterization in Richardson's fiction does not depend on convenience.[1] Nor do *Pamela* and *Clarissa* suggest to most of their readers any sense of overall design. Richardson's sequences of letters between characters contain no conspicuous signposts like those of *Tom Jones* that continually direct us to the novelist's deliberately constructed narrative scheme. Richardson's narrative schemes were actually contrived with scrupulous precision, one sign of which is the planned chronology of his novels; but Richardson differs from Fielding in generally directing his readers' attention away from his artifice, not towards it.[2]

Arguing that *Pamela* is an example of literature as process rather than product, Northrop Frye put one reader's response succinctly:

Johnson's well-known remark that if you read Richardson for the story you would

---

[1] Samuel Richardson, *Clarissa or the History of a Young Lady*, ed. Angus Ross (Harmondsworth: Penguin, 1985), p. 790, and cf. pp. 1,124, 1,205. Ross's text follows that of the first edition, 7 vols., 1747–48. Unless otherwise indicated, all my quotations from *Clarissa* refer to Ross's edition. The revised third edition of *Clarissa* (8 vols., 1751) is preferred by some scholars: this is the basis of the text printed in the easily accessible Everyman edition (4 vols., 1932). For a short discussion of the relative merits of these two differing texts, see Ross's introduction, pp. 16–18. For bibliographical and textual discussion, see Shirley Van Marter, 'Richardson's Revisions of *Clarissa* in the Second Edition', and 'Richardson's Revisions of *Clarissa* in the Third and Fourth Editions', *Studies in Bibliography*, 26 (1973), 107–32, and 28 (1975), 119–52. For a table that facilitates reference and comparison between the different editions, see Ross, p. 1512.

[2] On the chronology of *Clarissa*, see Ross, pp. 23–24. Ian Donaldson comments on a difference between *Tom Jones*, continually heading to its 'end', and *Clarissa*, apparently displaying the opposite tendency ('Fielding and Richardson', *Essays in Criticism*, 32 [1982], 26–47).

hang yourself indicates that Richardson is not interested in a plot with a quick-march rhythm. Richardson does not throw the suspense forward, but keeps the emotion at a continuous present. Readers of *Pamela* have become so fascinated by watching the sheets of Pamela's manuscript spawning and secreting all over her master's house, even into the recesses of her clothes, as she fends off assault with one hand and writes about it with the other, that they sometimes overlook the reason for an apparently clumsy device. The reason is, of course, to give the impression of literature as process, as created on the spot out of the events it describes.[3]

Whether or not *Pamela* was 'of course' conceived quite so conveniently for Frye's purpose, Richardson's narrative technique certainly discourages his readers from perceiving Fielding's kind of artfully devised, planned structure. As an isolated unit of narrative, the letter itself has an obvious connection not with design but only, as a means of 'communication', with other letters. Also, incidents accumulate, and often their reporters – the letter writers – do not, because they cannot, discriminate between the truly and the apparently significant. When Pamela characteristically writes to her parents, who are worried about whether or not she will stay at Mr B's, she adds to her letter a hurried afterthought: 'O! I forgot to say, that I would stay to finish the Waistcoat. I never did a prettier piece of Work; and I am up early and late to get it finish'd; for I long to come to you.'[4] Firstly, what Pamela's parents most want to know is relegated to a postscript. Secondly, Pamela seems not to have realized that her well-being depends on her staying or not. Thirdly, even when she does add this information, she is immediately distracted by the unimportant details of her workmanship and the flattery it has evoked. The narrative technique of this example is typical. Buried in the voluminous mass of words are the signs that may lead eventually to a revelation of overall design, but those signs are virtually indistinguishable from all other signs.

Richardson's characters and perhaps readers too do not recognize motives until they have more information, and do not understand the full implications of an incident until they see its place in some larger pattern. When Lovelace, speaking on paper as usual, anticipates his own narration by saying, 'The reason let it follow; if it will follow – no preparation for it, from me' (945), he could just as well be characterizing the narrative technique of *Clarissa* as a whole. In the first edition of *Clarissa* (1747–8) in seven volumes, only a short preface and a dramatis personae lead readers straight into the text of letter

---

[3] 'Towards Defining an Age of Sensibility', *ELH*, 23 (1956), 144–52, reprinted in *Eighteenth-Century English Literature: Modern Essays in Criticism*, ed. James L. Clifford (New York: Oxford University Press, 1959), pp. 312–13.

[4] Samuel Richardson, *Pamela, or Virtue Rewarded*, ed. T. C. Duncan Eaves and Ben D. Kimpel, Riverside edition (Boston: Houghton Mifflin, 1971), p. 51. Page numbers in parentheses after quotations refer to this edition. Arguments exist over the merits of the various texts of *Pamela*, too: I prefer the first edition, which the Eaves and Kimpel text follows. For textual matters, see Eaves and Kimpel, 'Richardson's Revisions of *Pamela*', *Studies in Bibliography*, 20 (1967), 61–88, and Peter Sabor, 'The Cooke-Everyman Edition of *Pamela*', *Library*, 5th series, 32 (1977), 360–66.

1. For the second edition (1749) Richardson provided a table of contents intended to indicate 'the connexion of the whole', but then he changed his mind again and broke up that table, distributing it among the eight volumes of the third edition (1751), each portion of the table being printed at the *end* of the volume to which it referred.[5] The unintrusive author is rarely in evidence, as an editor who very occasionally supplies summaries and cross-references. Only in the third paragraph before the end of the postscript does he let slip his mask and refer to himself as 'the author' (1,499). Until the end of the first and third editions, which are the ones read today, readers may not even perceive that any design has been imposed on the narrative at all. Design, then, was something with which Richardson did not encourage readers to engage, until they reached the end of his seven- or eight-volume narrative, when 'the complicated adjustment of the several parts to one another could be seen, or fully known'.[6]

In a traditional argument for *Pamela's* realism, William M. Sale, Jr. draws attention to 'the sobriety of rational discourse' in *Pamela's* 'common-place diction', which 'lends matter-of-factness to the incidents and to much of the dialogue'.[7] At least in the earliest edition of *Pamela*, before Richardson's later revisions began to gentrify the idiomatic language of the servant-girl's letters, the commonplace diction also suggests a sprawling world of parts that do not seem to make up a coherent or visible whole. For example:

And so, when I had din'd, up Stairs I went, and lock'd myself into my little Room. There I trick'd myself up as well as I could in my new Garb, and put on my round-ear'd ordinary Cap; but with a green Knot however, and my homespun Gown and Petticoat, and plain-leather Shoes; but yet they are what they call *Spanish* Leather, and my ordinary Hose, ordinary I mean to what I have been lately used to; tho' I shall think good Yarn may do very well for every Day, when I come home. A plain Muslin Tucker I put on, and my black Silk Necklace, instead of the *French* Necklace my Lady gave me, and put the Ear-rings out of my Ears; and when I was quite 'quip'd, I took my Straw Hat in my Hand with its two blue Strings, and look'd about me in the Glass, as proud as any thing. – To say Truth, I never lik'd myself so well in my Life. (60)

Pamela's purpose in locking herself in her own space is clear enough, and shows that her use of the space is intimately linked to the privacy of the action that she contemplates. Only in the paragraph that follows will Pamela reveal any hint of her purpose in dressing up like this. Nothing in Pamela's letter

---

[5] The second edition was little more than a partial reprint of the first: only the first four volumes were published. Cf. Van Marter (1973), 110.

[6] Postscript to the first edition (Ross, *Clarissa*, p. 1,495). In another sense there is virtually no 'end' to either *Pamela* or *Clarissa*, because Richardson revised them so often and so extensively that he had really never finished writing them by the time he died. (But the 1759 edition of *Clarissa* is hardly a serious revision of the third edition of 1751, so for the last ten years of his life Richardson worked little on *Clarissa*. Instead he worked on *Pamela*.) He did admit that *Clarissa* was too long (pp. 1,343, 1,423).

[7] *Pamela* (New York: Norton, 1958), introduction, pp. viii–ix.

anticipates the paragraph I quote: Pamela herself introduces it abruptly. There is such a delight in the details of the green knot, Spanish leather, two blue strings to her hat, and so on, that Pamela is apt to become submerged in her own words. And indeed, words generate other words in a description that wanders off into diffuseness when she starts qualifying 'ordinary' as an adjective to describe her hose. That erratic quality of Pamela's prose is central to Richardson's style in his two more important novels. Although Pamela might write lists of words as an inventory of her personal belongings, the 'whole' – that is, the space – that contains her possessions is often not signified in any detail at all. And although Clarissa and Lovelace do not write as diffusely as Pamela, their language similarly places no emphasis on wholes, only on parts, and so – since without anything much to connect them, the letters comprise sequences of discrete narrative units – the tendency of each entire novel is to show only parts, not wholes, for 'in the minutiae lie often the unfoldings of the Story, as well as of the heart'.[8] Instead of spatial conceptions of convenience and design, personal space and the politics of space give Richardson's fiction – especially *Clarissa* – its uniquely compelling power.

Clarissa relies much more extensively than *Pamela* on the politics of space for its cumulative dramatic effectiveness. The action of *Clarissa* occurs almost exclusively in enclosed spaces; the language of Clarissa and Lovelace, as they write their streams of letters, teems with spatial images; Clarissa's moral struggles are fought continually in spaces that have become her prisons. In addition to the spaces – gardens and parlours, mostly – in which such reported actions as Clarissa's struggles of will with her family have occurred, the situations that Richardson imagines for both these epistolary novels require another kind of interior space, that in which isolated characters write their many letters.[9]

When Clarissa is tricked into entering Mrs Sinclair's house, where she will shortly be drugged, she is told in a casual aside that Lovelace is in the next room, 'very busy in writing answers to his letters', as if that is an adequate, acceptable explanation for their tarrying, even though this is supposed to be only a flying visit (1,009). All things stop for letter writing. Writing letters is an archetypal eighteenth-century activity, a form of expression that Englishmen in the period virtually perfected, and one that emerged as an increasingly important means of communication for those conducting business. Writing letters is simultaneously an individual and a social act: individual because it expresses the self, social because it communicates with other

[8] Richardson to Lady Bradshaigh, 14 February 1754, *Selected Letters of Samuel Richardson*, ed. John Carroll (Oxford: Clarendon Press, 1964), p. 289. He added that few besides Lady Bradshaigh 'will read [*Grandison*] over once for Amusement, and a second time to examine into the unjustness or justness of its several parts, as they contribute to make one Whole!'

[9] The novels do not make unreasonable demands on readers' imagination of space, but of time they do: sometimes there could not be enough hours in a day for a character to undergo some experience and also write about it for as long as he or she is supposed to do.

'selves'. In this novel characters are obsessed with writing letters just as many people are enslaved by the telephone today: 'I will write!' says Lovelace to Belford, 'Can I do anything else?' (1,202). And as one may create a voice or a persona adopted solely for the telephone, so a writer may create a mask adopted for the pen: 'all gloom at heart, by Jupiter! although the pen and the countenance assume airs of levity!' (1,439). The words a writer uses to express himself, as Lovelace tells Belford, may change even according to where the writer is:

I imagine that thou wilt be apt to suspect that some passages of this letter were written in town. Why, Jack, I cannot but say that the Westminster air is a little grosser than that at Hampstead; and the conversation of Mrs Sinclair and the Nymphs less innocent than Mrs Moore's and Miss Rawlins's. And I think in my heart, that I can say and write those things at one place, which I cannot at the other; nor indeed anywhere else. (870)

Words therefore depend on place.

Places and spaces in Richardson's fiction also suggest class, relationships, and states of mind. Belford's description of the sponging house, to which Clarissa is committed, is a conspicuous example of a person occupying a space unsuited to her class (1,064–65, 1,068), but a more mundane illustration of Richardson's exploitation of space occurs earlier when Lovelace, insisting that he is 'so totally' Clarissa's, explains to Belford:

But now I hear the rusty hinges of my beloved's door give me creaking invitation. My heart creaks and throbs with respondent trepidations. Whimsical enough though! For what relation has a lover's heart to a rusty pair of hinges? – But they are the hinges that open and shut the door of my beloved's bed chamber! – Relation enough in that! (575)

This suggests more than a whimsical fancy, for Lovelace identifies his own desires with the physical environment. At the same time he surely knows that the function of the door is determined by the way someone uses it. No invitation is forthcoming, so Clarissa uses the door not to enclose both herself and him in her bedroom as he would like, but to enclose herself and exclude him. His fear of such rejection emerges in the next paragraph, as he ponders the two obvious possibilities – her escape, or his 'grand attempt':

She must be mine, let me do or offer what I will. Courage whenever I assume, all is over: for should she think of escaping from hence, whither can she fly to avoid me? Her parents will not receive her. Her uncles will not entertain her. Her beloved Norton is in their direction, and cannot. Miss Howe dare not. She has not one friend in town but me: is entirely a stranger to the town. And what then is the matter with me, that I should be thus unaccountably overawed and tyrannized over by a dear creature, who wants only to know how impossible it is that she should escape me, in order to be as humble to me as she is to her persecuting relations? (575)

This is an extraordinary piece of logic. Lovelace thinks that Clarissa would be humbled if she knew she could not escape: he has her trapped in his power, yet Clarissa's response is to enclose herself, and Lovelace interprets her action as a sign that *he* is in *her* thrall. He expresses her civil refusal to admit him 'to dine with her' simply: 'The door is again shut' (575). We have no sense of the actual room where she sits, but even so the relation between Clarissa and Lovelace is eloquently expressed by the door that helps to delimit and define its space. The room is thus not fully realized as an imagined spatial unit, but is still a metonymic spatial vehicle that expresses Lovelace's desires, Clarissa's opposition, and her isolation.

To a large extent *Clarissa* is obviously 'about' isolation. A servant or some other go-between is often Clarissa's only means of contact either with Lovelace, whose company she frequently rejects, or with her family, who reject her company. In the scene from which I have just quoted, Clarissa's self-imposed isolation in her bedroom reflects her political isolation, which Lovelace gloatingly describes. Likewise Pamela at an early stage prefers such isolation: hearing footsteps, she says, 'I . . . dread nothing so much as Company; for my heart was up at my Mouth now, for fear my Master was coming' (53). Like the menacing footsteps, which she hears but we do not, the space Pamela occupies is more metaphorical than actual, an image of the mind rather than a place that we see being put to any particular use, an abstract political instrument rather than a substantial physical entity.[10]

In a formulation that recalls the ambiguities of enclosure (in life as in Defoe's fictions), isolation can mean either desirable privacy or undesirable imprisonment, for both Clarissa and Pamela. When Clarissa prefers solitude to Lovelace's company, she asks, in frustration, 'Can I have no retirement uninvaded, sir?' (793), ironic phrasing that anticipates Lovelace's ultimate invasion of her personal space.[11] Lovelace thinks Clarissa is 'almost *eternally* shutting up [herself] from him', precisely because she expects 'to be uninvaded in [her] retirements' (457). Shortly after her rape, and still incoherent from being drugged, Clarissa desires to escape from Mrs Sinclair's brothel,

[10] This was (of course) by no means an unfamiliar conception of space: Swift, for one, customarily wrote of space in this way. See Hopewell R. Selby, 'The Cell and the Garret: Fictions of Confinement in Swift's Satires and Personal Writings', *Studies in Eighteenth-Century Culture*, vol. 6, ed. Ronald C. Rosbottom (Madison: University of Wisconsin Press, 1977), 133–56; C. J. Rawson, *Gulliver and the Gentle Reader* (London: Routledge & Kegan Paul, 1973), esp. pp. 66–83; and Carole Fabricant, *Swift's Landscape* (Baltimore and London: Johns Hopkins University Press, 1982), pp. 43–54.

[11] Cf. Christina Marsden Gillis, 'Private Room and Public Space: the Paradox of Form in *Clarissa*', *Studies on Voltaire and the Eighteenth Century*, 176 (1979), 153–68: the rape as an invasion of the body (thus an 'attack' on the 'private room') leads to the argument that *Clarissa* makes private places public, and so makes the writing process itself public. Gillis links the arrangement of letters to stage design and interior architectural space in *The Paradox of Privacy: Epistolary Form in 'Clarissa'* (Gainesville: University Presses of Florida, 1984). Marijke Rudnik offers close analysis of the language in *Samuel Richardson: Minute Particulars within the Large Design* (Leiden: Leiden University Press & E. J. Brill, 1983).

but only that she may be herself locked up in a private madhouse (896, 918). Then, restored to lucidity, she wants to go to her 'father's house', an orthodox image of the sanctuary of death: although this 'house' is Heaven, as she explains to Belford, it is also her term for the coffin she buys for herself.[12] Clarissa longs to be enclosed in her coffin, symbol of her earnest 'wish for the last closing scene' (1,018). Dunned for a debt she does not owe, Clarissa welcomes her ruin and death: 'Let my ruin, said she, lifting up her eyes, be LARGE, be COMPLETE, *in this life*! – for a *composition*, let it be COMPLETE – and there she stopped' (1,062). Indulging 'the thoughts of death', which, she admits, 'strictly speaking, I enjoy' (1,306), she welcomes the coffin with the same masochistic fervour that provokes some readers either to condemn her as narcissistic and sentimental or to dismiss her as unhealthily crazed. Once she is conscious of her ruin, Clarissa decides to die, and the coffin comes to be her ultimately inviolable personal space, so that her enclosure is, at the last, desirable.

When Pamela is Mr B's bride, she can say, 'Oh! my Prison is become my Palace' (293). Clarissa's perceptions of personal space vary in just the same way, according to her attitudes; locked up by her family, she realizes that her bedroom becomes her 'prison', and she repeatedly demands that Lovelace release her from 'imprisonment' in London. At the High Holborn sponging house (which she repeatedly calls a prison), Clarissa opts for 'the prisoner's room', that her 'wretchedness be complete', but her paradoxically self-abasing bravado falters because 'She found fault that all the fastenings were on the outside, and none within; and said she could not trust herself in a room where others could come in at their pleasure, and she not go out. She had not *been used* to it!' (1,055). Appalled by Clarissa's new degradation, Belford tries to persuade her to leave 'the wretched hole' and return to her lodgings in Russell Street, 'where', he promises, 'she should not be invaded . . . by anybody', but her initial response to his plea is just to say that death makes all places alike (1,071). Her concept of personal space seems to have been replaced at this point by her desire for death, which will be accompanied by her final desire to be enclosed.

One sign of the recurrent violation of personal space, in both *Pamela* and *Clarissa*, is that the heroine's correspondence is intercepted by her enemy or supposed enemy.[13] When Pamela is leaving Mr B's household, the pretended editor interrupts the narrative to explain Mr B's conduct. He tells us first

[12] Cf. pp. 1,114, 1,118, 1,273–74, 1,316, 1,351. The expression comes from John 14:2. Belford speaks of the coffin as Clarissa's 'palace' (1,306), and Lovelace thinks (as she intends him to think) that her 'father's house' means Harlowe Place. See Allan Wendt, 'Clarissa's Coffin', *Philological Quarterly*, 39 (1960), 481–95, and Anthony Kearney, '*Clarissa* and the Epistolary Form', *Essays in Criticism*, 16 (1966), 49. Van Marter (1975), 125, notes Richardson's efforts in the third edition to exonerate Clarissa from the possible charge of deceit.

[13] Illegal interception of letters for political purposes was also commonplace. Lovelace alludes to the practice once (p. 1,085).

how Pamela was abducted and second how her corrrespondence had been intercepted. The two points receive equal weight, to show that 'Thus every way was the poor Virgin beset', the verb suggesting a spatial image of siege. 'And the Whole', the editor continues, 'will shew the base Arts of designing Men to gain their wicked Ends' (89–90). The editorial intrusion concludes with a paragraph explaining 'the sequel': 'The intriguing Gentleman thought fit, however, to keep back from her Father her three last Letters . . . and to send himself a Letter to her Father' (90). Ironically, Mr B insists in this letter that he will keep Pamela 'safe and inviolate' (90). Neither Pamela nor Clarissa knows at first that her correspondence is being intercepted. Without even realizing that Lovelace is intercepting her letters, Clarissa calls him 'the vile encroacher' (381): because Lovelace wants to read all of her letters, he has Dorcas intercept and transcribe them, but Clarissa unwittingly tries to foil him by 'removing her papers from the mahogany chest into a wainscot box, which held her linen', and that box is itself to be enclosed, significantly, by being 'put into her dark closet' (676). Fearing that Clarissa may discover the violation of her privacy, Dorcas is 'uneasy upon it' (676), but she soon 'tried to get at the wainscot box in the dark closet. But it cannot be done without violence' (702). Such an attempt to do violence to Clarissa's letters would symbolize and anticipate doing violence not only to her property, but to her personal space, indeed to her person.

Lovelace's motives are expressed in such ways as these more than once. For instance Anna Howe tries to warn Clarissa (in a letter that Lovelace intercepts) because she has heard that Lovelace boasts 'that no woman shall keep him out of her bedchamber, when he has made a resolution to be in it' (859). While these words form a statement as explicit as politely evasive discourse would normally permit, Anna's words also reveal that the space is metonymy for the goal: getting into a bedroom is just a way of expressing what Lovelace will do to the room's occupant, just as 'to resist invasion of the room and the self, and to bolt oneself in to write letters, may be seen as synonymous acts in *Clarissa*'.[14] Lovelace himself declares his desire 'to trace human nature, and more particularly female nature, through its most secret recesses', which is simultaneously a spatial and a sexual metaphor (843). As ordinary examples like these show, space is constantly capable of representing desires, especially those motivated by sexual impulses.

Richardson invites an unusual form of intimacy between author and reader by having his readers emulate Lovelace, who looks voyeuristically over Clarissa's private correspondence, written, read, and now stored in

---

[14] Gillis, 'Private Room', p. 161.

private spaces.[15] Mediated through the letter, the relationship of writer to reader may be social, but the physical activities of writing and reading letters are unsocial, because they occur in isolated or enclosed, individual but not social spaces. Caused by a refusal of the weak to accede to the power of the strong, the strain on social relationships is expressed in part by Clarissa's (and, for a time, Pamela's) physical isolation in individual space. In different ways Pamela and Clarissa are individuals trying to find a means of giving shape and substance to their own subjectivity: once isolated from family or society, they have little option but to define themselves, in writing, by reference to their personal space.[16]

Richardson's inexorable accumulation of detail, which does much to define social relationships in *Clarissa* as in *Pamela*, serves the double function of defining self and space. *Clarissa* is not at all a descriptive novel: its extravagant length is not attributable to minute descriptions of things, such as curtains and clothes, nor exactly to what Gillis calls 'highly individualized experience', but to conversations, demands, and opinions.[17] The words spoken by characters account for the extremely slow pace of the narration, especially in the first two volumes, 'which are chiefly taken up with the altercations between Clarissa and the several persons of her family' (1,498), and are designed 'to suggest many interesting *personalities*, in which a good deal of the instruction essential to a work of this nature is conveyed' (1,499). These detailed 'altercations are the foundation of the whole' (1,499). Their direct result is to enclose Clarissa, and so lead to a succession of invasions of her space, and to the definition of her subjectivity.

The detail of *Pamela* is of a different kind, concentrating much more on material objects, and leading directly to a denotation of class and power. In an early letter Pamela notes that her 'old Lady's Cloaths', passed on after her death to Pamela are 'too rich and too good for me, to be sure' (30). In this and the almost identical opening paragraph of her next letter, Pamela specifies the materials and the quantities, but she also sees clothes as a vehicle for defining her own status: a mere maid cannot wear such fine things (31). In these instances, possessions enable Pamela to define herself, and although she shared a bed with Mrs Jervis, Pamela says (after yet another list of her clothes) that she kept her 'own little Apartment still for my Clothes, and nobody went thither but myself' (53). Pamela reserves her own space for her

---

[15] Cf. Preston, *The Created Self*, p. 59, and Bertrand H. Bronson, 'The Writer', in *Man versus Society in Eighteenth-Century Britain*, ed. James L. Clifford (Cambridge: Cambridge University Press, 1968), pp. 118–20. Since Fielding's famous letter to Richardson was first published in 1948, it has become a critical commonplace that the reader of the novel is put in the same position as the reader of each letter (see E. L. McAdam, Jr., 'A New Letter from Fielding', *Yale Review*, 38 [1948], 300–10). See *Clarissa*, pp. 1,068–69.

[16] Cf. Robert Sommer, *Personal Space: the Behavioral Basis of Design* (Englewood Cliffs, N.J.: Prentice-Hall, 1969), esp. pp. 26–38, and Gillis, 'Private Room' and *Paradox of Privacy*.

[17] Gillis, 'Private Room', p. 158.

possessions, and like Crusoe, she is what she possesses. Her space, no less than her clothes, therefore denotes her class.

Later, the forty-eight conditions or 'rules' which will determine the marital conduct of Pamela and Mr B, define marriage as a means of regulating social discourse between two people and between two classes.[18] The first of these rules involves a conception of violating space:

1. That I must not, when he is in great Wrath with any body, break in upon him, without his Leave – *Well I'll remember it, I warrant. But yet I fansy this Rule is almost peculiar to himself.* (469)

Marriage will remain a financial and social or, broadly, a political relationship, as it will in *Clarissa*: a discourse of power in practice, with a code to regulate it.[19] Class enables Mr B, and Lady Davers, to exercise their power as they please, and marrying into that class gives Pamela the same rights.[20] Lady Davers, whose scorn for Pamela derives entirely from their difference in class, expresses her contempt of Pamela and fury with Mr B for marrying her by violating their space: she forces her way into their bedroom, where she roundly insults Pamela. The thoroughly conventional wording of Mr B's response to all this shows how closely space and property are allied to social relationships: he demands, 'How dare you set a Foot into my House after the Usage I have receiv'd from you?' and physically carries Lady Davers out of the room (344). He warns that she must 'come not near my Apartment' until she has cooled off, and he then allows Pamela 'to go to write in [her] Closet' and to lock herself in the bedroom to prevent another encroachment (344–45). Lady Davers' violation of their space seems to matter more to Pamela and Mr B than the fury and insults they endure from her.

Before the marriage of Mr B and Pamela, the relationship between them is emphatically that of master and servant. Besides the warning of Pamela's parents about Mr B's power and authority 'as your Master' (32), Mr B's power is expressed repeatedly by means of spatial language. The 'editorial' intrusion, in which Richardson explains how Mr B's Lincolnshire coachman abducts Pamela instead of taking her home, reveals that Mr B imprisons her at his Lincolnshire estate, thus showing that if her liberty is restricted at all, it is actually destroyed, as it is for Booth in *Amelia*. Pamela is not even 'at

[18] Sweet kisses and 'obliging Terms' intermingle in a relationship between Pamela and Mr B that is simultaneously amatory and fiscal (306). Cf. Lovelace's remark that 'Mutual obligation is the very essence and soul of the social and commerical life' (760).

[19] Numerous writers portrayed marriage as a contract. A well known and striking example is in *The Beggar's Opera*, but more typical ones occur in newspapers (e.g. *Mist's Weekly Journal*, 21 August 1725).

[20] Pamela's scorn for Mr B's 'high condition' echoes the bourgeois creed of Crusoe's father: 'Much good may do them with their Pride of Birth, and Pride of Fortune, say I! – All it serves for, as far as I can see, is to multiply their Disquiets, and every body else's that has to do with them' (210).

Liberty' to walk in the garden (139). Under constant surveillance, every move
she makes is reported to Mr B. When she thinks of appealing to a clergyman,
she discovers that his living is in Mr B's power (123). When she makes her
abortive attempt to escape, she finds that Mr B has the law in his pocket: Mrs
Jewkes 'was provided with a Warrant from my Master (who is a Justice of
Peace in this County, as well as the other) to get me apprehended, if I *had*
got away, on suspicion of wronging him, let me have been where I would'
(156). Pamela gradually discovers the truth of what Parson Williams tells her:
'You don't know how you are surrounded' (118). In each case, the language
that expresses Mr B's power over her is spatial: as the common expression
has it, Mr B has got her where he wants her.

More explicitly still, Mr B instructs Pamela's 'wicked Bed-fellow' to enclose
Pamela for, she says, 'she locks me and herself in, and ties the two Keys (for
there is a double door to the Room) about her Wrist, when she goes to Bed'
(104). But before long Pamela chooses to enclose herself so that she may read
Parson Williams' letter in her own private space, and when she is put to bed
wet and bedraggled after her futile attempt to escape, she asks 'in my Closet,
to be left to myself; which she [Mrs Jewkes] consented to, it being double-
barr'd the Day before' (156). The closet is physically even more like a prison
now, but we learn nothing of Pamela's attitude towards this new curb on her
liberty. Her ensnarement and imprisonment are self-evident forms of spatial
restriction, but they are also evidence of Mr B's authority and power: his
power is manifested most of all by his control of space, which therefore
determines the nature of social relationships. To resist Mr B's power at all is
Pamela's attempt at self-determination.

In spite of the differences of description and detail between the two novels,
Clarissa too exploits the politics of space in a class society, and does so far
more effectively. Clarissa's family meets her challenge to their authority and
power by resorting to the only means they know: 'imprisonment' in her own
room at Harlowe Place. Clarissa is obliged to hand over her keys, to her
'officious gaoleress' at Harlowe Place (312–13, 366), where her family is
'watchful' over her walks (352). Her private space ceases to be attractive to
her once the function of her room is defined by what an authoritative
spokesman (her brother) says its function will be. With this, yet another
example of an 'official' assignation of a function to a space, Clarissa's room
becomes her prison (352, 367), where her 'spirit' is 'cramped' and where her
behaviour accordingly changes. When Aunt Hervey 'entered my chamber',
Clarissa 'told her that this visit was a high favour to a poor prisoner in her
hard confinement' (198). Both *Pamela* and *Clarissa* revolve around the politics
of authority and power: in each novel authority is expressed by enclosure,
entrapment, and imprisonment of the victim, though Mr B relents, changes
his tactics (without losing his tendency to be domineering), and prefers affec-
tionate persuasion to outright force. The tortures inflicted on Pamela and

Clarissa are not the physical brutalities of Newgate or Bridewell but the deprivation of the rights (some would say privileges) of liberty, movement, and choice. However, when the two heroines choose to enclose themselves, they show that privacy and imprisonment are divided by the narrowest of lines: what matters is who has control of the key. More importantly still, when Pamela and Clarissa voluntarily shut themselves in their rooms or closets, they give themselves the liberty of privacy (which Clarissa regards as safety [1,021]), but they are still trapped inside the larger space, such as the house or estate, controlled by their tormentors.[21] Then their privacy is not liberty at all, but only a gesture of self-determination. Their freedom of movement is still restricted by the power of their jailers.

Pamela embodies a relatively straightforward discourse of power, which is attenutated anyway by the evasive sentimentalism that allows Pamela to marry her oppressor and so dispense with all her problems. *Clarissa* raises the same issue since, after the rape, marriage is the course of action that Mrs Howe recommends and Lovelace expects as a means of concealing Clarissa's ruin and so saving her public reputation. Clarissa's resolute refusal to do anything of the sort is one sign that this novel will not follow *Pamela*'s easy solution.[22] *Clarissa* offers a far more challenging and complex treatment than *Pamela* does of such political relationships, at several levels.

Marriage was the time-honoured method of consolidating wealth and power by merging estates, as Fielding merges Allworthy's and Western's estates on the occasion of Jones's marriage to Sophia.[23] Pamela has no estate to bring to Mr B, but in *Clarissa* this customary political function of marriage looms much larger, as it clashes with Clarissa's self-determining act of rebellion against her family. Clarissa prefers to be 'buried alive' than marry the repugnant Solmes, whatever 'terms' he may offer, but her resolution not to marry the man her family has selected for her quickly becomes a challenge to power (101). Clarissa rejects Solmes because she dislikes his morals and his manners, not for any political reason, but her radical act of self-determination deprives her greedy family of the opportunity to 'increase [their] interest in this county' and climb to 'a footing with the principal [families] in the kingdom' (101), a motive that she finds has little to be said for it. Her brother James fulminates: 'It is *my* authority you defy' (125). The italicized possessive obviously locates the source of power, and may distract us from the wider statement, that her 'defiance' is defiance of authority *tout court*. Clarissa's family responds to her defiance at once by restricting the space in which she

---

[21] Clarissa, for example, double-locks herself in her room at Mrs Sinclair's (p. 951), and at the sponging house she sits all night on a chair set against the door (p. 1,055).

[22] For instance, p. 1,087. Lovelace speaks of a prospective marriage between her and him as 'atonement' (p. 1,039).

[23] See Christopher Hill, 'Clarissa Harlowe and Her Times', *Essays in Criticism*, 5 (1955), 315–40, reprinted in *Samuel Richardson: A Collection of Critical Essays*, ed. John Carroll (Englewood Cliffs, N.J.: Prentice-Hall, 1969), pp. 102–23.

may move: 'By your papa's and mamma's command', James says that he writes 'expressly to forbid you to come into their presence, or into the garden when they are there: nor when they are *not* there, but with Betty Barnes to attend you, except by particular licence or command . . . You are not to be seen in any apartment of the house you so lately governed as you pleased, unless you are commanded down. In short, are strictly to confine yourself to your chamber,' except to walk occasionally in the garden, which she must reach by the back stairs (120-21). The next assaults on her liberty are spatial too: first, to make this enclosure stricter still and, second, to threaten that she will '*be bricked up*' (306). James thus expresses the family's power over her by treating her as a commodity which they may dispose of – give away or shut away – as they choose.

In spite of differing social and economic status, Lovelace is just as willing as the Harlowes to treat Clarissa as a possession. Flattering himself that Clarissa is 'the dearest property I ever purchased' (736), he still thinks he has a 'right to her' when she is dead (1,384) and his principal tactic to gain possession of her is similarly spatial.[24] Unlike Lovelace, the Harlowes, though 'no contemptible family', are nouveaux riches (1,035). Since Clarissa's fortune comes from her late grandfather, her immediate family represents the second generation of new moneyed men, usually Whiggish and middle-class, who had risen to greater wealth and power since 1688.[25] Because it was built 'within every elderly person's remembrance' (161), Harlowe Place symbolizes the Harlowe family's social status. The house is simultaneously a symbol in a quite different sense, because it represents also the outrageous moral pressure that the family brings to bear on Clarissa. The Harlowe family likes to cast judgment, to 'correct' the behaviour of other people, or 'In other words, to employ itself rather in the *out-door* search than in the *in-door* examination', as Clarissa herself describes it in the language of 'convenience'.[26]

As critics habitually point out, Harlowe Place is indistinct but thoroughly real, and so it corresponds to the undetailed behaviour of Clarissa's father, whose furious fuming rumbles distantly somewhere downstairs, but whose power is no less menacing for that distance.[27] Lovelace's contempt for the

[24] As Hill notes, Lovelace is as dependent as anyone else on the property-marriage system, directly for his power if only indirectly for his money (p. 113). See *Clarissa*, pp. 1,160–61. Lovelace's aim is to triumph over the female sex, whose best representative Clarissa is (p. 1,175). Perhaps she sees herself that way when she refers to 'the offence given to virtue in my fall' (p. 1,426). Clarissa's resistance to Lovelace certainly becomes woman's opposition to man, as Clarissa's will poignantly underlines: her corpse 'shall not be touched but by those of my own sex' (p. 1,413).

[25] Ross (ed.), *Clarissa*, p. 19, suggests that the Harlowes might evoke a tendency towards Jacobitism, anathema to anyone with Richardson's political affiliation, despite his early flirtation with the movement. But the economic circumstances and ambitions of the Harlowes point to the bourgeois who stood to lose, not gain, by embracing Jacobitism.

[26] Cf. Lovelace: 'I intend to make every soul of the family mourn – *outside*, if not *in* –' (p. 941): the spatial language of 'convenience' once more suggests hypocrisy.

[27] For example, Ian Watt, *Rise of the Novel*, p. 27; J. S. Bullen, *Time and Space in the Novels of Samuel*

Harlowes and their house, which he says is 'sprung up from a dunghill' (161), neatly accents the class distinction between them, a distinction that Clarissa herself recognizes. Confronted with one of Lovelace's protestations that he will marry her, the now 'ruined' Clarissa asks him to 'imagine' hearing his distinguished relatives calling on him, 'the dead from their monuments, the living from their laudable pride; not to dishonour thy ancient and splendid house by entering into wedlock with a creature whom thou hast levelled with the dirt of the street and classed with the vilest of her sex' (912). Clarissa thinks of Lovelace's 'house' of course as his dynasty, yet the contrast between his 'ancient and splendid house' and her new degradation to 'the dirt of the street' connotes a vivid spatial conception too. For all its architectural vagueness in the novel, M. Hall, Lovelace's ancestral home, symbolizes his social status just as emphatically and publicly as Harlowe Place does for the Harlowe family, because, as Lovelace defiantly tells his uncle, 'People . . . fenced in by their quality and by their years, should not take freedoms that a man of spirit could not put up with, unless he were able heartily to despise the insulter': Lovelace himself is enclosed, 'fenced in' by his own class (1,033), and a house, as we have seen repeatedly, represents the class (as well as temperament) of its owner. Later, Lovelace too will be isolated for a short time, in 'the state part' of the house, the rest of his family occupying the rest of the building (1,182), and he is enraged when later he is excluded from the final, inexorable drama of Clarissa's dying. With another of his egocentric reversals of logic, he even speaks of his persecution of Clarissa as his own 'long imprisonment in my close attendance to so little purpose on the fair perverse' (1,085). Landed, semi-aristocratic, Lovelace belongs to a class that did not take kindly to the bourgeois invasion of its territorial 'rights', and yet it is Lovelace who has invaded Clarissa's territory.

The city, 'this great town, wicked as it is' (1,139), to which Lovelace drags Clarissa, is also a spatial emblem of his effort to control her body, for she is as much his prisoner there as she was her family's prisoner at Harlowe Place: Lovelace is one of those 'rakes and libertines' who 'get a young creature into their power' (1,015). Like Mr B, Lovelace has a whole army of minions to carry out his sadistic, near-Satanic strategies;[28] Lovelace's apparatus of power

Richardson, Monograph Series, vol. 12, no. 2 (Logan: Utah State University Press, 1965), pp. 34, 41; Gillis, 'Private Room', p. 155; Rachel Trickett, ' "Curious Eye": Some Aspects of Visual Description in Eighteenth-Century Literature', in *Augustan Studies: Essays in Honor of Irvin Ehrenpreis*, ed. Douglas Lane Patey and Timothy Keegan (Newark: University of Delaware Press, and London and Toronto: Associated University Presses, 1985), p. 247. Cf. Ross (ed.), *Clarissa*, p. 21. Clarissa's father maintains his power although he has delegated authority to his son.

[28] Lovelace is Satanic (e.g. pp. 1,037, 1,083), and Clarissa angelic (pp. 1,071, 1,106, 1,112). Lovelace's imagination can be excessively violent to the point of sadism (p. 1,069). The parallels between Lovelace's tactics and the Harlowes' are obvious. Mrs Howe, who loves her parental authority (p. 1,112), employs tactics which, though not often noticed, are not much different (pp. 1,017, 1,087).

includes his lies, manipulations, bribery, interception, impersonation and forgery, these last two being signs of the utmost iniquity to Clarissa when she discovers them (1,076). Predominant over all these methods of changing appearances is Lovelace's relentless, 'barbarous and illegal' confinement of Clarissa's body (1,019). When Clarissa has escaped finally from Lovelace and is 'enumerating' her few 'comforts' after her ordeal, she explains: 'I am no prisoner now in a vile house. I am not now in the power of that man's devices. I am not now obliged to hide myself in corners for fear of him' (1,088).

The discourse of power imposes spatial limitations, whether legal or illegal, civilized or barbarous, like the restrictions imposed by class, on Clarissa's individual liberty. She asks Lovelace, 'do you think I might not be *safe* and *private* in London?' but she is neither, since he has her surrounded, and in London she is entirely alienated, both from him and from the city: 'My case is a hard, a very hard one', she writes, 'I am quite bewildered! – I know not what to do! – I have not a friend in the world that can or will help me! – yet had none but friends till I knew *that man!*' (790), who, she adds later, has *made* her 'friendless' (911). Since she 'knows not a soul' in London, Lovelace assumes that he has her always in his power (736). Then, when she escapes to Hampstead, he recaptures her with an ease that, long after the event, 'must also remain wholly a mystery' to Clarissa (1,020). He knows, even if she does not, that Hampstead is 'not the *wide world*', and hopes 'to restore her to a *narrower*' (760). When he recaptures her, she protests, 'You have no right to invade me thus' (775), but he ignores her protest. When she asks 'Why am I to be imprisoned here?' she is saying the same thing: her confinement is his invasion of her space (905–06, 908, 911). Clarissa's manoeuvre of getting Lovelace's servant out of the way, to deliver a letter that is pure 'feint', prompts Lovelace to ask: 'Now, Jack, will not her *feints* justify mine? Does she not invade my province, thinkest thou?' (759). This language of invasion, heavy with sexual implications, accompanies actions that are restrictive, limiting: arms 'kemboed', Mrs Sinclair stands with her back to the door, and menaces Clarissa (898). Servants rush to block her exit if she tries to escape. Eventually Lovelace appoints a servant to stand guard at the street door like a sentry (913). 'Oh house!' Clarissa laments metonymically, 'contrived for my ruin!' (935). 'Lovelace', says John Preston, 'is in a position not of power but of fear', which may be true psychologically and in the novel's implied economics, but of course what Lovelace exerts over Clarissa is certainly power.[29]

The Harlowe family, obviously, also exerts power over Clarissa, with several consequences unforeseen and undesired by anyone. One of the less spectacular consequences is that Clarissa's first forced isolation, at Harlowe Place, prompts a significant change in her social conduct. When her Aunt Hervey comes into her room at Harlowe Place, Clarissa greets her with a

---

[29] *The Created Self*, pp. 83–84. Clarissa herself says: 'I am too much in your power . . . your prisoner' (p. 934).

distinctively cool gesture that creates formal space between them and at once reduces intimacy: she 'kissed her hand'. Recognizing the social and spatial implication, Aunt Hervey reacts at once with mild reproach: 'Why this distance to your aunt, my dear, who loves you so well?' (198). That gesture of Clarissa's points towards a spatial formality that will eventually become characteristic of her.[30] After she has shown a degree of willingness, in some circumstances, to touch Lovelace and be touched by him, she more frequently withdraws her hand and refuses to allow him any physical contact with her at all, and in the penknife scene where she threatens suicide, what she gains primarily is 'distance' (950).

Between these two episodes is Lovelace's campaign to reduce the physical distance between himself and Clarissa. One of his ruses is to administer ipecacuanha to himself with the object of playing on her sympathy for a sick person. When Clarissa thinks Lovelace's self-induced illness is serious and genuine, she tells Anna Howe that no one can 'hate people in danger of death, or who are in distress or affliction' (678), and expresses her sympathy for Lovelace 'obligingly', as he reports to Belford:

She suffered me to take her hand, and kiss it as often as I pleased. On Mrs. Sinclair's mentioning that I too much confined myself, she pressed me to take an airing . . . I asked if I might have the honour of her company in a coach; and this, that I might observe if she had an intention of going out in my absence. . . I kissed her hand again! She was all goodness! (678)

Clarissa's method of showing her concern for Lovelace is thus to allow him to touch her: the very antithesis of her usual desire to be alone in a locked room. Very soon after this incident, Lovelace perceives an excuse to touch her again, this time more boldly: as 'Captain Tomlinson' is about to arrive, she begs 'Good Mr Lovelace' to control his temper. As Lovelace replies, he embraces her ('such innocent freedoms as this from *good* Mr Lovelace too') (682). Apparently not resenting this new infringement of her personal space, Clarissa promptly retires to her room for fear of being seen by the visitor. However, she indignantly frees herself from Lovelace when he tries 'a still bolder freedom' (705). Love, he tells Belford 'is an encroacher', Clarissa's word for Lovelace as she struggles 'out of [his] encircling arms' (704). Lovelace describes this scene in language that constantly suggests his invasion of her space, his surrounding her, touching her. At first she gently 'repulse[s]' him by averting her eyes, but when he kisses her breast she is enraged; of course, he has gone too far or, to put it in another way, come too close. He expects her to marry him, when 'every inch of her person' will no longer be 'sacred', because 'all will be my own by deed of purchase and settlement' (705). Lovelace expects to own her, much as Mr B thinks he owns Pamela, and his method of expressing that expectation is to reduce the space between

[30] For example, pp. 928, 937.

them, to engage Clarissa in as much physical contact as she will tolerate. 'I would have whispered her about the treaty with her uncle, and the contents of the Captain's letter', Lovelace explains to Belford, 'but, retreating, and with a rejecting hand, Keep thy distance, *man*, cried the dear insolent' (794). 'The struggle', as Lovelace perceives it, is 'whether I am to have her in *my own way*, or in *hers*' (808). In a grotesque reminder of Mr B's treatment of Pamela as his property, Lovelace concludes that possession will give him the right to invade her personal space just as often, and with as extreme a violation of it, as he likes.

Unlike characters in a Sartre novel, who stare fully at one another's faces, characters in Defoe, Richardson, and Fielding novels habitually bridge physical gaps, like those Clarissa creates, only by speaking.[31] The theatrical scene in which 'Captain Tomlinson' comes on his sham mission to discover whether or not Clarissa has married Lovelace exemplifies the eighteenth century's habits of social behaviour: the aristocracy, gentry, and bourgeoisie are supposed to keep their distance, avoiding such rudeness as a direct gaze (though this would normally be rude only if directed at a lady). Modesty is expressed by averted eyes and silence, more often than not. It seems almost archetypally revealing of social custom that to 'make love' should mean only to give *verbal* expression to amorous desire, and paradoxically that there was no polite word for copulation. In such a milieu as that of polite eighteenth-century England, personal space is as likely to be violated by words and intentions as it is by physical disruption. This makes Lady Davers' intrusion all the more shocking for its impropriety and extremity, and Lovelace's rape of Clarissa a brutal act of paramount destructiveness.

The letter in which Lovelace – he who keeps a list of the women he ruins (1,030) – tells Belford that he has raped Clarissa is the shortest, most oblique, and most evasive in the novel. The entire letter reads: 'And now, Belford, I can go no further. The affair is over. Clarissa lives' (883). 'Words', as Anna Howe says, 'are poor' (1,015). The rape, 'the highest injury that can be offered to woman' (958), is the climax of the narrative, yet the event signified by Lovelace's terse words is dispersed into verbal unimportance, in contrast to the deluge of words that inundates all the other letters. It is a strange paradox that when Lovelace is in a hurry, he writes at length: now, with time to spare, he has no words to say. There are no available words to describe the 'black transaction', as the 'editor' calls it (883). Even though Lovelace has repeatedly violated her space, and so has gained control over Clarissa's body by imprisoning and then raping her, he has previously been rebuffed again and again, not as much by Clarissa's withdrawing her hand whenever he tries to kiss it, as by her words, the only weapon she has to defend herself through all her trials (e.g. 689). Lovelace is furious that 'a lady whom once I had bound to

---

[31] With the exception of *Amelia*, where eye-contact is an important weapon in the arsenal of seduction.

me in the silken cords of love' (1,144) concedes in her gracious last letter to him only that she 'once respected [him] with a preference'; he is insulted because she did not use a different form of words: 'To say I once loved you is the English; and there is truth and ease in the expression' (1,428). Reading this letter after her death, Lovelace is still vainly demanding a verbal admission from her. He always wants to break her will, which, he says with calculated effrontery after the rape, is unviolated (916), as she too seems to believe (1,162) until she tells him 'a will of my own has been long denied me' (1,191). He has used spatial restriction in his effort to force her to submit – that is, to give her verbal assent – to his desires: 'But here's the thing – I have given her cause enough of offence; but not enough to make her hold her tongue' (790). As his alternative to prospective defeat, he drugs her, certainly to render her body unresisting, but also to silence the torrent of her verbal resistance, the signifier of her 'unexampled vigilance and exalted virtue' (1,015). That way, he may then go on to violate the most intimate of all spaces, and so send Clarissa first to her ruin and then to 'the slowest of deaths' (1,341).

Lovelace does not desire Clarissa's death any more than he desired marriage with her, but he hopes that she may be pregnant: what he wants is 'the triumph of nature over principle, and to have a young Lovelace by such an angel' (1,147), and therefore he refuses to believe that rape caused Clarissa's death (1,439). Taken as a whole, whatever Lovelace wants is what Clarissa perceives as invasion of her space. Thinking spatially even as she approaches death, Clarissa begs Belford to ensure that Lovelace 'will not invade her in her last hours' (1,343), an expression that reminds Belford of her words when Lovelace did pursue her to her lodgings at Mrs Smith's: 'He will not let me die decently . . . He will not let me enter into my Maker's presence with the composure that is required in entering into the drawing room of an earthly prince!' (1,343). Then in her last letter to Lovelace, Clarissa urges her persecutor to reform, because 'A hardened insensibility is the only foundation on which your inward tranquillity is built' (1,426). In death she will not only 'slide quietly' into her grave, but be enclosed in a coffin, 'on the happy day that shall shut up all my sorrows' (1,013).

Clarissa's desire to be so enclosed is her final gesture of defiance because it is the last expression of self: in death she can assert that she is no longer a social being, no longer a prisoner.[32] Once Clarissa had made her previous gestures of defiance, the people wishing to exert their power over her began the processes of using space to break her will. Denied social space by her family, personal space by Lovelace, Clarissa has also been watched, so that, whether or not she has ever known it, she has been denied privacy too.

[32] I therefore see Clarissa tending towards closure rather than opening, even though the coffin becomes an object of public gaze and the doors of Harlowe Place finally re-open. But for the opposite view, see Gillis, 'Private Room', passim, esp. p. 163.

There is a fine line between this form of surveillance, with its overtones of institutional imprisonment, and voyeurism.[33]

Confinement, which Clarissa finally desires, is usually a weapon wielded by the strong over the weak. That Clarissa chooses confinement and isolation suggests that her defiance is unabated. At the end Clarissa does not defy James or Lovelace specifically, but an ideology, which these two both represent, and which customarily imposes spatial restriction to deny independence. Political life when Richardson was writing was largely a matter of 'dependence', and to opt out as Clarissa does is to challenge the prevailing demand for conformity by asserting herself. Her tormentors express their power over her by limiting or violating her space: her responses are no less spatial. Resisting verbally and enclosing herself are, in life and death, Clarissa's spatial acts of radical self-determination.

[33] Imprisonment in the 1740s, I must concede, did not involve techniques of surveillance such as those symbolized much later by the Panopticon.

8

The politics of space

'Twould cure an author for ever of the fuss and folly of opening his street-door, and calling in his neighbours and friends, and kinsfolk, with the devil and all his imps, with their hammers and engines, &c. only to observe how one sentence of mine follows another, and how the plan follows the whole.

Sterne, *Tristram Shandy*, volume 8, chapter 2

It has been a theme of this book that the disposition of space in eighteenth-century Britain was political, and that in a parallel development the major novelists exploited spatial conceptions in ways that make their novels political as well. The thinking which politicized space grew in a materialist culture that placed high value on self-interest and property. Defence of power, authority and property was only to be expected of the ruling (that is, mostly landowning) class. E. P. Thompson notices an 'increasing impersonality in the mediation of class relations', brought about in part by an increase in the number of offences against property.[1] Thompson sees this 'Whig state of mind' in the paradigmatic Waltham Black Act, which permitted the death penalty for numerous new offences against property.[2] Allied with the defence of property is a tendency to control that part of property that is specifically spatial: land. As I have suggested in part I, eighteenth-century polite society furnished the ideology of control and consumption of space. Together with their bourgeois imitators, the dominant classes had few qualms about crushing poorer people than themselves into small, cramped spaces, and then condemning the poor for living in such conditions. The rulers' ideological demand for conformity among the ruled could be – and was – expressed spatially.

The dominant classes very nearly perfected the politics of keeping distance, and not only in railed enclosures of city squares: one reason why a mob was ugly (apart from an inferred threat to property) was that its members paid no respect to spatial decorum. This lies behind even Sir John Blunt's account

[1] *Whigs and Hunters: the Origin of the Black Act* (New York: Pantheon, 1975), p. 208. See also H. T. Dickinson, *Liberty and Property* (London: Weidenfeld & Nicolson, 1977), and Neil McKendrick, John Brewer and J. H. Plumb in *The Birth of a Consumer Society: the Commercialization of Eighteenth-Century England* (London: Europa, 1982).

[2] *Whigs and Hunters*, pp. 188–89.

of the South Sea mania in 1720, when the prospect of fabulous wealth prompted 'Persons of all Ranks and Stations' to

lay aside all manner of distance, and almost Decency, to become the humble Suitors for Subscriptions: not only to the *Directors* of the *South Sea* Company, but also to the *meanest* and *vilest* of *People* . . .[3]

Blunt singles out the '*lower part* of the *People*', who 'deserted their *Shops* and *Trades*, and their usual Methods of Industry, and were strip'd of what by their former Diligence and Frugality they had acquired'.[4] 'Distance', then, means physical space, but it also means social space, which is rich with connotations of decorum. When the petty bourgeois desert their shops, they leave their designated physical space and their social space, and mix either with those as lofty as the South Sea directors (i.e. Blunt himself) or with those who occupy the lowest positions on the social scale. What seems to bother Blunt most of all is that if distinctions of social rank are so blurred in the crush of Exchange Alley, social hierarchy is threatened with collapse, which would in turn imply the collapse of the ideology supporting the hierarchy. Whig ideology was meant to keep the weaker and the poor in their places, as the ultimate price Walpole, Blunt and other predators willingly paid for the advancement of their own interest.

It is that ideology and its consequent alienating tendency that Moll Flanders resists when she tenaciously maintains her own space. In striving to achieve a higher social status, with its economic and political rewards, Defoe's characters establish a relationship between an individual and society: I have suggested that a sign of their consciousness of themselves as individuals is their desire for space that they can call their own. Moll's childish aspiration to be a gentlewoman, that is, to raise her social status, is later transformed into a desire for her own space.[5] As an urban rogue, Moll does not want just more space, in the sense of more rooms or a larger house: she desires space for herself because sharing her space with the other rogues would deprive her of her fragile identity. Moll's refusal to be incorporated even in a society of criminals is a radical refusal to conform.

Moll is not, of course, the only participant in such spatial politics. Demonstrably imitating their social superiors' tactics of persecution, the Harlowe family certainly alienate Clarissa, and threaten her with the dire penalty of enclosure – being 'bricked up' – because she challenges their pursuit of self-interest when she thwarts their desire for property by marriage. When Clarissa falls from community she no longer has an identifiable self, because her subjectivity has been defined previously by her dependent social role in her family. Before the rape Clarissa has constantly resisted the family's

---

[3] *A True State of the South Sea Scheme* (London, 1722), p. 41.
[4] *Ibid.*, p. 42.
[5] *Moll Flanders*, Shakespeare Head Edition, I, pp. 5–6.

oppressive desire to incorporate her, and after it she hopes, vainly, for a reconciliation. By resisting incorporation and yet identifying herself in it, Clarissa is at once socialized and alienated. Richardson expresses this paradox continually by means of the spatial politics that subject Clarissa to enclosure and surveillance. Although isolated by her family, Clarissa goes on to create a new, limited subjectivity for herself in her isolation, as do Moll Flanders and Robinson Crusoe. All these characters engage with these alienating aspects of the dominant ideology of the time and, in refusing to conform, all express the same desire to control their own space. Their desire for such control is continually opposed or threatened.

When Clarissa and Pamela are enclosed against their will, their movements are monitored. In some novels, surveillance of the kind to which Clarissa and Pamela are subjected can take the forms of regulating behaviour by rules and confinements, or even eavesdropping (listening at doors and watching through keyholes are two conventions of eighteenth-century fiction). In the long run, such surveillance may lead to physical violation of personal space, as it does for Clarissa, but its most immediate effect is always the violation of the privacy associated with personal space or, at an extreme, the violation of secrecy. Surveillance implies the desire of the powerful to regulate the weak in a hierarchic social system.

The conspicuous display of narrative structure indulged by Fielding, an aspect of regulatory control if not of surveillance, approvingly affirms that hierarchic social system, and so offers it as an image of a far more stable and ordered world than the world encountered by Defoe's or Richardson's characters. Only Fielding of these three writers parades his design: the narrator of *Tom Jones* is a controller, of words, of a plot, of a putative readership, and so is an obvious figure in whom the novelist vests authority. This designer's role is something of a literary analogue of John Wood's role as a designer of urban spaces and their surrounding buildings, whose purpose is to satisfy the taste of those who constitute a leisured class. It is difficult to say with confidence that the users of Wood's spaces in Bath were the same people, a mixture of aristocracy, gentry, and bourgeoisie, as those who are known to have read *Tom Jones*. But it was to the ideology of the dominant class that these two designers appealed. Previously associated in the main with hereditary ownership of land, but transformed by the politics of interest and dependence, that originally aristocratic ideology was largely adopted as a guide or model by the bourgeoisie. Both Fielding's literary space and Wood's urban space could serve to express an ideal of progressive history and, consequently, an emblem of the alleged order and stability of expanding British power.

As my early chapters have shown, the dominant architectural theory, which Fielding parallels in his design, is fundamentally conservative if not always aristocratic in upholding architecture as a supposedly permanent symbol of imperial achievement. If the narrator as designer suggests emblematically a system of control, Fielding's language of architecture to describe people suggests an equivalent system of perception. Fielding's use of 'convenience' also aligns him more closely than Defoe or Richardson with the distinctively architectural aspects of spatial discourse. Buildings acquire identity only from their place in the larger patterns of a street, village, town, or city. A country house like Paradise Hall or Prior Park gains its identity in the same way, its physical position in the surrounding estate suggesting its central political role in the relationship between its owner and the inhabitants of the houses both within and outside its estate. If people are like buildings, as many writers discussed in this book suggested they are, then people too can achieve identity only by means of their place among other people.[6] 'Convenience' leads once again to thinking of people as Locke did: as static individuals who are contiguous but whose opportunities for interaction are constricted and defined usually by the larger class pattern to which they belong. The individual is therefore always a social being, an identity that Fielding affirms when he installs his good-natured characters together in an intimate but exclusive social group at the end of every one of his novels. Fielding shows much less interest in the psychological development of his characters than in the patterns of their behaviour. If subjectivity is determined by one's place in a society, human interaction would be perceived like this, as more generalized, less individual, more a question of the class that a person represents. This, I think, is the meaning of Fielding's generalizing tendency at the expense of psychic exploration in *Tom Jones*. The opposite of Fielding's technique in this, as usual, is Richardson's.

Fielding's emphasis on social rather than personal space suggests his preference for incorporation, his ideological rejection of bourgeois self-consciousness. Few of Fielding's characters in any of his novels care very much about personal space: one or two have to resist a Lovelace's invasions, but even when one of them, Amelia, must do so, her response is rarely to withdraw her hand or retire to the privacy of her bedchamber. By contrast Defoe and Richardson both show that personal space creates a crucially important but undefinable, psychological boundary around the individual, best exemplified by Clarissa's horror of being touched, since touch is a destruction of that boundary and an invasion of personal space.

Eighteenth-century English fiction does not abound with tactile sensations. A conspicuous exception such as *Fanny Hill* proves why: it is salacious enough to be pornographic. By reducing personal space to nothing at all, touch distorts a social relationship between individuals, as many other contemporary examples amply demonstrate. For instance, on his return from Houyhnhnmland, Gulliver expresses his alienation from his own race by keeping physical distance between himself and his family. Swift's personal taste was for

[6] See chapter 2, above.

small, intimate gatherings, not crowds. For Sterne's Parson Yorick, touching a woman's hand, her wrist, or even her glove, is an ambigous substitute for more substantially erotic contact. Joseph Andrews finds his Fanny sexually attractive, but he keeps his hands to himself and only stares at her half-bared bosom. Tom Jones is occasionally ardent or chivalrous enough to take a woman in his arms (in public, that is), but his love for Sophia is expressed most commonly by earnest protestations delivered in a posture of supplication. Leaving aside the devotional implications of such genuflection, we might just observe that Jones *does not touch her*: he touches her muff instead. Social contact is not usually physical contact. Lovelace's rape of Clarissa is dreadful enough to provoke even Belford's reproach and condemnation of his friend, but the rape also violates a network of codes of social behaviour, which paradoxically underpin the hierarchical society that keeps Lovelace as socially high as he is: it is the hierarchical structure of Richardson's England.

In this widely accepted system of social relations, intimacy can usually be shared only by adults of the same class. 'Intimacy' meant close friendship but it certainly did not mean any reduction of physical distance between friends conversing in a drawing room. One written sign of that distance is the decorous form of address, normal for the time, by which a man writing to an 'intimate' friend would open a letter, 'Dear Sir'. Some used the old-fashioned familiar form of 'thou', like two friends such as Belford and Lovelace. Even a letter was supposed to express social relations spatially: the spaces between words in a letter conveyed intimacy or distance. Etiquette demanded that an 'inferiour' writing a letter to a 'superiour' must use a large sheet of paper, and leave a large blank space between the superior's title and the first line of the text.[7] Richardson's characters evidently know also that the physical document is itself an indication of rank, or of differences in rank. They should know: it was common knowledge.

Hannah Woolley's advice to gentlewomen includes the remark that 'If kindred write to one another, the greater may express the relation in the beginning of the Letter [of thanks for courtesies received]; but she that is of the meaner quality, must be content to specifie it in the Subscription.'[8] The political relationship between James and Clarissa is thus intensified in a way that might easily escape us, when, for instance, she addresses her brother: 'Sir, [text of letter], Your unhappy sister, Cl. Harlowe'.[9] Specifying her relation 'in the Subscription' is a sign that she recognizes her own 'meaner quality', which

---

[7] [Antoine de Courtin], *The Rules of Civility; or, Certain Ways of Deportment Observed amongst all Persons of Quality upon Several Occasions*, rev. edn (London, 1685), p. 170. Such advice was, one might say, generic: it was repeated for instance by Jean Puget de la Serre, *The Secretary in Fashion: or, an Elegant and Compendious Way of Writing all Manner of Letters*, 5th edn (London, 1673), n.p. I owe thanks to Carol Briggs for drawing my attention to these books.

[8] Hannah Woolley, *The Gentlewoman's Companion; or, a Guide to the Female Sex* (London, 1675), p. 227.

[9] *Clarissa*, ed. Angus Ross, p. 121.

will make her rebellion all the more daring. Arabella asserts her superiority
to her sister by omitting any mention of their relationship when she signs a
letter to Clarissa.[10] There was a whole catalogue of polite and proper forms
to be observed in the organization of space on a piece of paper, whose full
social force we necessarily miss because the printed text of *Clarissa* does not
reproduce the appearance of manuscripts.

Courtesy books laid down these and other rules for writing letters, for
appropriate style, proper forms of address, and so on. Among the many
fascinating pieces of advice is this: if one receives a letter when in company,
it is socially correct to absent oneself, read the letter alone, and then return
to the company and tell them what the letter contained.[11] To do otherwise is
impolite but this etiquette indicates also that an attempt to preserve privacy
is impolite. The authors said they devised these manuals of 'rules' either to
enable the bourgeois to imitate 'polite' society, or to give the gentry a code of
conduct when they approached the nobility.[12] The rules regulate privacy,
which means in this particular example denying it and so making the subject
demonstrably social. When one letter arrives for Clarissa from Anna Howe,
'She took the letter from old Grimes with her own hands, and retired to an
inner parlour to read it', but she does not return to relate the contents to
Lovelace, who has anyway already violated etiquette (as well as privacy) by
intercepting and reading the letter.[13] Later, Anna Howe and Clarissa willingly
organize correspondence which will be subject to the surveillance of Anna's
mother.[14] 'Privacy' is therefore a deformation of 'individualism'; their behaviour reinforces their status as social beings, as individual subjects for whom
'privacy' is not even an issue.

Not only is the form of a letter itself a spatial and organizational means of
expressing political relationships; it is also obviously a statement of distance
between two people, as Richardson himself was aware. He wrote to Sophia
Westcomb:

Who then shall decline the converse of the pen? The pen that makes distance, presence; and brings back to sweet remembrance all the delights of presence; which makes
even presence but body, while absence becomes the soul; and leaves no room for the

---

[10] *Clarissa*, p. 140; later, an indication that Arabella's severity may be relenting a little is her
signing one letter 'Your afflicted sister' (p. 1160).

[11] Courtin, *Rules*, pp. 252–53.

[12] Courtin, *Rules*, advertisement, n.p. Incidentally, this advertisement also described the book as
an addition 'to a Fabrick of intrensical [*sic*] Riches, and of incomparable Architecture'.

[13] *Clarissa*, pp. 808, 1,022. Anna Howe's mother does this, though (p. 975). Anne Elliott, however,
knew 'that her seeing the letter [from William Elliott] was a violation of the laws of honour, . . .
that no private correspondence could bear the eye of others' (*Persuasion*, ch. 21, *The Novels of
Jane Austen*, ed. R. W. Chapman, 2nd edn [Oxford: Clarendon Press, 1926], V, p. 204). It is,
of course, as both Algernon and Jack know, 'a very ungentlemanly thing to read a private
cigarette case' (*Importance of Being Earnest*, Act 1).

[14] *Clarisssa*, pp. 993ff.

intrusion of breakfast-calls, or dinner or supper direction, which often broke in upon us.[15]

Woolley explained that a letter 'is or ought to be the express image of the Mind, represented in writing to a friend at a distance; wherein is declared what He or She would do or have done', a definition that adequately denotes the epistolary correspondence between Clarissa and her jailers, James or Lovelace.[16] Consciously desired or not, such written communication – 'the discourse of the absent' – emphasizes physical distance (sometimes only slightly), and moral distance.[17] There are moments in *Clarissa* when communication by letter between people in the same house seems absurd or contrived. That Clarissa is reduced to special pleading by letter, when her family is downstairs, indicates the emotional and political abyss that separates them.[18] Since all letters must presuppose distance between writer and reader, *Clarissa* also depends on the Lockean concept of people as individual, contiguous, spatial entities. Intimacy without touching is possible either through social rites of conversation, perfected in this period in England, or through the medium of the letter. Either way, spoken or written, intimacy is verbal before it is physical.

Unlike personal spaces, social spaces, which express social relationships, imply a less intimate, more nearly public life, in the sense that a family or other group is a unit more social than an isolated individual can possibly be. A social space such as a drawing room can be a vehicle for revealing class, as it is at Harlowe Place when Solmes is the guest welcomed by Clarissa's family. Social spaces designed for 'the public' are also places of assembly: one such space, Bath's North Parade, was purposely designed to expose class – 'real and apparent People of Rank and Fortune', in Wood's phrase – in a more public light, and to a greater number of people, so that the spaces people occupy can easily determine their place in a social hierarchy.[19] If people of real and apparent fortune intermingle as Wood means them to, the upper classes (Defoe's 'great' and 'rich') are joined by the 'middle sort' in fulfilment of bourgeois aspirations. That is what happened, as Smollett's Matt Bramble attests: 'Every upstart of fortune, harnessed in the trappings of the mode, presents himself at Bath . . . and all of them hurry to Bath, because here, without any further qualification, they can mingle with the princes and nobles

[15] *Selected Letters of Samuel Richardson*, ed. John Carroll (Oxford: Clarendon Press, 1964), p. 65.

[16] Woolley, *Companion*, p. 218.

[17] Courtin, *Rules*, p. 169.

[18] And Clarissa's 'knack at writing' is so persuasive that she 'depended upon making everyone do what [she] wrote': *that* perhaps explains Arabella's jealousy of her sister, and also her family's subsequent refusal to read, open, or even accept Clarissa's letters.

[19] *Essay towards a Description of Bath* (1749), II, p. 446.

of the land', with the result that 'a very considerable proportion of genteel people are lost in a mob of impudent plebeians'.[20]

Smollett was recording, in 1771, a confusion of rank. In the hands of Wood or Richardson or Defoe, social space is an instrument that slightly modifies, but still affirms, hierarchical distinctions of rank, and therefore tends to conflict with personal space. For that reason the use of a space can be determined still, in eighteenth-century England as in first-century Rome, by the power of an authoritative verbal pronouncement, as Sterne's Parson Yorick realizes when he contemplates imprisonment in the Bastille, which is only a tower until someone chooses to call it a prison:

– And as for the Bastile! the terror is in the word – Make the most of it you can, said I to myself, the Bastile is but another word for a tower – and a tower is but another word for a house you can't get out of – . . . but with nine livres a day, and pen and ink and paper and patience, albeit a man can't get out, he may do very well within – at least for a month or six weeks.[21]

The characters in *Humphry Clinker*, too, recognize that the social spaces of Bath itself are similarly determined by words.[22] The second of Yorick's attitudes here – that one can make the best of it – is similar in principle to Crusoe's when he thinks of his first island shelter as his home, or to Emily's, in *The Mysteries of Udolpho*, when, ordered not to leave the peasants' cottage, she 'became fond' of her room in it, 'and began to experience in it those feelings of security, which we naturally attach to home.'[23] To acquire delimited personal space without actually desiring it is imprisonment, but to express a desire for personal space, as Defoe's outsiders do, or as Clarissa does, is to modify the demand for incorporation that social spaces usually express.

Moll, who is not born into the middle class, and Crusoe, who is, exemplify the paradoxical political aspirations of the bourgeois, emulating their socio-economic superiors, while displaying enough individualism to pose a challenge to the power of those superiors. Lovelace scorns this tendency of the petty bourgeois:

When I came into the shop, seeing no chair or stool, I went behind the counter and sat down under an arched kind of canopy of carved work, which these proud traders, emulating the royal niche-fillers, often give themselves, while a joint-stool perhaps serves those by whom they get their bread: such is the dignity of trade in this mercantile nation![24]

---

[20] *Humphry Clinker*, ed. Lewis M. Knapp, Oxford English Novels (London: Oxford University Press, 1966), pp. 36–37.

[21] *A Sentimental Journey through France and Italy*, ed. Gardner D. Stout (Berkeley and Los Angeles: University of California Press, 1968), p. 196.

[22] *Humphry Clinker*, pp. 32–33, 37, 40–41.

[23] Ann Radcliffe, *The Mysteries of Udolpho*, ed. Bonamy Dobrée, notes by Frederick Garber, World's Classics edition (London: Oxford University Press, 1980), p. 418.

[24] *Clarissa*, p. 1,213.

That bourgeois assertion of dignity, based on an uneasy mixture of measured hostility and obsequious flattery, can be perceived as hypocrisy. But while the petty bourgeoisie might be 'emulating the royal niche-fillers', it is no less true that the placemen and great predators at the highest levels are invading the space of those below them. Corruption, it was frequently alleged, spreads from the top, with the honest Puritan printer doing all he can to keep his hands clean. There was a real sense, detectable behind Lovelace's scorn, that the petty bourgeois tradesman who asserted his own 'dignity' somehow posed a threat to the class that controlled most of the power, authority, and property.

All the major novels I have discussed serve to entrench political convictions or aspirations such as these. As I have sought to show, space has a crucial social function in those novels, just as it has in the architectural theory and practice of the eighteenth century. The major consequence of this for the novel is that it is an expression of the politics of the author's world. The novelists exploited the two fundamental dynamics, time and space, to give verbal substance to their aspirations. Those aspirations naturally vary from one class to another, but they are all social.

Spatial discourse is therefore a discourse of social relationships in a class society, but, as Anne Elliott says in *Persuasion*, 'I will not allow books to prove any thing'.

Index

Page numbers in *italic* refer to illustrations